Testimonies

for the Church

Vol. 8

Ellen G. White

Copyright Notice

Copyright © 2022 by Waymark Books

Published by Waymark Books

All rights reserved. No part of this publication may be reproduced, distributed, or transmitted in any form or by any means, including photocopying, recording, or other electronic or mechanical methods, without the prior written permission of the publisher, except in the case of brief quotations embodied in critical reviews and certain other noncommercial uses permitted by copyright law. For permission requests, contact the publisher, addressed "Attention: Permissions Coordinator," at this address: WaymarkBooks@gmail.com.

TABLE OF CONTENTS

Section 1: Present Opportunities
1. Our Work 6
2. The Commission 10
   An Unchanging Promise 12
3. The Power Promised 14
4. Our Responsibility 18
5. The Work at Home & Abroad 22
6. The Work in Europe 28
7. A View of the Conflict 30

Section 2: Counsels Often Repeated
8. Warnings to Battle Creek Church ... 37
   The Time of the End 38
   Help in the Time of Trouble 39
   A Failure to Honor God 39
9. Our Duty to the World 41
   How to Gain Success 43
10. Mission Work at Home/Abroad ... 44
    Illustration of the Work We 45
    A Neglected Work 46
11. The Holy Spirit in our Schools ... 48
    The Will of God Concerning Us ... 49
    Working Against the Holy Spirit ... 51
12. A Departure from Right 52
13. Look to God for Help 54
    Medical Missionary Work 55
    A Word of Caution 58
14. An Appeal to Battle Creek 60

15. A Neglected Warning 64
16. The Result of Reformation 68
17. A Solemn Warning 70
18. The Review and Herald Fire 75
19. What Might Have Been 80
20. Forgetfulness 82
    A Hymn of the Promised Land 83
    A Hymn of the Captivity 86
    Song of the Redeemed 90
    "Call to Remember the Former..." ... 92
    "Written for our Admonition" 93
    The Message for this Time 94
    The Opposition of the Enemy 95
    The Loud Cry 96
    "And Hast Forgotten" 96
    "Choose You This Day Whom..." ... 97
    The Shield of Omnipotence 98
    Jehovah Reigneth 99

Section 3: Letters to Physicians
21. The Value of Trial 102
    Paul's Experience 104
    Resting in God's Love 104
    The Danger of Self-Sufficiency ... 105
    Our Burden Bearer 106
    Looking Away from Men 107
    An Eternal Weight of Glory 108

22. Centering Too Much in B.C. 110
   Unselfishness in Service 112
   Helping Those Who Need Help.. 112
   What One Institution Can Do 113
   A Reformation Needed................ 114
   Living Principle of Brotherhood .. 115
   The Only Safe Course 116
   The Danger from Enlargement.... 117
   The Question of Wages................ 117
23. Go Forth into Many Places 119
   The Need of Broader Plans.......... 121
   Build up New Centers 123
   Not Appreciating Responsibilities .. 124
24. God's Purpose for Institutions .. 125
   God's Purpose for the Sanitarium... 127
   Value of Study of God's Word..... 128
25. Medical Missionary Work......... 129
   Educate Medical Missionaries 129
   Our Work for Today 130
   No Change in God's Cause 131
   Words of Caution......................... 132
26. A Word of Caution 133
   A Danger to be Guarded Against... 133
   A High Standard......................... 135
   Teaching and Healing 135
27. Uphold the Medical Work 136
   The Need of Caution................... 137
   The Importance of M.M. Work .. 138
   Cause of Dearth in the Church.... 139
   To Every Man His Work 140
28. Unity of Effort........................... 140
   God's Building 141
   A Temple of Living Stones.......... 142

   Different Instrumentalities........... 142
   Truth a Unit 143
   Words of Cheer 143
29. Christ the Medium of Prayer..... 144
30. Words of Encouragement.......... 146
   Why God Made the Sanitarium ... 147
   A World-Wide Work.................. 148
   A Word of Caution...................... 149
   Helping or Hindering the Lord.... 150
   God's Purpose for His Workers.... 151
   The Need of Wise Counselors...... 152
   A Divine Helper 152
   Burdens that God Did Not Give 154
31. The Value of the Word of God 156
   Reward of Studying the Word.... 157
32. The Work for this Time 158
   Our Message................................ 160
   Sign of our Relationship to God... 160
33. A Broader View 162
   Christ's Victory over Unbelief 163
   Warning against Centralization.... 165
   A Neglected Field Near Us 165
34. Christ Our Example 166
   Self-Sacrifice................................ 168
   A Firm Stand for the Right.......... 170

Section 4: Be on Guard

35. Lessons from the Past 172
   Centralization 172
   An Educational Center 175
36. How Shall Youth be Trained? ... 177
   Words of Warning....................... 179
   No Time for Delay....................... 183

A Division of Responsibility 184
37. Leadership 187
    Early Experiences 188
    God Our Leader 188
38. One with Christ in God 189
39. Lay Members to Go Forth 192
40. Shall We Be Found Wanting? 195
    God's Purpose for His People 195
    "Repent, Do the First Works" 196
    A Failure to Honor God 197
    A Call for Reformation 198
41. Homeward Bound 198

Section 5: The Essential Knowledge

42. God in Nature 201
43. A Personal God 208
44. False & True Knowledge of God ... 226
    Speculative Theories 226
    The Greatness of Our God 228
    Warnings against Presumption 231
    Christ's Revelation of God 234
    The Glory of the Cross 235
    Knowledge Works Transformation 236
45. Danger in Speculative Knowledge 237
    Last-Day Deceptions 237
    Pantheistic Theories 238
    Fanaticism after 1844 239
    Past Experiences to be Repeated 240
    Beware of a Sensational Religion 241
    A Warning against False Teaching 241
    Diverting Minds from Present Duty .. 242
    Renewal of the Straight Testimony 243
    Seek the First Love 244

The Word of God our Safeguard ... 244
Study the Revelation 246
To the Church in Sardis 247
Message to Philadelphia Church 248
The Laodicean Message 248
46. The False & True in Education .. 249
    Philosophical Speculation 249
    Infidel Authors 250
    Historical and Theological Lore .. 251
    Myths and Fairy Tales 252
    A Purer Fountain 253
    Heart Education 254
47. Important to Seek True Knowledge .. 255
    Work that Requires Our Thought 255
    The Science to be Mastered 256
    No Time to Lose 257
    The Need for Self-Renunciation 258
    Highest Interests Demand Attention ... 258
    A Personal Knowledge of Christ . 259
48. Knowledge from God's Word ... 260
    To Be Given to Our Children 261
    An Experimental Knowledge 262
    Wonderful Possibilities 262
    Results of Receiving God's Word 264
    An Aid in the Study of Nature 266
    A Key to Divine Mysteries 267
    A Lesson of Obedience 268
    Education in the Life to Come 269
49. Our Great Need 269
    The Experience of Enoch 270
    Experience of John the Baptist 271
    God's Promises 274

— Section 1 —

Present Opportunities

"Israel shall blossom and bud, and fill the face of the world with fruit." Isaiah 27:6.

1. Our Work

What is our work? The same as that given to John the Baptist, of whom we read: "In those days came John the Baptist, preaching in the wilderness of Judea, and saying, Repent ye: for the kingdom of heaven is at hand. For this is he that was spoken of by the prophet Esaias, saying, The voice of one crying in the wilderness, Prepare ye the way of the Lord, make His paths straight." Matthew 3:1-3.

All who are truly engaged in the work of the Lord for these last days will have a decided message to bear. Read the first few verses of the fortieth chapter of Isaiah:

"The voice of him that crieth in the wilderness, Prepare ye the way of the Lord, make straight in the desert a highway for our God. Every valley shall be exalted, and every mountain and hill shall be made low: and the crooked shall be made straight, and the rough places plain: and the glory of the Lord shall be revealed, and all flesh shall see it together: for the mouth of the Lord hath spoken it." Isaiah 40:3-5.

"The voice said, Cry. And he said, What shall I cry? All flesh is grass, and all the goodliness thereof is as the flower of the field: the grass withereth, the flower fadeth: because the Spirit of the Lord bloweth upon it: surely the people is grass. The grass withereth, the flower fadeth: but the word of our God shall stand forever." Verses 6-8.

Section 1: Present Opportunities

This chapter is filled with instruction appropriate for us at this time. The word of the Lord to us is: "Repent ye; prepare the way for a revival of My work."

The removal to Washington of work hitherto carried on in Battle Creek is a step in the right direction. We are to continue to press into the regions beyond, where the people are in spiritual darkness. "Every valley shall be exalted, and every mountain and hill shall be made low: and the crooked shall be made straight, and the rough places plain." Verse 4. Every obstacle to the redemption of God's people is to be removed by the opening of His word and the presentation of a plain "Thus saith the Lord." The true light is to shine forth; for darkness covers the earth, and gross darkness the people. The truth of the living God is to appear in contrast with error. Proclaim the glad tidings. We have a Saviour who has given His life that those who believe in Him should not perish, but have everlasting life.

Obstacles to the advancement of the work of God will appear; but fear not. To the omnipotence of the King of kings, our covenant-keeping God unites the gentleness and care of a tender shepherd. Nothing can stand in His way. His power is absolute, and it is the pledge of the sure fulfillment of His promises to His people. He can remove all obstructions to the advancement of His work. He has means for the removal of every difficulty, that those who serve Him and respect the means He employs may be delivered. His goodness and love are infinite, and His covenant is unalterable.

The plans of the enemies of His work may seem to be firm and well established, but He can overthrow the strongest of these plans, and in His own time and way He will do this, when He sees that our faith has been sufficiently tested and that we are drawing near to Him and making Him our counselor.

In the darkest days, when appearances seem so forbidding, fear not. Have faith in God. He is working out His will, doing all things well in behalf of His people. The strength of those who love and serve Him will be renewed day by day. His understanding will be placed at their service, that they may not err in the carrying out of His purposes.

There is to be no despondency in God's service. Our faith is to endure the pressure brought to bear upon it. God is able and willing to bestow upon His servants all the strength they need. He will more than fulfill the highest expectations of those who put their trust in Him. He will give them the wisdom that their varied necessities demand.

Said the tried apostle Paul: "He said unto me, My grace is sufficient for thee: for My strength is made perfect in weakness. Most gladly therefore will I rather glory in my infirmities, that the power of Christ may rest upon me. Therefore I take pleasure in infirmities, in reproaches, in necessities, in persecutions, in distresses for Christ's sake: for when I am weak, then am I strong." 2 Corinthians 12:9, 10.

Oh, my brethren, hold the beginning of your confidence firm unto the end. The light of God's truth is not to be dimmed. It is to shine amidst the darkness of error that enshrouds our world. The word of God is to be opened to those in the high places of the earth, as well as to those in the more lowly.

The church of Christ is God's agency for the proclamation of truth; she is empowered by Him to do a special work; and if she is loyal to God, obedient to His commandments, there will dwell within her the excellence of divine power. If she will honor the Lord God of Israel, there is no power that can stand against her. If she will be true to her allegiance, the forces of the enemy will be no more able to overpower her than is the chaff to resist the whirlwind.

There is before the church the dawn of a bright, glorious day, if she will put on the robe of Christ's righteousness, withdrawing from all allegiance to the world.

The members of the church need now to confess their backslidings and press together. My brethren, allow nothing to come in that will separate you from one another or from God. Talk not of differences of opinion, but unite in the love of the truth as it is in Jesus. Come before God, and plead the shed blood of the Saviour as a reason why you should receive help in the warfare against evil. You will not plead in vain. As you draw near to God, with heartfelt contrition and in full assurance of faith, the enemy who seeks to destroy you will be overcome.

Turn to the Lord, ye prisoners of hope. Seek strength from God, the living God. Show an unwavering, humble faith in His power and His willingness to save. From Christ is flowing the living stream of salvation. He is the Fountain of life, the Source of all power. When in faith we take hold of His strength, He will change, wonderfully change, the most hopeless, discouraging outlook. He will do this for the glory of His name.

God calls upon His faithful ones, who believe in Him, to talk courage to those who are unbelieving and hopeless. May the Lord help us to help one another and to prove Him by living faith.

"Sing aloud unto God our strength: make a joyful noise unto the God of Jacob. Take a psalm, and bring hither the timbrel, the pleasant harp with the psaltery." Psalm 81:1, 2.

"It is a good thing to give thanks unto the Lord, and to sing praises unto Thy name, O Most High: to show forth Thy loving-kindness in the morning, and Thy faithfulness every night, upon an instrument of ten strings, and upon the psaltery; upon the harp with a solemn sound. For Thou, Lord, hast made me glad through Thy work: I will triumph in the works of Thy hands." Psalm 92:1-4.

"O come, let us sing unto the Lord: let us make a joyful noise to the Rock of our salvation. Let us come before His presence with thanksgiving, and make a joyful noise unto Him with psalms. For the Lord is a great God, and a great King above all gods. In His hand are the deep places of the earth: the strength of the hills is His also. The sea is His, and He made it: and His hands formed the dry land. O come, let us worship and bow down: let us kneel before the Lord our Maker." Psalm 95:1-6.

"O sing unto the Lord a new song: sing unto the Lord, all the earth. Sing unto the Lord, bless His name; show forth His salvation from day to day. Declare His glory among the heathen, His wonders among all people. For the Lord is great, and greatly to be praised: He is to be feared above all gods." Psalm 96:1-4.

"Make a joyful noise unto the Lord, all ye lands. Serve the Lord with gladness: come before His presence with singing. Know ye that the Lord He is God: it is He that hath made us, and not we ourselves; we are His people, and the sheep of His pasture. Enter into His gates with thanksgiving, and into His courts with praise: be thankful unto Him, and bless His name. For the Lord is good; His mercy is everlasting; and His truth endureth to all generations." Psalm 100.

2. The Commission

It is God's purpose that His people shall be a sanctified, purified, holy people, communicating light to all around them. It is His purpose that, by exemplifying the truth in their lives, they shall be a praise in the earth. The grace of Christ is sufficient to bring this about. But let God's people remember that only as they believe and work out the principles of the gospel can He make them a praise in the earth. Only as they use their God-given capabilities in His service will they enjoy the fullness and power of the promise whereon the church has been called to stand. If those who profess to believe in Christ as their Saviour reach only the low standard of worldly measurement, the church fails to bear the rich harvest that God expects. "Found wanting" is written upon her record.

The commission that Christ gave to His disciples just before His ascension is the great missionary charter of His kingdom. In giving it to the disciples, the Saviour made them His ambassadors and gave them their credentials. If, afterward, they should be challenged and asked by what authority they, unlearned fishermen, went forth as teachers and healers, they could reply: "He whom the Jews crucified, but who rose from the dead, appointed us to the ministry of His word, declaring, 'All power is given unto Me in heaven and in earth.'"

Christ gave this commission to His disciples as His chief ministers, the architects who were to lay the foundation of His church. He laid upon them, and upon all who should succeed them as His ministers, the charge of handing His gospel down from generation to generation, from age to age.

The disciples were not to wait for the people to come to them. They were to go to the people, hunting for sinners as a shepherd hunts for lost sheep. Christ opened the world before them as their field of labor. They were to go "into all the world, and preach the gospel to every creature." Mark 16:15. It was of the Saviour that they were to preach, of His life of unselfish service, His death of shame, His unparalleled, unchanging love. His name was to be their watchword, their band of union. In His name they were to subdue the strongholds of sin. Faith in His name was to mark them as Christians.

Section 1: Present Opportunities

Giving the disciples further directions, Christ said: "Ye shall receive power, after that the Holy Ghost is come upon you: and ye shall be witnesses unto Me both in Jerusalem, and in all Judea, and in Samaria, and unto the uttermost part of the earth." "But tarry ye in the city of Jerusalem, until ye be endued with power from on high." Acts 1:8; Luke 24:49.

In obedience to the word of their Master the disciples assembled in Jerusalem to wait for the fulfillment of God's promise. Here they spent ten days, days of deep heart searching. They put away all differences and drew close together in Christian fellowship.

At the end of ten days the Lord fulfilled His promise by a wonderful outpouring of His Spirit. "Suddenly there came a sound from heaven as of a rushing mighty wind, and it filled all the house where they were sitting. And there appeared unto them cloven tongues like as of fire, and it sat upon each of them. And they were all filled with the Holy Ghost, and began to speak with other tongues, as the Spirit gave them utterance." "And the same day there were added unto them about three thousand souls." Acts 2:2-4, 41.

"And they went forth, and preached everywhere, the Lord working with them, and confirming the word with signs following." Mark 16:20. Notwithstanding the fierce opposition that the disciples met, in a short time the gospel of the kingdom had been sounded to all the inhabited parts of the earth.

The commission given to the disciples is given also to us.

Today, as then, a crucified and risen Saviour is to be uplifted before those who are without God and without hope in the world. The Lord calls for pastors, teachers, and evangelists. From door to door His servants are to proclaim the message of salvation. To every nation, kindred, tongue, and people the tidings of pardon through Christ are to be carried.

Not with tame, lifeless utterance is the message to be given, but with clear, decided, stirring utterances. Hundreds are waiting for the warning to escape for their lives. The world needs to see in Christians an evidence of the power of Christianity. Not merely in a few places, but throughout the world, messengers of mercy are needed. From every country is heard the cry: "Come over, and help us." Rich and poor, high and low, are calling for light. Men and women are hungering for the truth as it is in Jesus. When they hear the gospel preached with power from on high, they will know that the banquet is spread for them, and they will respond to the call: "Come; for all things are now ready." Luke 14:17.

The words "Go ye into all the world, and preach the gospel to every creature" (Mark 16:15) are spoken to each one of Christ's followers. All who are ordained unto the life of Christ are ordained to work for the salvation of their fellow men. The same longing of soul that He felt for the saving of the lost is to be manifest in them. Not all can fill the same place, but for all there is a place and a work. All upon whom God's blessings have been bestowed are to respond by actual service; every gift is to be employed for the advancement of His kingdom.

• An Unchanging Promise

Christ made full provision for the prosecution of the work entrusted to the disciples, and took upon Himself the responsibility of its success. So long as they obeyed His word, and worked in connection with Him, they could not fail. Go to all nations, He bade them. Go to the farthest part of the habitable globe, but know that My presence will be there. Labor in faith and confidence, for the time will never come when I will forsake you.

To us also the promise of Christ's abiding presence is given. The lapse of time has wrought no change in His parting promise. He is with us today as truly as He was with the disciplines, and He will be with us "even unto the end."

"Go forth preaching the gospel to all nations," the Saviour says to us, "that they may become children of God. I am with you in this work, teaching, guiding, comforting, strengthening you, giving you success in your work of self-denial and sacrifice. I will move upon hearts, convincing them of sin, and turning them from darkness to light, from disobedience to righteousness. In My light they shall see light. You will meet the opposition of satanic agencies, but put your trust in Me. I will never fail you."

Think you not that Christ values those who live wholly for Him? Think you not that He visits those who, like the beloved John, are for His sake in hard and trying places? He finds His faithful ones, and holds communion with them, encouraging and strengthening them. And angels of God, that excel in strength, are sent forth by God to minister to His human workers who are speaking the truth to those who know it not.

To the minister of the gospel God has given the work of guiding to Christ those who have wandered from the narrow way. He is to be wise and earnest in his efforts. At the end of each year he should be able to look back and see souls saved as the result of his labors. Some he is to save with fear, "pulling them out of the fire; hating even the garment spotted by the flesh," "holding fast the faithful word as he hath been taught." Jude 23; Titus 1:9. Paul's charge to Timothy comes to the ministers of today: "I charge thee therefore before God, and the Lord Jesus Christ; ... Preach the word; be instant in season, out of season; reprove, rebuke, exhort with all long-suffering and doctrine." 2 Timothy 4:1, 2.

But it is not only upon those who preach the word that God has placed the responsibility of seeking to save sinners. He has given this work to all. Our hearts are to be so filled with the love of Christ that our words of thanksgiving shall warm other hearts. This is service that all can perform, and the Lord accepts it as offered to Himself. He makes it efficacious, imparting to the earnest worker the grace that reconciles man to God.

May the Lord help His people to realize that there is earnest work to be done. May He help them to remember that in the home, in the church, and in the world they are to work the works of Christ. They are not left to labor alone. The angels are their helpers. And Christ is their helper. Then let them labor faithfully and untiringly. In due season they will reap if they faint not.

The Christian pilgrim does not yield to his desire to rest. He moves steadily forward, saying: "The night is far spent, the day is at hand." This is his motto: "Not as though I had already attained, either were already perfect: but I follow after... I count not myself to have apprehended: but this one thing I do, forgetting those things which are behind, and reaching forth unto those things which are before, I press toward the mark for the prize of the high calling of God in Christ Jesus." Philippians 3:12-14.

3. The Power Promised

God does not ask us to do in our own strength the work before us. He has provided divine assistance for all the emergencies to which our human resources are unequal. He gives the Holy Spirit to help in every strait, to strengthen our hope and assurance, to illuminate our minds and purify our hearts.

Just before His crucifixion the Saviour said to His disciples: "I will not leave you comfortless." "I will pray the Father, and He shall give you another Comforter, that He may abide with you forever." "When He, the Spirit of truth, is come, He will guide you into all truth: for He shall not speak of Himself; but whatsoever He shall hear, that shall He speak: and He will show you things to come." "He shall teach you all things, and bring all things to your remembrance, whatsoever I have said unto you." John 14:18, 16; 16:13; John 14:26.

Christ has made provision that His church shall be a transformed body, illumined with the light of heaven, possessing the glory of Immanuel. It is His purpose that every Christian shall be surrounded with a spiritual atmosphere of light and peace. There is no limit to the usefulness of the one who, putting self aside, makes room for the working of the Holy Spirit upon his heart and lives a life wholly consecrated to God.

What was the result of the outpouring of the Spirit upon the Day of Pentecost? The glad tidings of a risen Saviour were carried to the utmost bounds of the inhabited world. The hearts of the disciples were surcharged with a benevolence so full, so deep, so far-reaching, that it impelled them to go to the ends of the earth, testifying: "God forbid that I should glory, save in the cross of our Lord Jesus Christ." Galatians 6:14. As they proclaimed the truth as it is in Jesus, hearts yielded to the power of the message.

The church beheld converts flocking to her from all directions. Backsliders were reconverted. Sinners united with Christians in seeking the pearl of great price. Those who had been the bitterest opponents of the gospel became its champions. The prophecy was fulfilled: The weak shall be "as David," and the house of David "as the angel of the Lord." Every Christian saw in his brother the divine similitude of love and benevolence. One interest prevailed.

Section 1: Present Opportunities

One subject of emulation swallowed up all others. The only ambition of the believers was to reveal the likeness of Christ's character and to labor for the enlargement of His kingdom.

"With great power gave the apostles witness of the resurrection of the Lord Jesus: and great grace was upon them." Acts 4:33. Under their labors there were added to the church chosen men, who, receiving the word of life, consecrated their lives to the work of giving to others the hope that had filled their hearts with peace and joy. Hundreds proclaimed the message: "The kingdom of God is at hand." They could not be restrained or intimidated by threatenings. The Lord spoke through them; and, wherever they went, the sick were healed, and the poor had the gospel preached unto them.

So mightily can God work when men give themselves up to the control of His Spirit.

To us today, as verily as to the first disciples, the promise of the Spirit belongs. God will today endow men and women with power from above, as He endowed those who on the Day of Pentecost heard the word of salvation. At this very hour His Spirit and His grace are for all who need them and will take Him at His word.

Notice that it was after the disciples had come into perfect unity, when they were no longer striving for the highest place, that the Spirit was poured out. They were of one accord. All differences had been put away. And the testimony borne of them after the Spirit had been given is the same. Mark the word: "The multitude of them that believed were of one heart and of one soul." Acts 4:32. The Spirit of Him who died that sinners might live animated the entire congregation of believers.

The disciples did not ask for a blessing for themselves. They were weighted with the burden of souls. The gospel was to be carried to the ends of the earth, and they claimed the endowment of power that Christ had promised. Then it was that the Holy Spirit was poured out, and thousands were converted in a day.

So it may be now. Let Christians put away all dissension and give themselves to God for the saving of the lost. Let them ask in faith for the promised blessing, and it will come. The outpouring of the Spirit in the days of the apostles was "the former rain," and glorious was the result. But the latter rain will be more abundant. What is the promise to those living in these last days? "Turn you to the stronghold, ye prisoners of hope: even today do I declare that I will render double unto thee." "Ask ye of the Lord rain in the time of the latter rain; so the Lord shall make bright clouds, and give them showers of rain, to every one grass in the field." Zechariah 9:12; 10:1.

Christ declared that the divine influence of the Spirit was to be with His followers unto the end. But the promise is not appreciated as it should be; and therefore its fulfillment is not seen as it might be. The promise of the Spirit is a matter little thought of; and the result is only what might be expected—spiritual drought, spiritual darkness, spiritual declension and death. Minor matters occupy the attention, and the divine power which is necessary for the growth and prosperity of the church, and which would bring all other blessings in its train, is lacking, though offered in its infinite plenitude.

It is the absence of the Spirit that makes the gospel ministry so powerless. Learning, talent, eloquence, every natural or acquired endowment, may be possessed; but, without the presence of the Spirit of God, no heart will be touched, no sinner won to Christ. On the other hand, if they are connected with Christ, if the gifts of the Spirit are theirs, the poorest and most ignorant of His disciples will have a power that will tell upon hearts. God makes them channels for the outflowing of the highest influence in the universe.

Why do we not hunger and thirst for the gift of the Spirit, since this is the means by which we are to receive power? Why do we not talk of it, pray for it, preach concerning it? The Lord is more willing to give the Holy Spirit to us than parents are to give good gifts to their children. For the baptism of the Spirit every worker should be pleading with God. Companies should be gathered together to ask for special help, for heavenly wisdom, that they may know how to plan and execute wisely. Especially should men pray that God will baptize His missionaries with the Holy Spirit.

The presence of the Spirit with God's workers will give the presentation of the truth a power that not all the honor or glory of the world could give. The Spirit furnishes the strength that sustains striving, wrestling souls in every emergency, amidst the unfriendliness of relatives, the hatred of the world, and the realization of their own imperfections and mistakes.

Section 1: Present Opportunities

Zeal for God moved the disciples to bear witness to the truth with mighty power. Should not this zeal fire our hearts with a determination to tell the story of redeeming love, of Christ and Him crucified? Is not the Spirit of God to come today, in answer to earnest, persevering prayer, and fill men with power for service? Why, then, is the church so weak and spiritless?

It is the privilege of every Christian, not only to look for, but to hasten the coming of our Lord Jesus Christ. Were all who profess His name bearing fruit to His glory, how quickly the whole world would be sown with the seed of the gospel. Quickly the last harvest would be ripened, and Christ would come to gather the precious grain.

My brethren and sisters, plead for the Holy Spirit, God stands back of every promise He has made. With your Bibles in your hands, say: "I have done as Thou hast said, I present Thy promise, 'Ask, and it shall be given you; seek, and ye shall find; knock, and it shall be opened unto you.'" Christ declares: "What things soever ye desire, when ye pray, believe that ye receive them, and ye shall have them." "Whatsoever ye shall ask in My name, that will I do, that the Father may be glorified in the Son." Matthew 7:7; Mark 11:24; 14:13.

The rainbow about the throne is an assurance that God is true; that in Him is no variableness, neither shadow of turning. We have sinned against Him and are undeserving of His favor; yet He Himself has put into our lips that most wonderful of pleas: "Do not abhor us, for Thy name's sake, do not disgrace the throne of Thy glory: remember, break not Thy covenant with us." Jeremiah 14:21. He has pledged Himself to give heed to our cry when we come to Him confessing our unworthiness and sin. The honor of His throne is staked for the fulfillment of His word to us.

Christ dispatches His messengers to every part of His dominion to communicate His will to His servants. He walks in the midst of His churches. He desires to sanctify, elevate, and ennoble His followers. The influence of those who believe in Him will be in the world a savor of life unto life. Christ holds the stars in His right hand, and it is His purpose to let His light shine forth through them to the world. Thus He desires to prepare His people for higher service in the church above. He has given us a great work to do. Let us do it faithfully. Let us show forth in our lives what divine grace can do for humanity.

4. Our Responsibility

There are times when a distinct view is presented to me of the condition of the remnant church, a condition of appalling indifference to the needs of a world perishing for lack of a knowledge of the truth for this time. Then I have hours, and sometimes days, of intense anguish. Many to whom have been committed the saving truths of the third angel's message fail of realizing that the salvation of souls is dependent upon the consecration and activity of God's church. Many are using their blessings in the service of self. Oh, how my heart aches because Christ is put to shame by their un-Christlike behavior! But, after the agony is past, I feel like working harder than ever to arouse them to put forth unselfish effort for the saving of their fellow men.

God has made His people stewards of His grace and truth, and how does He regard their neglect to impart these blessings to their fellow men? Let us suppose that a distant colony belonging to Great Britain is in great distress because of famine and threatened war. Multitudes are dying of starvation, and a powerful enemy is gathering on the frontier, threatening to hasten the work of death. The government at home opens its stores; public charity pours forth; relief flows through many channels.

A fleet is freighted with the precious means of life and is sent to the scene of suffering, accompanied by the prayers of those whose hearts are stirred to help. And for a time the fleet sails directly for its destination. But, having lost sight of land, the ardor of those entrusted with carrying food to the starving sufferers abates. Though engaged in a work that makes them colaborers with angels, they lose the good impressions with which they started forth. Through evil counselors, temptation enters.

A group of islands lies in their course, and, though far short of their destination, they decide to call. The temptation that has already entered grows stronger. The selfish spirit of gain takes possession of their minds. Mercantile advantages present themselves. Those in charge of the fleet are prevailed on to remain on the islands. Their original purpose of mercy fades from their sight. They forget the starving people to whom they were sent. The stores entrusted to them are used for their own benefit. The means of beneficence is diverted into channels of selfishness. They barter the means of life for selfish gain, and leave their fellow beings to die. The cries of the perishing ascend to heaven, and the Lord writes in His record the tale of robbery.

Think of the horror of human beings dying because those placed in charge of the means of relief proved unfaithful to their trust. It is difficult for us to realize that man could be guilty of so terrible a sin. Yet I am instructed to say to you, my brother, my sister, that Christians are daily repeating this sin.

In Eden, man fell from his high estate and through transgression became subject to death. It was seen in heaven that human beings were perishing, and the compassion of God was stirred. At infinite cost He devised a means of relief. He "so loved the world, that He gave His only-begotten Son, that whosoever believeth in Him should not perish, but have everlasting life." John 3:16. There was no hope for the transgressor except through Christ. God saw that "there was no man, and wondered that there was no intercessor: therefore His arm brought salvation unto Him; and His righteousness, it sustained Him." Isaiah 59:16.

The Lord chose a people and made them the depositories of His truth. It was His purpose that by the revelation of His character through Israel, men should be drawn to Him. To all the world the gospel invitation was to be given. Through the teaching of the sacrificial service, Christ was to be uplifted before the nations, and all who would look unto Him should live.

But Israel did not fulfill God's purpose. They forgot God and lost sight of their high privilege as His representatives. The blessings that they had received brought no blessing to the world. All their advantages were appropriated for their own glorification. They robbed God of the service He required of them, and they robbed their fellow men of religious guidance and a holy example.

God finally sent His Son to reveal to men the character of the Unseen. Christ came and lived on this earth a life of obedience to God's law. He gave His precious life to save the world and made His servants His stewards. With the gift of Christ all the treasures of heaven were given to man. The church was freighted with the food of heaven for starving souls. This was the treasure that the people of God were commissioned to carry to the world. They were faithfully to perform their duty, continuing their work until the message of mercy had encircled the world.

Christ ascended to heaven and sent His Holy Spirit to give power to the work of His disciples. Thousands were converted in a day. In a single generation the gospel was carried to every nation under heaven. But little by little a change came. The church lost her first love. She became selfish and ease-loving. The spirit of worldliness was cherished. The enemy cast his spell upon those to whom God had given light for a world in darkness, light which should have shone forth in good works. The world was robbed of the blessings that God desired men to receive.

Is not the same thing repeated in this generation? Many in our day are keeping back that which the Lord has entrusted to them for the salvation of a world unwarned, unsaved. In the word of God an angel is represented as flying in the midst of heaven, "having the everlasting gospel to preach unto them that dwell on the earth, and to every nation, and kindred, and tongue, and people, saying with a loud voice, Fear God, and give glory to Him; for the hour of His judgment is come: and worship Him that made heaven, and earth, and the sea, and the fountains of waters." Revelation 14:6, 7.

The message of Revelation 14 is the message that we are to bear to the world. It is the bread of life for these last days. Millions of human beings are perishing in ignorance and iniquity. But many of those to whom God has committed the stores of life look upon these souls with indifference. Many forget that to them has been entrusted the bread of life for those starving for salvation.

Oh, for consecrated Christians, for Christlike consistency, for the faith that works by love and purifies the soul! May God help us to repent and change our sluggish movements into consecrated activity. May He help us to show in our words and works that we make the burden of perishing souls our own.

Let us be thankful every moment for God's forbearance with our tardy, unbelieving movements. Instead of flattering ourselves with the thought of what we have done, after doing so little, we are to labor still more earnestly. We are not to cease our efforts or relax our vigilance. Never is our zeal to grow less. Our spiritual life must be daily revived by the stream that makes glad the city of our God. We must be always on the watch for opportunities to use for God the talents He has given us.

Section 1: Present Opportunities

The world is a theater; the actors, its inhabitants, are preparing to act their part in the last great drama. With the great masses of mankind there is no unity, except as men confederate to accomplish their selfish purposes. God is looking on. His purposes in regard to His rebellious subjects will be fulfilled. The world has not been given into the hands of men, though God is permitting the elements of confusion and disorder to bear sway for a season. A power from beneath is working to bring about the last great scenes in the drama—Satan coming as Christ, and working with all deceivableness of unrighteousness in those who are binding themselves together in secret societies. Those who are yielding to the passion for confederation are working out the plans of the enemy. The cause will be followed by the effect.

Transgression has almost reached its limit. Confusion fills the world, and a great terror is soon to come upon human beings. The end is very near. We who know the truth should be preparing for what is soon to break upon the world as an overwhelming surprise.

John writes: "And I saw a great white throne, and Him that sat on it, from whose face the earth and the heaven fled away; and there was found no place for them. And I saw the dead, small and great, stand before God; and the books were opened: and another book was opened, which is the book of life: and the dead were judged out of those things which were written in the books, according to their works." Revelation 20:11, 12.

Are we as a people asleep? Oh, if the young men and young women in our institutions who are now unready for the Lord's appearing, unfitted to become members of the Lord's family, could only discern the signs of the times, what a change would be seen in them! The Lord Jesus is calling for self-denying workers to follow in His footsteps, to walk and work for Him, to lift the cross, and to follow where He leads the way.

Many are readily satisfied with offering the Lord trifling acts of service. Their Christianity is feeble. Christ gave Himself for sinners. With what anxiety for the salvation of souls we should be filled as we see human beings perishing in sin! These souls have been bought at an infinite price. The death of the Son of God on Calvary's cross is the measure of their value. Day by day they are deciding whether they will have eternal life or eternal death. And yet men and women professing to serve the Lord are content to occupy their time and attention with matters of little importance. They are content to be at variance with one another.

If they were consecrated to the work of the Master, they would not be striving and contending like a family of unruly children. Every hand would be engaged in service. Everyone would be standing at his post of duty, working with heart and soul as a missionary of the cross of Christ. The spirit of the Redeemer would abide in the hearts of the laborers, and works of righteousness would be wrought. The workers would carry with them into their service the prayers and sympathy of an awakened church. They would receive their directions from Christ and would find no time for strife and contention.

Messages would come from lips touched with a live coal from the divine altar. Earnest, purified words would be spoken. Humble, heartbroken intercessions would ascend to heaven. With one hand the workers would take hold of Christ, while with the other they would grasp sinners and draw them to the Saviour.

"This gospel of the kingdom shall be preached in all the world for a witness unto all nations; and then shall the end come." Matthew 24:14.

"If thou forbear to deliver them that are drawn unto death, and those that are ready to be slain; if thou sayest, Behold, we knew it not; doth not He that pondereth the heart consider it? and He that keepeth thy soul, doth not He know it? and shall not He render to every man according to his works?" Proverbs 24:11, 12.

5. The Work at Home and Abroad

St. Helena, California, August 7, 1902.

"Say not ye, There are yet four months, and then cometh harvest? behold, I say unto you, Lift up your eyes, and look on the fields; for they are white already to harvest. And he that reapeth receiveth wages, and gathered fruit unto life eternal: that both he that soweth and he that reapeth may rejoice together. And herein is that saying true, One soweth, and another reapeth." John 4:35-37.

Section 1: Present Opportunities

After sowing the seed, the husbandman is compelled to wait for months for it to germinate and develop into grain ready to be harvested. But in sowing it he is encouraged by the expectation of fruit in the future. His labor is lightened with the hope of good returns in the time of reaping.

Not so with the seeds of truth sown by Christ in the mind of the Samaritan woman during His conversation with her at the well. The harvest of His seed sowing was not remote, but immediate. Scarcely were His words spoken, before the seed thus sown sprang up and produced fruit, awakening her understanding, and enabling her to know that she had been conversing with the Lord Jesus Christ. She let the rays of divine light shine into her heart.

Forgetting her water pitcher, she hastened away to communicate the good news to her Samaritan brethren. "Come," she said, "see a man, which told me all the things that ever I did." Verse 29. And they came out at once to see Him. It was then that He likened the souls of these Samaritans to a field of grain. "'Lift up your eyes,' He said to His disciples, and look on the fields; for they are white already to harvest."

"So when the Samaritans were come unto Him, they besought Him that He would tarry with them: and He abode there two days." And what busy days these were! What is the record of the result? "And many more believed because of His own word; and said unto the woman, Now we believe, not because of thy saying: for we have heard Him ourselves, and know that this is indeed the Christ, the Saviour of the world." Verses 40-42.

Christ, in opening to the minds of the Samaritans the word of life, sowed many seeds of truth and showed the people how they, too, could sow seeds of truth in the minds of others. How much good might be accomplished if all who know the truth would labor for sinners, for those who need so much to know and understand Bible truth and who would respond to it as readily as the Samaritans responded to the words of Christ! How little do we enter into sympathy with God on the point that should be the strongest bond of union between us and Him-compassion for depraved, guilty, suffering souls, dead in trespasses and sins! If men shared the sympathies of Christ, they would have constant sorrow of heart over the condition of many needy fields, so destitute of workers.

The work in foreign fields is to be carried forward earnestly and intelligently. And the work in the home field is in no wise to be neglected. Let not the fields lying in the shadow of our doors, such as the great cities in our land, be lightly passed over and neglected. These fields are fully as important as any foreign field.

God's encouraging message of mercy should be proclaimed in the cities of America. Men and women living in these cities are rapidly becoming more and still more entangled in their business relations. They are acting wildly in the erection of buildings whose towers reach high into the heavens. Their minds are filled with schemes and ambitious devisings. God is bidding every one of His ministering servants: "Cry aloud, spare not, lift up thy voice like a trumpet, and show My people their transgression, and the house of Jacob their sins." Isaiah 58:1.

Let us thank the Lord that there are a few laborers doing everything possible to raise up some memorials for God in our neglected cities. Let us remember that it is our duty to give these workers encouragement. God is displeased with the lack of appreciation and support shown our faithful workers in our large cities by His people in our own land. The work in the home field is a vital problem just now. The present time is the most favorable opportunity that we shall have to work these fields. In a little while the situation will be much more difficult.

Jesus wept over Jerusalem because of the guilt and obstinacy of His chosen people. He weeps also over the hardheartedness of those who, professing to be co-workers with Him, are content to do nothing. Are those who should appreciate the value of souls carrying, with Christ, a burden of heaviness and constant sorrow, mingled with tears, for the cities of the earth? The destruction of these cities, almost wholly given up to idolatry, is impending. In the great day of final reckoning what answer can be given for neglecting to enter these cities now?

While carrying forward the work in America, may the Lord help us to give to other countries the attention that they ought to have, so that the workers in these fields will not be bound about, unable to leave memorials for God in many places. Let us not allow too many advantages to be absorbed in this country. Let us not continue to neglect our duty toward the millions living in other lands. Let us gain a better understanding of the situation and redeem the past.

My brethren and sisters in America, it may be that in lifting up your eyes to see afar off the fields white unto the harvest, you will receive into your own hearts the abundant grace of God. You who through unbelief have been spiritually poor will, through personal labor, become rich in good works. You will no longer starve your souls in the midst of plenty, but will appropriate the good things God has in store for you. When you begin to realize how destitute of means the laborers are to carry forward the work in foreign fields, you will do what you can to help, and your souls will begin to revive, your spiritual appetite will become healthy, and your mind will be refreshed with the word of God, which is a leaf from the tree of life for the healing of the nations.

In answer to the Lord's inquiry, "Whom shall I send?" Isaiah responded, "Here am I; send me." Isaiah 6:8. You, my brother, my sister, may not be able to go into the Lord's vineyard yourself, but you may furnish the means to send others. Thus you will be putting your money out to the exchangers; and when the Master comes, you will be able to return to Him His own with usury. Your means can be used to send forth and sustain the messengers of God, who by voice and by influence will give the message: "Prepare ye the way of the Lord, make His paths straight." Matthew 3:3. Plans are being made for the advancement of the cause, and now is your time to work.

If you work with self-denial, doing what you can to further the advancement of the cause in new fields, the Lord will help and strengthen and bless you. Trust in the assurance of His presence, which sustains you, and which is light and life. Do all for love of Jesus and the precious souls for whom He has died. Work with a pure, divinely inwrought purpose to glorify God. The Lord sees and understands, and He will use you, despite your weakness, if you offer your talent as a consecrated gift to His service; for in active, disinterested service the weak become strong and enjoy His precious commendation. The joy of the Lord is an element of strength. If you are faithful, the peace that passeth all understanding will be your reward in this life, and in the future life you will enter into the joy of your Lord.

January 23, 1903

I must write something in regard to the way in which our cities in America have been passed by and neglected, cities in which the truth has not been proclaimed. The message must be given to the thousands of foreigners living in these cities in the home field.

I cannot understand why our people have so little burden to take up the work that the Lord has for years been keeping before me, the work of giving the message of present truth in the Southern States. Few have felt that upon them rested the responsibility of taking hold of this work. Our people have failed to enter new territory and to work the cities in the South. Over and over again the Lord has presented the needs of this field, without any special results. I have sometimes felt as if I could no longer bear the burden of this work. I thought that, if men should continue to neglect this work, I would let matters drift and pray that the Lord would have mercy upon the ignorant and those who are out of the way.

But the Lord has a controversy with our ministers and people, and I must speak, placing upon them the burden of the Southern work and of the cities of our land. Who feels heavily burdened to see the message proclaimed in Greater New York and in the many other cities as yet unworked? Not all the means that can be gathered up is to be sent from America to distant lands, while in the home field there exist such providential opportunities to present the truth to millions who have never heard it. Among these millions are the representatives of many nations, many of whom are prepared to receive the message. Much remains to be done within the shadow of our doors—in the cities of California, New York, and many other states.

God says to His people: "Arise, shine; for thy light is come, and the glory of the Lord is risen upon thee." Isaiah 60:1. Why, then, do they feel so little burden to plant the standard of truth in new places? Why do they not obey the word: "Sell that ye have, and give alms; provide yourselves bags which wax not old, a treasure in the heavens that faileth not"? Luke 12:33. Why do they not return to the Lord His own, to be invested in heavenly merchandise? Why is there not a more earnest call for volunteers to enter the whitening harvest field? Unless more is done than has been done for the cities of

Section 1: Present Opportunities

America, ministers and people will have a heavy account to settle with the One who has appointed to every man his work.

We repeat the prayer: "Thy kingdom come. Thy will be done in earth, as it is in heaven." Matthew 6:10. Are we doing our part to answer this prayer? We profess to believe that the commission which Christ gave to His disciples is given also to us. Are we fulfilling it? May God forgive our terrible neglect in not doing the work that as yet we have scarcely touched with the tips of our fingers. When will this work be done? It makes my heart sick and sore to see such blindness on the part of the people of God.

There are thousands in America perishing in ignorance and sin. And looking afar off to some distant field, those who know the truth are indifferently passing by the needy fields close to them. Christ says: "Go work today in My vineyard." "Say not ye, There are yet four months, and then cometh harvest? behold, I say unto you, Lift up your eyes, and look on the fields; for they are white already to harvest." Matthew 21:28; 4:35.

Wake up, wake up, my brethren and sisters, and enter the fields in America that have never been worked. After you have given something for foreign fields, do not think your duty done. There is a work to be done in foreign fields, but there is a work to be done in America that is just as important. In the cities of America there are people of almost every language. These need the light that God has given to His church.

The Lord lives and reigns. Soon He will arise in majesty to shake terribly the earth. A special message is now to be borne, a message that will pierce the spiritual darkness and convict and convert souls. "Haste thee, flee for thy life," is the call to be given to those dwelling in sin. We must now be terribly in earnest. We have not a moment to spend in criticism and accusation. Let those who have done this in the past fall on their knees in prayer, and let them beware how they put their words and their plans in the place of God's words and God's plans.

We have no time for dwelling on matters that are of no importance. Our time should be given to proclaiming the last message of mercy to a guilty world. Men are needed who move under the inspiration of the Spirit of God. The sermons preached by some of our ministers will have to be much more powerful than they are now, or many backsliders will carry a tame, pointless message, which lulls people to sleep. Every discourse should be given under a sense of the awful judgments soon to fall on the world. The message of truth is to be proclaimed by lips touched with a live coal from the divine altar.

My heart is filled with anguish when I think of the tame messages borne by some of our ministers, when they have a message of life and death to bear. The ministers are asleep; the lay members are asleep; and a world is perishing in sin. May God help His people to arouse and walk and work as men and women on the borders of the eternal world. Soon an awful surprise is coming upon the inhabitants of the world. Suddenly, with power and great glory, Christ will come. Then there will be no time to prepare to meet Him. Now is the time for us to give the warning message.

We are stewards, entrusted by our absent Lord with the care of His household and His interests, which He came to this world to serve. He has returned to heaven, leaving us in charge, and He expects us to watch and wait for His appearing. Let us be faithful to our trust, lest coming suddenly He find us sleeping.

6. The Work in Europe

St. Helena, California
December 7, 1902.
To My Brethren in Europe—

I have words to speak to you. The time has come for much to be accomplished in Europe. A large work, such as has been done in America, can be done in Europe. Let sanitariums be established, let hygienic restaurants be started. Let the light of present truth shine forth from the press. Let the work of translating our books go forward. I have been shown that in the European countries lights will be kindled in many places.

There are many places where the Lord's work has not a proper showing. Help is needed in Italy, in France, in Scotland, and in many other countries. A larger work should be done in these places. Laborers are needed. There is talent among God's people in Europe, and the Lord desires this talent to be employed in establishing all through Great Britain and the continent, centers from which the light of His truth may shine forth.

Section 1: Present Opportunities

There is a work to be done in Scandinavia. God is just as willing to work through Scandinavian believers as through American believers.

My brethren, bind up with the Lord God of hosts. Let Him be your fear, and let Him be your dread. The time has come for His work to be enlarged. Troublous times are before us, but if we stand together in Christian fellowship, none striving for supremacy, God will work mightily for us.

Let us be hopeful and courageous. Despondency in God's service is sinful and unreasonable. He knows our every necessity. He has all power. He can bestow upon His servants the measure of efficiency that their need demands. His infinite love and compassion never weary. With the majesty of omnipotence He unites the gentleness and care of a tender shepherd. We need have no fear that He will not fulfill His promises. He is eternal truth. Never will He change the covenant that He has made with those that love Him. His promises to His church stand fast forever. He will make her an eternal excellence, a joy of many generations.

Study the forty-first chapter of Isaiah, and strive to understand it in all its significance. God declares: "I will open rivers in high places, and fountains in the midst of the valleys: I will make the wilderness a pool of water, and the dry land springs of water. I will plant in the wilderness the cedar, the shittah tree, and the myrtle, and the oil tree; I will set in the desert the fir tree, and the pine, and the box tree together: that they may see, and know, and consider, and understand together, that the hand of the Lord hath done this, and the Holy One of Israel hath created it." Isaiah 41:18-20.

He who has chosen Christ has joined himself to a power that no array of human wisdom or strength can overthrow. "Fear thou not; for I am with thee," He declares; "be not dismayed; for I am thy God: I will strengthen thee; yea, I will help thee; yea, I will uphold thee with the right hand of My righteousness." "I the Lord thy God will hold thy right hand, saying unto thee, Fear not; I will help thee." Verses 10, 13.

"To whom then will ye liken Me, or shall I be equal? saith the Holy One. Lift up your eyes on high, and behold who hath created these things, that bringeth out their host by number: He calleth them all by names by the greatness of His might, for that He is strong in power; not one faileth. Why sayest thou, O Jacob, and speakest, O Israel, My way is hid from the Lord, and my judgment is passed over from my God? Hast thou not known? hast thou not heard, that the everlasting God, the Lord, the Creator of the ends of the earth, fainteth not, neither is weary? there is no searching of His understanding. He giveth power to the faint; and to them that have no might He increaseth strength. Even the youths shall faint and be weary, and the young men shall utterly fall: but they that wait upon the Lord shall renew their strength; they shall mount up with wings as eagles; they shall run, and not be weary; and they shall walk, and not faint." Isaiah 40:25-31.

The light of truth is to shine to the ends of the earth. Greater and still greater light is beaming with celestial brightness from the Redeemer's face upon His representatives, to be diffused through the darkness of a benighted world. As laborers together with Him, let us pray for the sanctification of His Spirit, that we may shine more and more brightly.

The light of truth for this time is now shining upon the cabinets of kings. The attention of statesmen is being called to the Bible,—the statute book of the nations,—and they are comparing their national laws with its statutes. As representatives for Christ we have no time to lose. Our efforts are not to be confined to a few places where the light has become so abundant that it is not appreciated. The gospel message is to be proclaimed to all nations and kindreds and tongues and peoples.

7. A View of the Conflict

In vision I saw two armies in terrible conflict. One army was led by banners bearing the world's insignia; the other was led by the bloodstained banner of Prince Immanuel. Standard after standard was left to trail in the dust as company after company from the Lord's army joined the foe and tribe after tribe from the ranks of the enemy united with the commandment-keeping people of God. An angel flying in the midst of heaven put the standard of Immanuel into many hands, while a mighty general cried out with a loud voice: "Come into line. Let those who are loyal to the commandments of God and the testimony of Christ now take their position. Come out from among them, and be ye separate, and touch not the unclean, and I will receive you, and will be a Father unto you, and ye shall be My sons and daughters. Let all

Section 1: Present Opportunities

who will come up to the help of the Lord, to the help of the Lord against the mighty."

The battle raged. Victory alternated from side to side. Now the soldiers of the cross gave way, "as when a standardbearer fainteth." Isaiah 10:18. But their apparent retreat was but to gain a more advantageous position. Shouts of joy were heard. A song of praise to God went up, and angel voices united in the song, as Christ's soldiers planted His banner on the walls of fortresses till then held by the enemy. The Captain of our salvation was ordering the battle and sending support to His soldiers. His power was mightily displayed, encouraging them to press the battle to the gates. He taught them terrible things in righteousness as He led them on step by step, conquering and to conquer.

At last the victory was gained. The army following the banner with the inscription, "The commandments of God, and the faith of Jesus," was gloriously triumphant. The soldiers of Christ were close beside the gates of the city, and with joy the city received her King. The kingdom of peace and joy and everlasting righteousness was established.

Now the church is militant. Now we are confronted with a world in midnight darkness, almost wholly given over to idolatry. But the day is coming in which the battle will have been fought, the victory won. The will of God is to be done on earth, as it is done in heaven. Then the nations will own no other law than the law of heaven. All will be a happy, united family, clothed with the garments of praise and thanksgiving —the robe of Christ's righteousness. All nature, in its surpassing loveliness, will offer to God a constant tribute of praise and adoration. The world will be bathed in the light of heaven. The years will move on in gladness. The light of the moon will be as the light of the sun, and the light of the sun will be sevenfold greater than it is now. Over the scene the morning stars will sing together, and the sons of God will shout for joy, while God and Christ will unite in proclaiming: "There shall be no more sin, neither shall there be any more death."

This is the scene that is presented to me. But the church must and will fight against seen and unseen foes. Satan's agencies in human form are on the ground. Men have confederated to oppose the Lord of hosts. These confederacies will continue until Christ shall leave His place of intercession before the mercy seat and shall put on the garments of vengeance. Satanic agencies are in every city, busily organizing into parties those opposed to the law of God. Professed saints and avowed unbelievers take their stand with these parties. This is no time for the people of God to be weaklings. We cannot afford to be off our guard for one moment.

"Be strong in the Lord, and in the power of His might. Put on the whole armor of God, that ye may be able to stand against the wiles of the devil. For we wrestle not against flesh and blood, but against principalities, against powers, against the rulers of the darkness of this world, against spiritual wickedness in high places. Wherefore take unto you the whole armor of God, that ye may be able to withstand in the evil day, and having done all, to stand. Stand therefore, having your loins girt about with truth, and having on the breastplate of righteousness; and your feet shod with the preparation of the gospel of peace; above all, taking the shield of faith, wherewith ye shall be able to quench all the fiery darts of the wicked. And take the helmet of salvation, and the sword of the Spirit, which is the word of God." Ephesians 6:10-17.

"This I pray, that your love may abound yet more and more in knowledge and in all judgment; that ye may approve things that are excellent; that ye may be sincere and without offense till the day of Christ; being filled with the fruits of righteousness, which are by Jesus Christ, unto the glory and praise of God." Philippians 1:9-11.

"Let your conversation be as it becometh the gospel of Christ: ... stand fast in one spirit, with one mind striving together for the faith of the gospel; and in nothing terrified by your adversaries: which is to them an evident token of perdition, but to you of salvation, and that of God. For unto you it is given in the behalf of Christ, not only to believe on Him, but also to suffer for His sake." Verses 27-29.

There are revealed in these last days visions of future glory, scenes pictured by the hand of God, and these should be dear to His church. What sustained the Son of God in His betrayal and trial? He saw of the travail of His soul and was satisfied. He caught a view of the expanse of eternity and saw the happiness of those who through His humiliation should receive pardon and everlasting life. He was wounded for their transgressions, bruised for their iniquities. The chastisement of their peace was upon Him, and with His stripes they were healed. His ear caught the shout of the redeemed. He heard the ransomed ones singing the song of Moses and the Lamb.

We must have a vision of the future and of the blessedness of heaven. Stand on the threshold of eternity, and hear the gracious welcome given to those who in this life have cooperated with Christ, regarding it as a privilege and an honor to suffer for His sake. As they unite with the angels, they cast their crowns at the feet of the Redeemer, exclaiming: "Worthy is the Lamb that was slain to receive power, and riches, and wisdom, and strength, and honor, and glory, and blessing... Honor, and glory, and power, be unto Him that sitteth upon the throne, and unto the Lamb for ever and ever." Revelation 5:12, 13.

There the redeemed ones greet those who directed them to the uplifted Saviour. They unite in praising Him who died that human beings might have the life that measures with the life of God. The conflict is over. All tribulation and strife are at an end. Songs of victory fill all heaven as the redeemed stand around the throne of God. All take up the joyful strain: "Worthy, worthy is the Lamb that was slain, and lives again, a triumphant conqueror."

"I beheld, and, lo, a great multitude, which no man could number, of all nations, and kindreds, and people, and tongues, stood before the throne, and before the Lamb, clothed with white robes, and palms in their hands; and cried with a loud voice, saying, Salvation to our God which sitteth upon the throne, and unto the Lamb." Revelation 7:9, 10.

"These are they which came out of great tribulation, and have washed their robes, and made them white in the blood of the Lamb. Therefore are they before the throne of God, and serve Him day and night in His temple: and He that sitteth on the throne shall dwell among them. They shall hunger no more, neither thirst any more; neither shall the sun light on them, nor any heat. For the Lamb which is in the midst of the throne shall feed them, and shall lead them unto living fountains of waters: and God shall wipe away all tears from their eyes." "And there shall be no more death, neither sorrow, nor crying, neither shall there be any more pain: for the former things are passed away." Verses 14-17; 21:4.

Will you catch the inspiration of the vision? Will you let your mind dwell upon the picture? Will you not be truly converted, and then go forth to labor in a spirit entirely different from the spirit in which you have labored in the past, displacing the enemy, breaking down every barrier to the advancement of the gospel, filling hearts with the light and peace and joy of the Lord? Shall not the miserable spirit of faultfinding and murmuring be buried, never to have a resurrection? Shall not the incense of praise and thanksgiving ascend from hearts purified and sanctified and glorified by the presence of Christ? Shall we not in faith lay hold of sinners and bring them to the cross?

Who will now consecrate themselves to the service of the Lord? Who will now pledge themselves not to affiliate with the world, but to come out from the world and be separate, refusing to pollute the soul with the worldly schemes and practices that have been keeping the church under the enemy's influence?

We are in this world to lift the cross of self-denial. As we lift this cross we shall find that it lifts us. Let every Christian stand in his place, catching the inspiration of the work that Christ did for souls while in this world. We need the ardor of the Christian hero, who can endure the seeing of Him who is invisible. Our faith is to have a resurrection. The soldiers of the cross are to exert a positive influence for good. Christ says: "He that is not with Me is against Me; and he that gathereth not with Me scattereth abroad." Matthew 12:30. Indifference in the Christian life is a manifest denial of the Saviour.

Should we not see in the world today Christians who in all the features of their work are worthy of the name they bear? Who aspire to the doing of deeds worthy of valiant soldiers of the cross? We are living near the close of the great conflict, when many souls are to be rescued from the slavery of sin. We are living in a time when to Christ's followers the promise specially belongs: "Lo, I am with you alway, even unto the end." Matthew 28:20. He who commanded the light to shine out of darkness, He who has called us out of darkness into His marvelous light, bids us let our light shine brightly before men, that they may see our good works and glorify our Father who is in heaven. In such rich measure has light been given to God's people that Christ is justified in telling them that they are to be the light of the world.

Section 1: Present Opportunities

To our physicians and ministers I send the message: Lay hold of the Lord's work as if you believed the truth for this time. Medical missionary workers and workers in the gospel ministry are to be bound together by indissoluble ties. Their work is to be done with freshness and power. Throughout our churches there is to be a reconversion and a reconsecration to service. Shall we not, in our work in the future and in the gatherings that we hold, be of one accord? Shall we not wrestle with God in prayer, asking for the Holy Spirit to come into every heart?

The presence of Christ, manifest among us, would cure the leprosy of unbelief that has made our service so weak and inefficient. We need the breath of the divine life breathed into us. We are to be channels through which the Lord can send light and grace to the world. Backsliders are to be reclaimed. We are to put away our sins, by confession and repentance humbling our proud hearts before God. Floods of spiritual power are to be poured forth upon those prepared to receive it.

If we but realized how earnestly Jesus worked to sow the world with gospel seed, we, living at the very close of probation, would labor untiringly to give the bread of life to perishing souls. Why are we so cold and indifferent? Why are our hearts so unimpressible? Why are we so unwilling to give ourselves to the work to which Christ consecrated His life? Something must be done to cure the terrible indifference that has taken hold upon us. Let us bow our heads in humiliation as we see how much less we have done than we might have done to sow the seeds of truth.

My dear brethren and sisters, I speak to you in words of love and tenderness. Arouse and consecrate yourselves unreservedly to the work of giving the light of truth for this time to those in darkness. Catch the spirit of the great Master Worker. Learn from the Friend of sinners how to minister to sin-sick souls. Remember that in the lives of His followers must be seen the same devotion, the same subjection to God's work, of every social claim, every earthly affection, that was seen in His life. God's claims must always be made paramount. Christ's example is to inspire us to put forth unceasing effort for the good of others.

God calls upon every church member to enter His service. Truth that is not lived, that is not imparted to others, loses its life-giving power, its healing virtue. Everyone must learn to work and to stand in his place as a burden bearer. Every addition to the church should be one more agency for the carrying out of the great plan of redemption. The entire church, acting as one, blending in perfect union, is to be a living, active missionary agency, moved and controlled by the Holy Spirit.

It is not alone by men in high positions of responsibility, not alone by men holding positions on boards or committees, not alone by the managers of our sanitariums and publishing houses, that the work is to be done which will cause the earth to be filled with the knowledge of the Lord as the waters cover the sea. This work can be accomplished only by the whole church acting their part under the guidance and in the power of Christ.

— Section 2 —

Counsels Often Repeated

"The Lord God of their fathers sent to them by His messengers, rising up betimes, and sending; because He had compassion on His people, and on His dwelling place." 2 Chronicles 36:15.

8. Warnings and Counsels Given to Battle Creek Church

Granville, N. S. W.
July 20, 1894.

I wish to remind my brethren of the cautions and warnings that have been given me in reference to constantly investing means in Battle Creek in order to make a little more room or to make things more convenient. New fields are to be entered; the truth is to be proclaimed as a witness to all nations. The work is hindered so that the banner of truth cannot be uplifted, as it should be, in these new fields. While our brethren in America feel at liberty to invest means in buildings which time will reveal that they would do just as well and even better without, thousands of dollars are thus absorbed that the Lord called for to be used in "regions beyond."

I have presented the warnings and the caution, as the word of the Lord; but my heart has been made sad to see that, notwithstanding all these, means has been swallowed up to satisfy these supposed wants; building has been added to building so the money could not be used in places where they have no conveniences, no building for the public worship of God or to give character to the work, no place where the banner of truth could be uplifted. These things I have set before you; and yet you have gone on just the same, absorbing means, God's means, in one locality, when the Lord has spoken that too much was already invested in one place, which meant that there was nothing in other places, where there should be buildings and facilities, to make even a beginning.

What call had you to invest thousands of dollars in additional school buildings? You supposed that this outlay was needed, but did not entreaties come to you not to invest money thus?

- **The Time of the End**

I was shown that a terrible condition of things exists in our world. The angel of mercy is folding her wings, ready to depart. Already the Lord's restraining power is being withdrawn from the earth, and Satan is seeking to stir up the various elements in the religious world, leading men to place themselves under the training of the great deceiver, who work with all deceivableness of unrighteousness in the children of disobedience. Already the inhabitants of the earth are marshaling under the leading of the prince of darkness, and this is but the beginning of the end.

The law of God is made void. We see and hear of confusion and perplexity, want and famine, earthquakes and floods; terrible outrages will be committed by men; passion, not reason, bears sway. The wrath of God is upon the inhabitants of the world, who are fast becoming as corrupt as were the inhabitants of Sodom and Gomorrah. Already fire and flood are destroying thousands of lives and the property that has been selfishly accumulated by the oppression of the poor. The Lord is soon to cut short His work and put an end to sin.

Oh, that the scenes which have come before me of the iniquities practiced in these last days, might make a deep impression on the minds of God's professing people. As it was in the days of Noah, so shall it be when the Son of man shall be revealed. The Lord is removing His restrictions from the earth, and soon there will be death and destruction, increasing crime, and cruel, evil working against the rich who have exalted themselves against the poor. Those who are without God's protection will find no safety in any place or position. Human agents are being trained and are using their inventive power to put in operation the most powerful machinery to wound and to kill.

Instead of our enlarging and erecting additional buildings in Battle Creek or other places where our institutions are already established, there should be a limiting of the wants. Let the means and the workers be scattered to represent the truth and give the warning message in "regions beyond."

- ## Help in Time of Trouble

When the children of Israel were journeying through the wilderness, the Lord protected them from venomous serpents; but the time came when, because of Israel's transgression, impenitence, and stubbornness, the Lord removed His restraining power from these reptiles, and many of the people were bitten and died. Then it was that the brazen serpent was uplifted, that all who repented and looked to it in faith might live.

In the time of confusion and trouble before us, a time of trouble such as has not been since there was a nation, the uplifted Saviour will be presented to the people in all lands, that all who look to Him in faith may live.

- ## A Failure to Honor God

In view of the terrible crisis before us what are those doing who profess to believe the truth? I was called by my Guide, who said, "Follow Me," and I was shown things among our people that were not in accordance with their faith. There seemed to be a bicycle craze. Money was spent to gratify an enthusiasm in this direction that might better, far better, have been invested in building houses of worship where they are greatly needed. There were presented before me some very strange things in Battle Creek. A bewitching influence seemed to be passing as a wave over our people there, and I saw that this would be followed by other temptations. Satan works with intensity of purpose to induce our people to invest their time and money in gratifying supposed wants. This is a species of idolatry. The example will be followed, and while hundreds are starving for bread, while famine and pestilence are seen and felt, because God cannot, according to His own name's glory, protect those who are working contrary to His will, shall those who profess to love and serve God act as did the people in the days of Noah, following the imagination of their hearts?

While you have been gratifying your inclination in the appropriation of money-God's money-for which you must give an account, missionary work has been hindered and bound about for want of means and workers to plant the banner of truth in places where the people have never heard the message of warning. Will God say to those who are selfishly pleasing their own imagination and gratifying their own desires: "Well done, good and faithful servant; thou hast been faithful over a few things, I will make thee ruler over many things: enter thou into the joy of thy Lord"? Matthew 25:23.

My brethren and sisters in Battle Creek, what kind of witness are you bearing to an unbelieving world? I have been shown that the Lord does not look upon your course with favor, for your practice contradicts your profession. You are not doers of the words of Christ.

I was told by my Guide: "Look ye, and behold the idolatry of My people, to whom I have been speaking, rising up early, and presenting to them their dangers. I looked that they should bring forth fruit." There were some who were striving for the mastery, each trying to excel the other in the swift running of their bicycles. There was a spirit of strife and contention among them as to which should be the greatest. The spirit was similar to that manifested in the baseball games on the college ground. Said my Guide: "These things are an offense to God. Both near and afar off souls are perishing for the bread of life and the water of salvation." When Satan is defeated in one line, he will be all ready with other schemes and plans which will appear attractive and needful, and which will absorb money and thought, and encourage selfishness, so that he can overcome those who are so easily led into a false and selfish indulgence.

The question arises: What burden do these persons carry for the advancement of the work of God? Wherein do they realize the importance of the work for this time? Christ said to His disciples: "Ye are the light of the world... Let your light so shine before men, that they may see your good works, and glorify your Father which is in heaven." Matthew 5:14-16. Is this investment of means and this spinning of bicycles through the streets of

Battle Creek giving evidence of the genuineness of your faith in the last solemn warning to be given to human beings standing on the very verge of the eternal world?

My brethren and sisters in America, I make my appeal to you. "Be not deceived; God is not mocked: for whatsoever a man soweth, that shall he also reap." Galatians 6:7. The lives of many are too delicate and dainty. They know nothing of bearing hardship as good soldiers of Christ. They are hindrances to the work of soul saving. They have many wants; everything must be convenient and easy, to suit their taste. They will not do anything themselves, and those who would do something they hinder by their suppositions and imaginary wants, and their love of idols. They think themselves Christians, but they do not know what practical Christian life signifies. What does it mean to be a Christian? It means to be Christlike.

When the Lord sees His people restricting their imaginary wants and practicing self-denial, not in a mournful, regretful spirit, as Lot's wife left Sodom, but joyfully, for Christ's sake, and because it is the right thing to do, the work will go forward with power. Let nothing, however dear, however loved, absorb your mind and affections, diverting you from the study of God's word or from earnest prayer. Watch unto prayer. Live your own requests. Co-operate with God by working in harmony with Him. Expel from the soul-temple everything that assumes the form of an idol. Now is God's time, and His time is your time. Fight the good fight of faith, refusing to think or to talk unbelief. The world is to hear the last warning message.

9. Our Duty to the World

Granville, N. S. W. 1894.

There should be a decided change in the spirit and character of the work in the places where men and women have received increased light. What are they doing to warn those who do not understand that the Lord is soon coming? "Behold, the Lord cometh out of His place to punish the inhabitants of the earth for their iniquity: the earth also shall disclose her blood, and shall no more cover her slain." Isaiah 26:21. Who, I ask, is carrying a burden for the souls that are perishing out of Christ? Who will go forth without the camp, bearing the reproach? Who will leave pleasant homes and dear ties of relationship, and carry the precious light of truth to far-off lands? Every day, every moment, comes to those to whom have been entrusted the light of truth, weighted with the terrible significance that men and women in every land are preparing themselves for weal or for woe, fixing their destiny for eternity.

God has made amazing sacrifices for human beings. He has expended mighty energy to reclaim man from transgression and sin to loyalty and obedience, but I have been shown that He does nothing without the cooperation of human agencies. Every endowment of grace and power and efficiency has been liberally provided. The strongest motives have been presented to arouse and keep alive in the human heart the missionary spirit, that efforts of divine and human agencies may be combined.

But what have our people done in regard to moving out of Battle Creek, to carry the light to regions where the standard has never yet been planted? Did not the Lord at the recent Conference open the windows of heaven and pour you out a blessing? What use have you made of the gift of God? He has supplied you with the motive force of action, that with patience and hope and untiring vigilance you might set forth Christ and Him crucified, calling men to repent of their sins, sounding the note of warning that Christ is soon to come with power and great glory.

If the members of the Battle Creek church do not arouse now and go to work in missionary fields, they will fall back into deathlike slumber. How did the Holy Spirit work upon your hearts? ... Were you not inspired to exercise the talents God has given you, that every man and woman and youth should employ them to set forth the truth for this time, making personal efforts, going into the cities where the truth has never been proclaimed, and lifting up the standard?

Have not your energies been quickened by the blessing that God has bestowed upon you? Has not the truth been more deeply impressed upon your soul? Can you not see more clearly its relative importance to those who are perishing out of Christ? Since the manifest revealing of God's blessing, are you witnessing for Christ more distinctly and decidedly than ever before?

The Holy Spirit has brought decidedly to your minds the important, vital truths for this time. Is this knowledge to be bound up in a napkin and hidden in the earth? No, no. It is to be put out to the exchangers. As man uses his talents, however small, with faithfulness, the Holy Spirit takes the things of God, and presents them anew to the mind. Through His Spirit God makes His word a vivifying power. It is quick and powerful, exerting a strong influence upon minds, not because of the learning or intelligence of the human agent, but because divine power is working with the human power. And it is to the divine power that all praise is to be given.

Shall the selfishness and the ease of those who have earthly comforts and attractive homes allure us? Shall we cease as moral agencies to use our powers to the saving of souls? Shall our voices be indistinct? Then God will put His curse upon us who have had so great light, and inscribe upon the walls of our homes: "Lovers of pleasures more than lovers of God." 2 Timothy 3:4. He will put a tongue in the stones, and they will speak; but God commands of you in Battle Creek to go forth.

- **How to Gain Success**

Resolve, not in your own strength, but in the strength and grace given of God, that you will consecrate to Him now, just now, every power, every ability. You will then follow Jesus because He bids you, and you will not ask where, or what reward will be given. It will be well with you as you obey the word: "Follow Me." Your part is to lead others to the light by judicious, faithful efforts. Under the guardianship of the divine Leader, will to do, resolve to act, without a moment's hesitation.

When you die to self, when you surrender to God, to do His work, to let the light that He has given you shine forth in good works, you will not labor alone. God's grace stands forth to co-operate with every effort to enlighten the ignorant and those who do not know that the end of all things is at hand. But God will not do your work. Light may shine in abundance, but the grace given will convert your soul only as it arouses you to co-operate with divine agencies. You are called upon to put on the Christian armor and enter the Lord's service as active soldiers. Divine power is to co-operate with human effort to break the spell of worldly enchantment that the enemy has cast upon souls.

Again I call for the help that we ought to have had, the means that we must have, if anything is accomplished in this country. Let your hearts be drawn out in love for perishing souls. Obey the impulse given by High Heaven. Grieve not the Holy Spirit by delay. Resist not God's methods of recovering souls from the thralldom of sin. To every man, according to his several ability, is given his work. Do your best, and God will accept your efforts.

10. Missionary Work at Home and Abroad

God's field is the world. Jesus said to His disciples: "Ye shall receive power, after that the Holy Ghost is come upon you: and ye shall be witnesses unto Me both in Jerusalem, and in all Judea and in Samaria, and unto the uttermost part of the earth." "And that repentance and remission of sins should be preached in His name among all nations, beginning at Jerusalem." Acts 1:8; Luke 24:47. Peter said to the believers: "The promise is unto you, and to your children, and to all that are afar off, even as many as the Lord our God shall call." Acts 2:39.

God declares: "I will sow her unto Me in the earth; and I will have mercy upon her that had not obtained mercy; and I will say to them which were not My people, Thou art My people; and they shall say, Thou art my God." Hosea 2:23. "And He said, It is a light thing that Thou shouldest be My Servant to raise up the tribes of Jacob, and to restore the preserved of Israel: I will also give Thee for a light to the Gentiles, that Thou mayest be My salvation unto the end of the earth." Isaiah 49:6.

God has poured out richly of His Holy Spirit upon the believers in Battle Creek. What use have you made of these blessings? Have you done as did the men upon whom the Holy Spirit came on the Day of Pentecost? Then "they that were scattered abroad went everywhere preaching the word." Acts 8:4. Has this fruit been seen in Battle Creek? Have the church been taught of God to know their duty, and to reflect the light which they have received?

Section 2: Counsels Often Repeated

- **An Illustration of the Work We Are to Do**

"When the apostles which were at Jerusalem heard that Samaria had received the word of God, they sent unto them Peter and John." Verse 14. The Spirit of God was waiting to enlighten souls and convert them to the truth.

Notice how much effort was put forth for just one man, an Ethiopian. "The angel of the Lord spake unto Philip, saying, Arise, and go toward the south unto the way that goeth down from Jerusalem unto Gaza, which is desert. And he arose and went: and, behold, a man of Ethiopia, an eunuch of great authority under Candace queen of the Ethiopians, who had the charge of all her treasure, and had come to Jerusalem for to worship, was returning, and sitting in his chariot read Esaias the prophet."

"Then the Spirit said unto Philip, Go near, and join thyself to this chariot. And Philip ran thither to him, and heard him read the prophet Esaias, and said, Understandest thou what thou readest? And he said, How can I, except some man should guide me? And he desired Philip that he would come up and sit with him..."

"Then Philip ... began at the same scripture, and preached unto him Jesus. And as they went on their way, they came unto a certain water: and the eunuch said, See, here is water; what doth hinder me to be baptized? And Philip said, If thou believest with all thine heart, thou mayest. And he answered and said, I believe that Jesus Christ is the Son of God."

"And he commanded the chariot to stand still: and they went down both into the water, both Philip and the eunuch; and he baptized him."

"And when they were come up out of the water, the Spirit of the Lord caught away Philip, that the eunuch saw him no more: and he went on his way rejoicing. But Philip was found at Azotus: and passing through he preached in all the cities, till he came to Caesarea." Acts 8:26-40.

In the experience of Philip and the Ethiopian is presented the work to which the Lord calls His people. The Ethiopian represents a large class who need missionaries like Philip, missionaries who will hear the voice of God and go where He sends them. There are those in the world who are reading the Scriptures, but who cannot understand their import. The men and women who have a knowledge of God are needed to explain the word to these souls.

• A Neglected Work

In the parable of the good Samaritan the priest and the Levite looked on the wretched man who had been robbed and wounded, but it did not seem to them desirable to help the one who, because he was helpless and forsaken, most needed help. The priest and the Levite represent many, many in Battle Creek.

Many souls can be saved if the Southern field can have but a small part of the means so lavishly expended in Battle Creek to make things more convenient.

The Lord's heritage has been strangely neglected, and God will judge His people for this thing. Pride and the love of display are gratified by the accumulated advantages, while new fields are left untouched. The rebuke of God is upon the managers for their partiality and selfish appropriation of His goods.

Something has been done in foreign missions, and something in home missions; but altogether too much territory has been left unworked. The work is too much centralized. The interests in Battle Creek are overgrown, and this means that other portions of the field are robbed of facilities which they should have had. The larger and still larger preparations, in the erection and enlargement of buildings, which have called together and held so large a number in Battle Creek, are not in accordance with God's plan, but in direct contravention of His plan.

It has been urged that there were great advantages in having so many institutions in close connection, that they would be a strength to one another and could afford help to those seeking education and employment. This is according to human reasoning; it will be admitted that, from a human point of view, many advantages are gained by crowding so many responsibilities in Battle Creek; but the vision needs to be extended.

These interests should be broken up into many parts in order that the work may start in cities which it will be necessary to make centers of interest.

Buildings should be erected and responsibilities centered in many localities that are now robbed of vital, spiritual interest in order to swell the overplus already in Battle Creek. The Lord is not glorified by this management on the part of those who are in responsible positions. "The earth shall be filled with the knowledge of the glory of the Lord, as the waters cover the sea." "And this is life eternal, that they might know Thee the only true God, and Jesus Christ, whom Thou hast sent." Habakkuk 2:14; John 17:3.

The salvation of the heathen has long been deemed a matter that should engage the interest of Christians, and it is not more than justice to bring light to their dark borders. But home missionary work is just as much needed. The heathen are brought to our very doors. Idolatrous ignorance is within the very shadow of our homes. Something is being done for the colored people, but next to nothing compared with what others receive who already have a knowledge of the truth, who have had opportunities innumerable, but who have not half appreciated their advantages. To those who know not the truth, let the love of Jesus be presented, and it will work like leaven for the transformation of character.

What are we doing for the Southern field? I have looked most anxiously to see if some plan would not be set in operation to redeem the sinful neglect of that field, but I see not a proposition or a resolution to do anything. Perhaps something has been planned that I have not seen. I hope so, and praise the Lord if it is so. But though for years our duty has been laid out in a most decided manner, yet the Southern field has been touched only with the tips of our fingers. I now feel deeply in earnest in again bringing before you this neglected portion of the Lord's vineyard. This matter is brought before me again and again. I have been awakened in the night season, and the command has come: Write the things that I have opened before you, whether men will hear or whether they will forbear.

11. The Holy Spirit in our Schools

Cooranbong, N. S. W.
May 10, 1896.

I ask you who are living at the very heart of the work to review the experience of years and see if the well "done" can be truthfully spoken of you. I ask the teachers in our schools to consider carefully, prayerfully: Have I individually watched for my own soul as one who is co-operating with God for its purification from all sin and its entire sanctification? Can you by precept and example teach the youth sanctification, through the truth, unto holiness?

Have you not been afraid of the Holy Spirit? At times this Spirit has come with all-pervading influence into the school at Battle Creek and into the schools at other places. Did you recognize His presence? Did you accord Him the honor due to a heavenly messenger? When the Spirit seemed to be striving with the youth, did you say: "Let us put aside all study, for it is evident that we have among us a heavenly guest? Let us give praise and honor to God." Did you, with contrite hearts, bow in prayer with your students, pleading that you might receive the blessing that the Lord was presenting to you?

The Great Teacher Himself was among you. Did you honor Him? Was He a stranger to some of the educators? Was there need to send for someone of supposed authority to welcome or repel this Messenger from heaven? Though unseen, His presence was among you. But was not the thought expressed that in school the time ought to be given to study, and that there was a time for everything, as if the hours devoted to common study were too precious to be given up for the working of the heavenly messenger?

If you have in any way restricted or repulsed the Holy Spirit, I entreat you to repent as quickly as possible. If any of our teachers have not opened the door of the heart to the Spirit of God, but have closed and padlocked it, I urge them to unlock the door and pray with earnestness: "Abide with me." When the Holy Spirit reveals His presence in your school room, say to your students: "The Lord signifies that He has for us today a lesson of heavenly import, of more value than our lessons in ordinary lines. Let us listen; let us bow before God and seek Him with the whole heart."

Let me tell you what I know of this heavenly Guest. The Holy Spirit was brooding over the youth during the school hours; but some hearts were so cold and dark that they had no desire for the Spirit's presence, and the light of God was withdrawn. That heavenly Visitant would have opened all understanding, would have given wisdom and knowledge in all lines of study that could be employed to the glory of God. The Lord's messenger came to convince of sin and to soften hearts hardened by long estrangement from God. He came to reveal the great love wherewith God has loved those youth. They are God's heritage, and educators need the "higher education" before they are qualified to be teachers and guides of youth.

The teacher may understand many things in regard to the physical universe; he may know all about the structure of living things, the inventions of mechanical art, the discoveries of natural science; but he cannot be called educated unless he has a knowledge of the only true God and of Jesus Christ, whom He has sent.

A principle of divine origin must pervade our conduct and bind us to God. This will not be in any way a hindrance to the study of true science. The fear of the Lord is the beginning of wisdom, and the man who consents to be molded and fashioned after the divine similitude is the noblest specimen of the work of God. All who live in communion with our Creator will have an understanding of His design in their creation, and they will realize that God holds them accountable to employ their faculties to the very best purpose. They will seek neither to glorify nor to depreciate themselves.

- **The Will of God Concerning Us**

The knowledge of God is obtained from His word. The experimental knowledge of true godliness, found in daily consecration and service, ensures the highest culture of body, mind, and soul. This consecration of all our powers to God prevents self-exaltation. The impartation of divine power honors our sincere striving after wisdom that will enable us to use our highest faculties in a way that will honor God and bless our fellow men. As these faculties are derived from God, and not self-created, they should be appreciated as talents from God to be employed in His service.

The heaven-entrusted faculties of the mind are to be treated as the higher powers, to rule the kingdom of the body. The natural appetites and passions are to be brought under the control of the conscience and the spiritual powers.

The religion of Christ never degrades the receiver; it never makes him coarse or rough, discourteous or self-important, passionate or hardhearted. On the contrary, it refines the taste, sanctifies the judgment, and purifies and ennobles the thoughts, bringing them into captivity to Christ. God's ideal for His children is higher than the highest human thought can reach. He has given in His holy law a transcript of His character.

Christ is the greatest Teacher that the world has ever known. And what is the standard that He holds before all who believe in Him? "Be ye therefore perfect, even as your Father which is in heaven is perfect." Matthew 5:48. As God is perfect in His sphere, so man may be perfect in his sphere.

The ideal of Christian character is Christlikeness. There is opened before us a path of constant advancement. We have an object to gain, a standard to reach, that includes everything good and pure and noble and elevated. There should be continual striving and constant progress onward and upward toward perfection of character.

Paul says: "I count not myself to have apprehended: but this one thing I do, forgetting those things which are behind, and reaching forth unto those things which are before, I press toward the mark for the prize of the high calling of God in Christ Jesus." Philippians 3:13, 14.

This is the will of God concerning human beings, even their sanctification. In urging our way upward, heavenward, every faculty must be kept in the most healthy condition, prepared to do faithful service. The powers with which God has endowed man are to be put to the stretch. "Thou shalt love the Lord thy God with all thy heart, and with all thy soul, and with all thy strength, and with all thy mind; and thy neighbor as thyself." Luke 10:27. Man cannot possibly do this of himself; he must have divine aid. What part is the human agent to act? "Work out your own salvation with fear and trembling. For it is God which worketh in you both to will and to do of His good pleasure." Philippians 2:12, 13.

Without the divine working, man could do no good thing. God calls every man to repentance, yet man cannot even repent unless the Holy Spirit works upon his heart. But the Lord wants no man to wait until he thinks that he has repented before he takes steps toward Jesus. The Saviour is continually drawing men to repentance; they need only to submit to be drawn, and their hearts will be melted in penitence.

Man is allotted a part in this great struggle for everlasting life; he must respond to the working of the Holy Spirit. It will require a struggle to break through the powers of darkness, and the Spirit works in him to accomplish this. But man is no passive being, to be saved in indolence. He is called upon to strain every muscle and exercise every faculty in the struggle for immortality; yet it is God that supplies the efficiency. No human being can be saved in indolence. The Lord bids us: "Strive to enter in at the strait gate: for many, I say unto you, will seek to enter in, and shall not be able." "Wide is the gate, and broad is the way, that leadeth to destruction, and many there be which go in thereat: because strait is the gate, and narrow is the way, which leadeth unto life, and few there be that find it." Luke 13:24; Matthew 7:13, 14.

- **Working Against the Holy Spirit**

I entreat the students in our schools to be sober-minded. The frivolity of the young is not pleasing to God. Their sports and games open the door to a flood of temptation. In your intellectual faculties you are in possession of God's heavenly endowment, and you should not allow your thoughts to be cheap and low. A character formed in accordance with the precepts of God's word will reveal steadfast principles, pure, noble aspirations. When the Holy Spirit co-operates with the powers of the human mind, high, holy impulses are the sure result...

God sees that which the blind eyes of educators cannot discern, that immorality of every kind and degree is striving for the mastery, working against the manifestations of the power of the Holy Spirit. The commonest of conversation, and cheap, perverted ideas, are woven into the texture of the character.

Parties for frivolous, worldly pleasure, gatherings for eating, drinking, and singing, are inspired by a spirit that is from beneath. They are an oblation to Satan. The exhibitions in the bicycle craze are an offense to God. His wrath is kindled against those who do such things. In these gratifications the mind becomes besotted, even as in liquor drinking. The door is opened to vulgar associations. The thoughts, allowed to run in a low channel, soon pervert all the powers of the being. Like Israel of old, the pleasure lovers eat and drink, and rise up to play. There is mirth and carousing, hilarity and glee. In all this the youth follow the example of the authors of the books placed in their hands for study. The greatest evil of it all is the permanent effect that these things have upon the character.

Those who take the lead in these things bring upon the cause a stain not easily effaced. They wound their own souls, and through their lifetime will carry the scars. The evildoer may see his sins and repent; God may pardon the transgressor; but the powers of discernment, which ought ever to be kept keen and sensitive to distinguish between the sacred and the common, are in a great measure destroyed. Too often human devices and imaginations are accepted as divine. Some souls will act in blindness and insensibility, ready to grasp cheap, common, and even infidel sentiments, while they turn against the demonstrations of the Holy Spirit.

12. A Departure from Right

Cooranbong, N. S. W.
January 12, 1898.

I am pleased that the Lord is in mercy again visiting the church. My heart trembles as I think of the many times He has come in, and His Holy Spirit has worked in the church; but after the immediate effect was over, the merciful dealings of God were forgotten. Pride, spiritual indifference, was the record made in heaven. Those who were visited by the rich mercy and grace of God dishonored their Redeemer by their unbelief...

The Saviour has oft visited you in Battle Creek. Just as verily as He walked in the streets of Jerusalem, longing to breathe the breath of spiritual life into the hearts of those discouraged and ready to die, has He come to you. The cities that were so greatly blessed by His presence, His pardon, His gifts of healing, rejected Him; and just as great, yea, greater, evidence of unrequited love has been given in Battle Creek. Has Christ not loaded down His church with benefits and blessings? Has He not sent His servants with messages of pardon and righteousness, to be freely given to all who will receive them?

Jerusalem is a representation of what the church will be if it refuses to walk in the light that God has given. Jerusalem was favored of God as the depositary of sacred trusts. But her people perverted the truth, and despised all entreaties and warnings. They would not respect His counsels. The temple courts were polluted with merchandise and robbery. Selfishness and love of mammon, envy and strife, were cherished. Everyone sought for gain from his quarter. Christ turned from them, saying: "O Jerusalem, Jerusalem," how can I give thee up? "How often would I have gathered thy children together, even as a hen gathereth her chickens under her wings, and ye would not!" Matthew 23:37.

So Christ sorrows and weeps over our churches, over our institutions of learning, that have failed to meet the demand of God. He comes to investigate in Battle Creek, which has been moving in the same track as Jerusalem. The publishing house has been turned into desecrated shrines, into a place of unholy merchandise and traffic. It has become a place where injustice and fraud have been carried on, where selfishness, malice, envy, and passion have borne sway. Yet the men who have been led into this working upon wrong principles are seemingly unconscious of their wrong course of action. When warnings and entreaties come to them, they say: "Doth she not speak in parables?" Words of warning and reproof have been treated as idle tales.

When Christ looked down from the crest of Olivet, He saw this state of things existing in every church. The warnings come down to all that are following in the tread of the people of Jerusalem, who had such great light. This people is before us as a warning. By rejecting God's warnings in this our day, men are repeating the sin of Jerusalem. The Lord sees what the human agent does not see and will not see—the outcome of all the human devising in Battle Creek. He has done all that a God could do. He has flashed light before the eyes of the people, that their sins might not reach the boundary where repentance cannot be felt. But by a long process of departure from just and righteous principles, men have placed themselves where light and truth, justice and mercy, are not discerned. This course has become part of their very nature.

I call upon all who have united in a course of action that is wrong in principle, to make a decided reformation and forever after walk humbly with God...

These are no idle tales, but truth. Again I ask: On which side are you standing? "If the Lord be God, follow Him: but if Baal, then follow him." 1 Kings 18:21.

13. Look to God for Help

There are times when the truth must be spoken, whether men will hear or whether they will forbear. The Lord is greatly dishonored when those who profess to believe the truth fail to harmonize among themselves, and make appeals to lawyers. Will you study the word of God and heed the instruction given on this point? The interests of the cause of God are not to be committed to men who have no connection with heaven.

Matters have been presented before me that have filled my soul with keen anguish. I saw men linking up arm in arm with lawyers, but God was not in their company. Having many ideas regarding the work, they go to the lawyers for help to carry out their plans. I am commissioned to say to such that they are not moving under the inspiration of the Spirit of God.

"Is it not because there is not a God in Israel, that ye go to inquire of Baal-zebub the god of Ekron?" 2 Kings 1:3. Men in responsible positions are uniting with those in the church and out of the church, whose counsel is misleading. Is it necessary for the Lord to come to you with a rod to show you that you need a higher experience before you can be fitted for connection with the family above? Will you link up with men who have a faculty for accusing, for thinking and speaking evil of the things that God approves? In the name of the Lord I tell you that you need clearer discernment and clearer spiritual eyesight.

If the light which God has given you over and over again, that missionary centers should be established in many cities, and that the labor and the means centered in Battle Creek should be divided and planted in many places, had been followed, the present state of confusion and the dearth of means would never have been.

Men located in Battle Creek have disregarded the counsels of the Lord because it was more convenient for them to have the work centered there. God has left these to the results of their human wisdom, and its fruit is seen in the present perplexities.

"Who is among you that feareth the Lord, that obeyeth the voice of His servant, that walketh in darkness, and hath no light? let him trust in the name of the Lord, and stay upon his God. Behold, all ye that kindle a fire, that compass yourselves about with sparks: walk in the light of your fire, and in the sparks that ye have kindled. This shall ye have of Mine hand; ye shall lie down in sorrow." Isaiah 50:10, 11.

"Now therefore go to, speak to the men of Judah, and to the inhabitants of Jerusalem, saying, Thus saith the Lord; Behold, I frame evil against you, and devise a device against you: return ye now everyone from his evil way, and make your ways and your doings good. And they said, There is no hope: but we will walk after our own devices, and we will everyone do the imagination of his evil heart. Therefore thus saith the Lord; Ask ye now among the heathen, who hath heard such things: the virgin of Israel hath done a very horrible thing. Will a man leave the snow of Lebanon which cometh from the rock of the field? or shall the cold flowing waters that come from another place be forsaken? Because My people have forgotten Me, they have burned incense to vanity, and they have caused them to stumble in their ways from the ancient paths, to walk in paths, in a way not cast up." Jeremiah 18:11-15.

- **Medical Missionary Work**

Again and again the Lord has pointed out the work which the church in Battle Creek and those all through America are to do. They are to reach a much higher standard in spiritual advancement than they have yet reached. They are to awake out of sleep and go without the camp, working for souls that are ready to perish.

The medical missionary workers are doing the long-neglected work which God gave to the church in Battle Creek —they are giving the last call to the supper which He has prepared.

My brethren, why do you keep so many things bound up in Battle Creek? Why do you not take the tract and missionary work into other cities, where there is much missionary work to be done?

The many interests centering in Battle Creek should be divided and subdivided, and placed in other cities. You who think you are wise men may say: "It will cost too much. We can do the work here in Battle Creek at less expense." Well, does not the Lord know all this? Is not He a God who understands all the unbelieving reasoning that holds so many interests in Battle Creek? He has revealed to you that centers should be made in all the cities. This would call many out of Battle Creek to work in other places.

In order to be carried forward aright, the medical missionary work needs talent. It requires strong, willing hands, and wise, discriminating management. But can this be while those in responsible places—presidents of conferences and ministers —bar the way?

The Lord says to the presidents of conferences and to other influential brethren: "Remove the stumbling blocks that have been placed before the people."

Our people in Battle Creek have not exercised their talents in planning and devising how to plant the standard of truth in regions where the message has not been proclaimed and where decided efforts should be made; and the Lord has moved upon Dr. Kellogg and his associates to do the work which belongs to the church and which was offered to them, but which they did not choose to accept. Some in Battle Creek, instead of taking up the work given them of God, have, by following their own selfish way, blinded their spiritual eyesight and the spiritual eyesight of others; and God has placed His precious work in the hands of those who will take it up and carry it forward.

God is in His holy place, and He dwells also with him who is of a humble and contrite spirit, to revive the spirit of the humble and to revive the heart of the contrite ones. Those who are doing medical missionary work should have the full sanction and co-operation of the church. If they do not have this they are hindered. Nevertheless, they will advance. It is not in God's plan that there shall be two churches in Battle Creek because of the want of co-

Section 2: Counsels Often Repeated

operation. How much better it is to seek for unity of action. If the medical missionary workers will carry this line of effort into the churches everywhere, if they will work in the fear of God, they will find many doors opened before them, and angels will work with them.

Please read the invitation to the supper, and the last call to be made. Study what is being done to meet the command of Jesus. I cannot understand why such indifference is manifested, why you should stand afar off and criticize and draw away. The gospel net is to be cast into the sea, and it draws both good and bad. But because this is so, shall men and women ignore the efforts made to save those who will believe and who will unite in reaching that class of whom Christ spoke in His rebuke to the Pharisees? Sinners and harlots, He said, "go into the kingdom of God before you." Will you not see that even in the church there are those who have no connection with God? But Christ says: "Let the tares and the wheat grow together until the harvest: and in the time of harvest I will say to the reapers, Gather ye together first the tares, and bind them in bundles to burn them: but gather the wheat into My barn."

When the Lord moves upon the churches, bidding them do a certain work, and they refuse to do that work; and when some, their human efforts united with the divine, endeavor to reach to the very depths of human woe and misery, God's blessing will rest richly upon them. Even though but few accept the grace of our Lord Jesus Christ, their work will not be in vain; for one soul is precious, very precious, in the sight of God. Christ would have died for one soul in order that that one might live through the eternal ages.

Let us study the eighteenth chapter of Matthew. This chapter should enlighten our eyes. "Take heed," Christ says: "that ye despise not one of these little ones; for I say unto you, That in heaven their angels do always behold the face of My Father which is in heaven. For the Son of man is come to save that which was lost. How think ye? if a man have an hundred sheep, and one of them be gone astray, doth he not leave the ninety and nine, and goeth into the mountains, and seeketh that which is gone astray? And if so be that he find it, verily I say unto you, he rejoiceth more of that sheep, than of the ninety and nine which went not astray. Even so it is not the will of your Father which is in heaven, that one of these little ones should perish." Matthew 18:10-14.

Many souls are being rescued, wrenched from Satan's hand, by faithful workers. Someone must have a burden of soul to find those who have been lost to Christ. The rescue of one soul over whom Satan has triumphed causes joy among the heavenly angels. There are those who have destroyed in themselves the moral image of God. The gospel net must gather in these poor outcasts. Angels of God will co-operate with those who are engaged in this work, who make every effort to save perishing souls, to give them opportunities which many have never had. There is no other way of reaching them but in Christ's way. He ever worked to relieve suffering and teach righteousness. Only thus can sinners be raised from the depths of degradation.

The workers must labor in love, feeding, cleansing, and clothing those who need their help. In this way these outcasts are prepared to know that someone cares for their souls. The Lord has shown me that many of these poor outcasts from society will, through the ministration of human agencies, co-operate with divine power and seek to restore the moral image of God in others for whom Christ has paid the price of His own blood. They will be called the elect of God, precious, and will stand next to the throne of God.

- **A Word of Caution**

"Then shall appear the sign of the Son of man in heaven: and then shall all the tribes of the earth mourn, and they shall see the Son of man coming in the clouds of heaven with power and great glory. And He shall send His angels with a great sound of a trumpet, and they shall gather together His elect from the four winds, from one end of heaven to the other."

"Watch therefore: for ye know not what hour your Lord doth come. But know this, that if the goodman of the house had known in what watch the thief would come, he would have watched, and would not have suffered his house to be broken up. Therefore be ye also ready: for in such an hour as ye think not the Son of man cometh. Who then is a faithful and wise servant, whom his lord hath made ruler over his household, to give them meat in due season? Blessed is that servant, whom his lord when he cometh shall find so doing. Verily I say unto you, That he shall make him ruler over all his goods.

But and if that evil servant shall say in his heart, My lord delayeth his coming; and shall begin to smite his fellow servants, and to eat and drink with the drunken; the lord of that servant shall come in a day when he looketh not for him, and in an hour that he is not aware of, and shall cut him asunder, and appoint him his portion with the hypocrites: there shall be weeping and gnashing of teeth." Matthew 24:30, 31, 42-51.

Brethren, be careful, very careful. There is a work being done by the medical missionaries which answers to the description given in verses 48-51. The Lord is working to reach the most depraved. Many will know what it means to be drawn to Christ, but will not have moral courage to war against appetite and passion. But the workers must not be discouraged at this; for it is written: "In the latter times some shall depart from the faith, giving heed to seducing spirits, and doctrines of devils." 1 Timothy 4:1.

Is it only those rescued from the lowest depths that backslide? There are those in the ministry who have had light and a knowledge of the truth, who will not be overcomers. They do not restrict their appetites and passions or deny themselves for Christ's sake. Many poor outcasts, even publicans and sinners, will grasp the hope set before them in the gospel and will go into the kingdom of heaven before the ones who have had great opportunities and great light, but who have walked in darkness. In the last great day many will say: "Lord, Lord, open unto us." But the door will be shut, and their knock will be in vain.

We should feel deeply over these things, for they are true. We should have a high estimate of truth and of the value of souls. Time is short, and there is a great work to be done. If you feel no interest in the work that is going forward, if you will not encourage medical missionary work in the churches, it will be done without your consent; for it is the work of God, and it must be done. My brethren and sisters, take your position on the Lord's side and be earnest, active, courageous co-workers with Christ, laboring with Him to seek and save the lost.

14. An Appeal to the Brethren in Battle Creek

Why is it, brethren, that you continue to keep so many interests bound up in Battle Creek? Why do you not listen to the counsels and the warnings that have been given you regarding this matter? Why do you not take decisive steps to establish centers of influence in many of the large cities? Why do you not encourage the Michigan Tract Society and the International Tract Society to establish their offices in cities where there is much missionary work to do, and where their secretaries and other workers may engage personally in missionary work, acting as leaders in important enterprises? Move out, brethren, move out, and educate your workers to labor for those outside the camp. Why do you hide your light by continuing to remain in Battle Creek? Go out, brethren, go out into the regions beyond.

There is much work to be done, and our experienced workers should strive to place themselves where they will come in direct contact with those needing help. They can do comparatively little in Battle Creek. Is it right, brethren, for you to keep your light hid under a bushel or under a bed? Is it not better that you do that which the Lord has plainly indicated you should do? Resolve now that you will give up your preference, your way, and that you will obey His voice. Seek the Lord most earnestly, with humble, fervent prayer for wisdom and for success in this endeavor. Then take the light from under the bushel, away from the place that seems most favorable for your financial interests, and from under the bed, away from the place most convenient for your comfort, and put it on a candlestick, that it may give light to all that are in the house.

A crisis in missionary effort is upon us. There is a great work to be done, and if this work is earnestly done in Battle Creek, if it is faithfully done throughout the churches in Michigan, if it is vigorously prosecuted in all our older churches and strongholds of influence, we may hope that its influence will leaven the churches throughout all the conferences, many of whom are now standing as if paralyzed.

The institutions which God has established as centers of influence for the dissemination of light are not blending their interests and working together as God would have them. The managers of these institutions should know that their very first work is to harmonize with their fellow workers. Our ministers must awake to understand the situation. The gospel is the sanctifying influence in our world. Its influence upon hearts will bring harmony. The standard of truth is to be uplifted and the atonement of Christ presented as the grand, central theme for consideration.

The medical missionary work is to be to the work of the church as the right arm to the body. The third angel goes forth proclaiming the commandments of God and the faith of Jesus. The medical missionary work is the gospel in practice. All lines of work are to be harmoniously blended in giving the invitation: "Come; for all things are now ready."

To those in Battle Creek has been given the message that many should move into places where they may engage in this very work in connection with their temporal business. Had they moved out by faith, willing to endure wearing labor and privation for the work's sake, they would have obtained a rich experience in the things of God.

But they thought that they would find things a little more convenient in Battle Creek, that the work there would be less taxing than elsewhere, and therefore they remained. Many who crowd into Battle Creek get no good there because they do not make use of the knowledge they receive. They do no good in Battle Creek, but are swelling the number who need conversion. They have not the spirit of sacrifice. They have much of self and a little of Christ, a little faith and a few good works. They think that they have religion, but it all amounts to nothing.

God speaks to you in His word, saying: "Forasmuch as this people draw near Me with their mouth, and with their lips do honor Me, but have removed their heart far from Me, and their fear toward Me is taught by the precept of men: therefore, behold, I will proceed to do a marvelous work among this people, even a marvelous work and a wonder: for the wisdom of their wise men shall perish, and the understanding of their prudent men shall be hid."

"In that day shall the deaf hear the words of the book, and the eyes of the blind shall see out of obscurity, and out of darkness. The meek also shall increase their joy in the Lord, and the poor among men shall rejoice in the Holy One of Israel." Isaiah 29:13, 14, 18, 19.

My brethren, the Lord has called upon you to do a certain work, but you have not done it; and in the place where you are there is discord and contention and strife. But this need not be. God does not design that His workmen shall stand apart as separate atoms. All have a great and solemn work to do, and it is to be done under God's supervision.

God will do great things for His people if they will co-operate with Him. He will work upon the minds of men, so that there will be seen in their lives, even in this world, a fulfillment of the promise of the future state:

The wilderness and the dry land shall be glad;
And the desert shall rejoice, and blossom as the rose.
It shall blossom abundantly, and rejoice even with joy and singing;
The glory of Lebanon shall be given unto it,
The excellency of Carmel and Sharon:
They shall see the glory of Jehovah,
The excellency of our God.
Strengthen ye the weak hands,
And confirm the feeble knees.
Say to them that are of a fearful heart, Be strong, fear not:
Behold, your God will come with vengeance,
With the recompense of God;
He will come and save you.
Then the eyes of the blind shall be opened,
And the ears of the deaf shall be unstopped.
Then shall the lame man leap as a hart,
And the tongue of the dumb shall sing;
For in the wilderness shall waters break out,
And streams in the desert.
And the glowing sand shall become a pool,
And the thirsty ground springs of water:
In the habitation of jackals, where they lay,
Shall be grass with reeds and rushes.
And a highway shall be there, and a way,
And it shall be called The way of holiness;
The unclean shall not pass over it; but it shall be for the redeemed:

The wayfaring men, yea fools, shall not err therein.
No lion shall be there,
Nor shall any ravenous beast go up thereon;
They shall not be found there;
But the redeemed shall walk there:
And the ransomed of Jehovah shall return,
And come with singing unto Zion;
And everlasting joy shall be upon their heads:
They shall obtain gladness and joy,
And sorrow and sighing shall flee away.
Isaiah 35, A. R. V.

The wilderness itself has neither glory nor excellence, and to the Lord is to be ascribed all the honor for the transformation wrought. This great work is of God. Therefore magnify not the men who are under the special working of His power. Glorify God, and He will continue to work.

The Lord has a special work for His people to do at this time. He says: "Strengthen ye the weak hands, and confirm the feeble knees." This is the very work that the apostle Paul charges the churches to do. "Lift up the hands which hang down, and the feeble knees," he says, "and make straight paths for your feet, lest that which is lame be turned out of the way; but let it rather be healed. Follow peace with all men, and holiness, without which no man shall see the Lord: looking diligently lest any man fail of the grace of God; lest any root of bitterness springing up trouble you, and thereby many be defiled." Hebrews 12:12-15.

I pray that now as never before both ministers and church members may come up to the help of the Lord, to the help of the Lord against the mighty powers of darkness. Study prayerfully the seventeenth chapter of John. This chapter is not only to be read again and again; its truths are to be eaten and assimilated.

"For their sakes," Christ prayed: "I sanctify Myself, that they also might be sanctified through the truth. Neither pray I for these alone, but for them also which shall believe on Me through their word; that they all may be one; as Thou, Father, art in Me, and I in Thee, that they also may be one in Us: that the world may believe that Thou hast sent Me. And the glory which

Thou gavest Me I have given them; that they may be one, even as We are one: I in them, and Thou in Me, that they may be made perfect in one; and that the world may know that Thou hast sent Me, and hast loved them, as Thou hast loved Me." John 17:19-23.

Are these words, of such wonderful import to us, to be always neglected? God calls upon those who profess to be His children to study these words, to eat them, to live them. He calls upon them to seek for unity and love, else the candlestick will be moved out of its place.

15. A Neglected Warning

St. Helena, California
November, 1901.

"Behold, I set before you this day a blessing and a curse; a blessing, if ye obey the commandments of the Lord your God, which I command you this day: and a curse, if ye will not obey." Deuteronomy 11:26-28.

"And it shall come to pass, if ye shall hearken diligently unto My commandments which I command you this day, to love the Lord your God, and to serve Him with all your heart and with all your soul, that I will give you the rain of your land in his due season, the first rain and the latter rain, that thou mayest gather in thy corn, and thy wine, and thine oil. And I will send grass in thy fields for thy cattle, that thou mayest eat and be full. Take heed to yourselves, that your heart be not deceived, and ye turn aside, and serve other gods, and worship them; and then the Lord's wrath be kindled against you, and He shut up the heaven, that there be no rain, and that the land yield not her fruit; and lest ye perish quickly from off the good land which the Lord giveth you." Verses 13-17.

"Therefore shall ye lay up these My words in your heart and in your soul, and bind them for a sign upon your hand, that they may be as frontlets between your eyes. And ye shall teach them your children, speaking of them when thou sittest in thine house, and when thou walkest by the way, when thou liest down, and when thou risest up. And thou shalt write them upon the doorposts of thine house, and upon thy gates: that your days may be multiplied, and the days of your children, in the land which the Lord sware

Section 2: Counsels Often Repeated

unto your fathers to give them, as the days of heaven upon the earth." Verses 18-21.

If Seventh-day Adventists had walked in the way of the Lord, refusing to allow selfish interests to control them, the Lord would greatly have blessed them. Those who have remained in Battle Creek contrary to the will of the Lord have lost the valuable experience and the spiritual knowledge they might have gained through obedience. Many of them have forfeited the favor of God. The heart of the work has become congested. For a long time the warning has been given, but it has not been heeded. The reason for this disobedience is that the hearts and minds of many in Battle Creek are not under the influence of the Holy Spirit. They do not realize how much work there is to do. They are asleep.

When Seventh-day Adventists move into cities where there is already a large church of believers, they are out of place, and their spirituality becomes weaker and weaker. Their children are exposed to many temptations. My brother, my sister, unless you are absolutely needed in carrying forward the work in such a place, it would be wise for you to go to some place where the truth has not yet been proclaimed, and there strive to give proof of your ability to work for the Master. Make earnest efforts to arouse an interest in present truth. House-to-house work is effectual when conducted in a Christlike manner. Hold meetings, and be sure to make them interesting. Remember that this requires something more than preaching.

Many who have lived so long in one place are spending their time criticizing those who are working in Christ's lines to convict and convert sinners. They criticize the motives and intentions of others, as if it were not possible for anyone else to do the unselfish work they themselves refuse to do. They are stumbling blocks. If they would go to places where there are no believers, and work to win souls to Christ, they would soon be so busy proclaiming the truth and helping the suffering that they would have no time to dissect character, no time to surmise evil and then report the results of their supposed keenness in seeing beneath the surface.

Let those who have lived so long in places where there are large churches of believers go out into the harvest field to sow and reap for the Master. They will forget self in the desire to save souls. They will see so much work to do, so many fellow beings to help, that they will have no time to look for faults in others. They will have no time to work on the negative side.

Bringing so many believers together in one place tends to encourage evil surmising and evilspeaking. Many become absorbed in looking and listening for evil. They forget what a great sin they are committing. They forget that the words they speak can never be unsaid and that by their suspicions they are sowing seeds that will spring up to bear a harvest of evil. How great this harvest is no one will know until the last great day, when every thought, word, and action will be brought into judgment.

The thoughtless, unkind words that are spoken grow with every repetition. One and another adds a word, until the false report assumes large proportions. Great injustice is done. By their unrighteous suspicions and unrighteous judgments the talebearers hurt their own experience and sow the seeds of discord in the church. If they could see things as God sees them they would change their attitude. They would realize how they have neglected the work He has given them to do as they have found fault with their brethren and sisters.

The time spent in criticizing the motives and works of Christ's servants might better be spent in prayer. Often if those who find fault knew the truth in regard to those with whom they find fault, they would have an altogether different opinion of them. How much better it would be if, instead of criticizing and condemning others, everyone would say: "I must work out my own salvation. If I co-operate with Him who desires to save my soul, I must watch myself diligently. I must cut away every evil from my life. I must become a new creature in Christ. I must overcome every fault. Then, instead of weakening those who are striving against evil, I can strengthen them by encouraging words."

Let those who have used the talent of speech to discourage and dishearten God's servants, who are striving to advance God's cause, planning and working to master hindrance, ask God to forgive them for the injury they have done to His work by their wicked prejudices and unkind words. Let them think of the harm they have done by spreading false reports, by judging those they have no right to judge.

In the word of God we are given plain directions as to the course we are to follow when we think a brother is in the wrong. Christ says:

Section 2: Counsels Often Repeated

"If thy brother shall trespass against thee, go and tell him his fault between thee and him alone: if he shall hear thee, thou hast gained thy brother. But if he will not hear thee, then take with thee one or two more, that in the mouth of two or three witnesses every word may be established. And if he shall neglect to hear them, tell it unto the church: but if he neglect to hear the church, let him be unto thee as an heathen man and a publican." And again the Saviour says: "If thou bring thy gift to the altar, and there rememberest that thy brother hath aught against thee; leave there thy gift before the altar, and go thy way; first be reconciled to thy brother, and then come and offer thy gift." Matthew 18:15-17; 5:23, 24.

"Lord, who shall abide in Thy tabernacle? who shall dwell in Thy holy hill? He that walketh uprightly, and worketh righteousness, and speaketh the truth in his heart. He that backbiteth not with his tongue, nor doeth evil to his neighbor, nor taketh up a reproach against his neighbor. In whose eyes a vile person is contemned; but he honoreth them that fear the Lord. He that sweareth to his own hurt, and changeth not. He that putteth not out his money to usury, nor taketh reward against the innocent. He that doeth these things shall never be moved." Psalm 15.

"Judge not, that ye be not judged. For with what judgment ye judge, ye shall be judged: and with what measure ye mete, it shall be measured to you again. And why beholdest thou the mote that is in thy brother's eye, but considerest not the beam that is in thine own eye? Or how wilt thou say to thy brother, Let me pull out the mote out of thine eye; and, behold, a beam is in thine own eye? Thou hypocrite, first cast out the beam out of thine own eye; and then shalt thou see clearly to cast out the mote out of thy brother's eye." Matthew 7:1-5.

Much is involved in the matter of judging. Remember that soon your life record will pass in review before God. Remember, too, that He has said: "Thou art inexcusable, O man, whosoever thou art that judgest: for wherein thou judgest another, thou condemnest thyself; for thou that judgest doest the same things. But we are sure that the judgment of God is according to truth against them which commit such things. And thinkest thou this, O man, that judgest them which do such things, and doest the same, that thou shalt escape the judgment of God?" Romans 2:1-3.

Those who came to Battle Creek when they had a work to do in the church that they left, lost their missionary spirit and their spiritual discernment in coming to Battle Creek. There they came in contact with a pharisaism, a self-righteousness, that is always a snare. It is the form of godliness without the power thereof.

When the power of the truth is felt in the heart, when the principles of truth are brought into the daily life, there will be a great movement of reform in the Battle Creek church. Soon will be fulfilled the words: "I will turn and overturn." We know not now just when this will be accomplished, but the time will come when there will be a scattering from Battle Creek. Those who moved to Battle Creek without any call from the Lord will move away.

Earnest workers have no time to dwell upon the defects of others. They behold the Saviour, and by beholding become changed into His likeness. He is the One whose example we are to follow in our character building. In His life upon the earth He plainly revealed the divine nature. We should strive to be perfect in our sphere, as He was perfect in His sphere. No longer are the members of the church to remain unconcerned in regard to the formation of right characters. Placing themselves under the molding influence of the Holy Spirit, they are to form characters that are a reflection of the divine character.

16. The Result of Reformation

Dear Brother Daniells: Yesterday morning I read your letter, in which you express your ardent desire to see a strong corps of workers sent to India and China and other Oriental countries. Last night instruction was given me that at present our principal efforts are not to be made especially for China or other fields similar to China. We first have a work to do at home. All our institutions—our sanitariums, publishing houses, and schools—are to reach a higher standard. Then the workers sent to foreign fields will reach a higher standard. They will be more earnest, more spiritual, and their labors will be more effective.

Years ago the Lord gave me special directions that buildings should be erected in various places in America, Europe, and other lands for the publication of literature containing the light of present truth. He gave

Section 2: Counsels Often Repeated

instruction that every effort should be made to send forth to the world from the press the messages of invitation and warning. Some will be reached by our literature who would not be reached in any other way. From our books and papers bright beams of light are to shine forth to enlighten the world in regard to present truth.

Workers who are not benefited by the advantages they receive in connection with the cause of God should not be brought into our offices of publication. Neither should matter of an objectionable character be introduced into these institutions, for by so doing the sacred truth of God is placed on a level with common matters. And when outside work is brought in, a correspondingly large number of workers must be employed. This brings care and perplexity.

I have been shown that mistakes are being made in our publishing houses. There is a constant increase of expensive machinery for the doing of commercial work. A large amount of work has been brought in that has no relation to the work which in faith and love is to be accomplished for the salvation of human beings. Time and talent have been used in doing a class of work that has brought no glory to God. Much effort has been put forth in lines that do nothing to spread a knowledge of the truth.

It is high time that consideration be given to this matter. This mistake must be corrected. It is not wisdom to use money to establish enterprises that consume without producing. It is said that more room is needed in the publishing houses. But there is ample room in them, and when the right thing is done, it will be seen that there is sufficient room.

Far less commercial work should be received into our offices of publication, and not a line of matter containing Satan's sentiments should be received. The introduction of such matter destroys all sense of the sacredness of the institution. The whole institution is cheapened. There is always danger, when the common is mingled with the sacred, that the common will be allowed to take the place of the sacred.

How does the Lord regard the using of the presses in His institutions to print the errors of the enemy? When objectionable matter is mingled with sacred matter coming from the presses, His blessing cannot rest upon the work done. Said the divine Teacher: "What have you gained by bringing in this outside work? It has brought you much vexation of spirit; and the workers have had to hurry and rush to get the matter finished in the specified time. This has occasioned confusion and strife. Harsh words have been spoken, and an unpleasant spirit has been brought into the office. The financial gain in no way compares with the loss which has come through rushing and driving and scolding and fretting."

May the Lord help His people to see that this is not wisdom and that far more is lost than is gained. If less machinery and fewer workers had been brought together in one place while other portions of the vineyard were destitute of facilities; if more money had been spent in making plants in various places, God would have been better pleased. It is not sanctified ambition that has led to the investment of so much money in one place. It is a mistake for our brethren to run so many presses for the printing of merely secular matter. We are fast approaching the end. The printing and circulation of the books and papers that contain the truth for this time are to be our work.

There is a marked neglect of the cautions and warnings that have been given from time to time. When there is a seeking of the Lord and a confession of sin, when the needed reformation takes place, united zeal and earnestness will be shown in restoring what has been withheld. The Lord will manifest His pardoning love, and means will come to cancel the debts on our institutions.

17. A Solemn Warning

To the Managers of the Review and Herald—

Dear Brethren: God's design in the establishment of the publishing house at Battle Creek was that from it light should shine forth as a lamp that burneth. This has been kept before the managers. Again and again they have been told of the sacredness of God's office of publication and of the importance of maintaining its purity. But they have lost true understanding and have united with the force of the enemy by consenting to print papers and books containing the most dangerous errors that can be brought into existence. They have failed to see the evil influences of such erroneous sentiments on typesetters, proofreaders, and all others engaged in the printing of such matter. They have been spiritually asleep.

Section 2: Counsels Often Repeated

By some of the outside work brought into this institution the science of Satan has been presented to the minds of the workers. The printing of such matter is a dishonor to God. It has done its part in deteriorating the minds of the workers. The managers have agreed to print it at a low figure. The gain would have been loss if the very highest figure had been asked for the work.

I have received a letter from Elder Daniells regarding the addition of another building to the Review and Herald office. The answer I make to this is: No, no, no. Instead of making any additions to the buildings already erected, cleanse the office of the trash of satanic origin, and you will gain room in every way.

God is not pleased with the congested state of things in Battle Creek. If the workers were divided and plants made in other places, God would be better pleased, and the standard of truth would be planted in regions which have never heard the message. Before you add another building to the office in Battle Creek, make thorough restitution to the Southern field. This has not yet been done as it should be done. Every step has been forced.

The five thousand dollars which would be used in adding to the Review and Herald buildings should now be invested in the work in other places where the gospel of truth has not yet been preached.

I feel a terror of soul as I see to what a pass our publishing house has come. The presses in the Lord's institution have been printing the soul-destroying theories of Romanism and other mysteries of iniquity. The office must be purged of this objectionable matter. I have a testimony from the Lord for those who have placed such matter in the hands of the workers. God holds you accountable for presenting to young men and young women the fruit of the forbidden tree of knowledge. Can it be possible that you have not a knowledge of the warnings given to the Pacific Press on this subject? Can it be possible that with a knowledge of these warnings you are going over the same ground, only doing much worse? It has often been repeated to you that angels of God are passing through every room in the office. What impression has this made on your minds?

You have given matter containing Satan's sentiments into the hands of the workers, bringing his deceptive, polluting principles before their minds. The Lord looks upon this action on your part as helping Satan to prepare his snare to catch souls. God will not hold guiltless those who have done this thing.

He has a controversy with the managers of the publishing house. I have been almost afraid to open the Review, fearing to see that God has cleansed the publishing house by fire.

The Lord has instructed me that those who cannot see the wickedness of co-operating with Satan by publishing his falsehoods might better seek some work in which they will not ruin our youth, body and soul. There is danger that the standard of truth and righteousness will be so lowered that God will bring His judgments upon the wrongdoers.

It is high time that we understood what spirit has for years been controlling matters at the Review and Herald office. I am horrified to think that the most subtle phase of spiritualism should be placed before the workers, and that in a way calculated to confuse and perplex the mind. Be assured that Satan will follow up the advantage thus given him.

The Review and Herald office has been defiled as the temple was defiled, only the result has been tenfold more disastrous. Overturning the tables of the money-changers, Christ drove the sheep and cattle from the precincts of the temple, saying: "It is written, My house shall be called the house of prayer; but ye have made it a den of thieves." Matthew 21:13. Worse even than the defilement of the temple has been the defilement of the publishing house by the printing of matter which should never have been placed in the hands of the workers in God's institution.

God's law has been transgressed, His cause betrayed, and His institution made a den of thieves. The work of printing and circulating stirring appeals for the truth, which should have been placed first, to which the time and the talent of the workers should have been devoted, has received little or no attention. The commercial work, some of it of a most objectionable character, has gradually assumed the supremacy.

This work has absorbed the energies which should have been devoted to the publication of literature of the purest quality and the most elevating character. Time has been wasted, talent misapplied, and money misappropriated. The work which ought to have been done has been left undone. Satan's sentiments have been exalted. His theories have been printed by presses which should have been used to prepare the truth of God for circulation. Men have coveted promotion when their principles were under the ban of God's displeasure. Loss is infinitely better than dishonorable gain.

Section 2: Counsels Often Repeated

Oh, what will God do with the timeservers? Think you that Jesus will stand in the printing establishment, to work through human minds by His ministering angels, to make the truth coming from the press a power to warn the world that the end of all things is at hand, while Satan is allowed to pervert the minds of the workers right in the institution? The light I have is: Refuse to print another line of this pernicious matter. Those who have had to do with its introduction into the publishing house need to repent before God in contrition of soul, for His wrath is kindled against them. Let this class of work be forever excluded from our publishing houses. Give more time to the publication and circulation of the books containing present truth. See that your work in this line reaches perfection. Do all in your power to diffuse throughout the world the light of heaven.

The apprentices and the other workers must not be so rushed and hurried that they have no time to pray. The youth in our publishing houses should be educated as were the youth in the schools of the prophets. They should be prepared to take hold of the work in new places.

If the men who heard the message given at the time of the Conference—the most solemn message that could be given—had not been so unimpressionable, if in sincerity they had asked, "Lord, what wilt Thou have me to do?" the experience of the past year would have been very different from what it is. But they have not made the track clean behind them. They have not confessed their mistakes, and now they are going over the same ground in many things, following the same wrong course of action, because they have destroyed their spiritual eyesight.

The message of the third angel is to prepare a people to stand in these days of peril. It is to be proclaimed with a loud voice and is to accomplish a work which few realize.

John writes: "I saw another angel fly in the midst of heaven, having the everlasting gospel to preach unto them that dwell on the earth, and to every nation, and kindred, and tongue, and people, saying with a loud voice, Fear God, and give glory to Him; for the hour of His judgment is come: and worship Him that made heaven, and earth, and the sea, and the fountains of waters. And there followed another angel, saying, Babylon is fallen is fallen, that great city, because she made all nations drink of the wine of the wrath of her fornication." Revelation 14:6-8. How is this done? By forcing men to accept a spurious sabbath. In the thirty-first chapter of Exodus we are plainly told which day is the Sabbath of the Lord. The keeping of the Sabbath is declared to be a sign of the loyalty of God's people.

God means just what He says. Man has interposed between God and the people, and the Lord has sent forth the third angel with the message: "If any man worship the beast and his image, and receive his mark in his forehead, or in his hand, the same shall drink of the wine of the wrath of God, which is poured out without mixture into the cup of His indignation; and he shall be tormented with fire and brimstone in the presence of the holy angels, and in the presence of the Lamb." Verses 9, 10.

God's people are to keep His commandments, discarding all worldly policy. Having adopted right principles of action, they are to reverence these principles; for they are heaven-born. Obedience to God is of more value to you than gold or silver. Yoking up with Christ, learning His meekness and lowliness, cuts short many a conflict; for when the enemy comes in like a flood, the Spirit of the Lord lifts up a standard against him.

I address those who in accepting positions of trust in the publishing house have taken upon themselves the responsibility of seeing that the workers receive the right education. Seek to realize the importance of your work. Those who show by their actions that they make no effort to distinguish between the sacred and the common may know that, unless they repent, God's judgments will fall upon them. These judgments may be delayed, but they will come. If, because your own minds are not clear and elevated, you give the wrong bias to other minds, God will call you to account. He will ask: "Why did you do the devil's work when you were supposed to be doing a good work for the Master?"

In the great day of final accounts the unfaithful servant will meet the result of his unfaithfulness.

I send you this because I am afraid for you. Your continually increasing force of workers might better be sent into the work in other places. In the night season I have been talking earnestly to you in your meetings, presenting the truth as it is in Jesus. But by some it was rejected. They had passed beyond conviction. They had sinned against great light and knowledge, stifling conscience until it could no longer penetrate the callous heart.

Some have so long sacrificed principle that they cannot see the difference between the sacred and the common. Those who refuse to give heed to the Lord's instruction will go steadily downward in the path of ruin. The day of test and trial is just before us. Let every man put on his true colors. Do you choose loyalty or rebellion? Show your colors to men and an angels. We are safe only when we are committed to the right. Then the world knows where we shall be found in the day of trial and trouble.

If the work begun at the General Conference had been carried forward to perfection, I should not be called upon to write these words. There was opportunity to confess or deny wrong, and in many cases the denial came to avoid the consequences of confession.

Unless there is a reformation, calamity will overtake the publishing house, and the world will know the reason. I have been shown that there has not been a turning to God with full purpose of heart. The Lord is dishonored in the institutions erected for His honor. The marked disregard of God's commandments in the publishing house has placed its impress on the workers. God asks: "Shall I not judge for these things?" I saw heavenly angels turning away with grieved countenances. God has been mocked by your hardness of heart, which is continually increasing. According to their responsibility will be the punishment of those who know the truth and yet disregard God's commands.

18. The Review and Herald Fire

To the Brethren in Battle Creek—

Today I received a letter from Elder Daniells regarding the destruction of the Review office by fire. I feel very sad as I consider the great loss to the cause. I know that this must be a very trying time for the brethren in charge of the work and for the employees of the office. I am afflicted with all who are afflicted. But I was not surprised by the sad news, for in the visions of the night I have seen an angel standing with a sword as of fire stretched over Battle Creek. Once, in the daytime, while my pen was in my hand, I lost consciousness, and it seemed as if this sword of flame were turning first in one direction and then in another. Disaster seemed to follow disaster because God was dishonored by the devising of men to exalt and glorify themselves.

This morning I was drawn out in earnest prayer that the Lord would lead all who are connected with the Review and Herald office to make diligent search, that they may see wherein they have disregarded the many messages God has given.

Sometime ago the brethren at the Review office asked my counsel about the erection of another building. I then said that if those who were in favor of adding another building to the Review and Herald office had the future mapped out before them, if they could see what would be in Battle Creek, they would have no question about putting up another building there. God said: "My word has been despised; and I will turn and overturn."

At the General Conference, held in Battle Creek in 1901, the Lord gave His people evidence that He was calling for reformation. Minds were convicted, and hearts were touched; but thorough work was not done. If stubborn hearts had then broken in penitence before God, there would have been seen one of the greatest manifestations of the power of God that has ever been seen. But God was not honored. The testimonies of His Spirit were not heeded. Men did not separate from the practices that were in decided opposition to the principles of truth and righteousness, which should ever be maintained in the Lord's work.

The messages to the church of Ephesus and to the church in Sardis have been often repeated to me by the One who gives me instruction for His people. "Unto the angel of the church of Ephesus write; These things saith He that holdeth the seven stars in His right hand, who walketh in the midst of the seven golden candlesticks; I know thy works, and the labor, and thy patience, and how thou canst not bear them which are evil: and thou hast tried them which say they are apostles, and are not, and hast found them liars: and hast borne, and hast patience, and for My name's sake hast labored, and hast not fainted. Nevertheless I have somewhat against thee, because thou hast left thy first love. Remember therefore from whence thou art fallen, and repent, and do the first works; or else I will come unto thee quickly, and will remove thy candlestick out of his place, except thou repent." Revelation 2:1-5.

Section 2: Counsels Often Repeated

"And unto the angel of the church in Sardis write; These things saith He that hath the seven Spirits of God, and the seven stars; I know thy works, that thou hast a name that thou livest, and art dead. Be watchful, and strengthen the things which remain, that are ready to die: for I have not found thy works perfect before God. Remember therefore how thou hast received and heard, and hold fast, and repent. If therefore thou shalt not watch, I will come on thee as a thief, and thou shalt not know what hour I will come upon thee." Revelation 3:1-3.

We are seeing the fulfillment of these warnings. Never have scriptures been more strictly fulfilled than these have been.

Men may erect the most carefully constructed, fireproof buildings, but one touch of God's hand, one spark from heaven, will sweep away every refuge.

It has been asked if I have any advice to give. I have already given the advice that God has given me, hoping to prevent the falling of the fiery sword that was hanging over Battle Creek. Now that which I dreaded has come—the news of the burning of the Review and Herald building. When this news came, I felt no surprise, and I had no words to speak. What I have had to say from time to time in warnings has had no effect except to harden those who heard, and now I can only say: I am so sorry, so very sorry, that it was necessary for this stroke to come. Light enough has been given. If it were acted upon, further light would not be needed.

To our people, ministers and lay members, I am instructed to say: "Seek ye the Lord while He may be found, call ye upon Him while He is near: let the wicked forsake his way, and the unrighteous man his thoughts: and let him return unto the Lord,"—for many ministers and people are walking in strange paths,—"and He will have mercy upon him; and to our God, for He will abundantly pardon." Isaiah 55:6, 7.

Let every soul be on the alert. The adversary is on your track. Be vigilant, watching diligently lest some carefully concealed and masterly snare shall take you unawares. Let the careless and indifferent beware lest the day of the Lord come upon them as a thief in the night. Many will wander from the path of humility, and, casting aside the yoke of Christ, will walk in strange paths. Blinded and bewildered, they will leave the narrow path that leads to the city of God.

A man cannot be a happy Christian unless he is a watchful Christian. He who overcomes must watch; for, with worldly entanglements, error, and superstition, Satan strives to win Christ's followers from Him. It is not enough that we avoid glaring dangers and perilous, inconsistent moves. We are to keep close to the side of Christ, walking in the path of self-denial and sacrifice. We are in an enemy's country. He who was cast out of heaven has come down with great power. With every conceivable artifice and device he is seeking to take souls captive. Unless we are constantly on guard we shall fall an easy prey to his unnumbered deceptions.

The experience of the disciples in the Garden of Gethsemane contains a lesson for the Lord's people today. Taking with Him Peter and James and John, Christ went to Gethsemane to pray. He said to them: "My soul is exceeding sorrowful unto death: tarry ye here, and watch. And He went forward a little, and fell on the ground, and prayed that, if it were possible, the hour might pass from Him. And He said, Abba Father, all things are possible unto Thee; take away this cup from Me: nevertheless not what I will, but what Thou wilt. And He cometh, and findeth them sleeping, and saith unto Peter, Simon, sleepest thou? couldest not thou watch one hour? Watch ye and pray, lest ye enter into temptation." Mark 14:34-38.

Read these words carefully. Many today are asleep, as were the disciples. They are not watching and praying lest they enter into temptation. Let us read and study those portions of God's word that have special reference to these last days, pointing out the dangers that will threaten God's people.

We need keen, sanctified perception. This perception is not to be used in criticizing and condemning one another, but discerning the signs of the times. We are to keep our hearts with all diligence, that we may not make shipwreck of faith. Many who were once firm believers in the truth have become careless in regard to their spiritual welfare and are yielding, without the slightest opposition, to Satan's well-laid plots. It is time for our people to take their families from the cities into more retired localities, else many of the youth, and many also of those older in years, will be ensnared and taken by the enemy.

January 7, 1903.

Section 2: Counsels Often Repeated

We have all been made very sad by the news of the terrible loss that has come to the cause in the burning of the Review and Herald office. In one year two of our largest institutions have been destroyed by fire. The news of this recent calamity has caused us to mourn deeply, but it was permitted by the Lord to come upon us, and we should make no complaint, but learn from it the lesson that the Lord would teach us.

The destruction of the Review and Herald building should not be passed over as something in which there is no meaning. Everyone connected with the office should ask himself: "Wherein do I deserve this lesson? Wherein have I walked contrary to a 'Thus saith the Lord,' that He should send this lesson to me? Have I heeded the warnings and reproofs that He has sent, or have I followed my own way?"

Let the heart-searching God reprove the erring, and let each one bow before Him in humility and contrition, casting aside all self-righteousness and self-importance, confessing and forsaking every sin, and asking God, in the name of the Redeemer, for pardon. God declares, "Him that cometh to Me I will in no wise cast out" (John 6:37); and those who in sincerity present themselves before Him will be pardoned and justified, and will receive power to become the sons of God.

I pray that those who have resisted light and evidence, refusing to listen to God's warnings, will see in the destruction of the Review and Herald office an appeal to them to turn to God with full purpose of heart. Will they not realize that God is in earnest with them? He is not seeking to destroy life, but to save life. In the recent destruction the lives of the workers were graciously preserved, that all might have an opportunity to see that God was correcting them by a message coming not from a human source, but from above. God's people have departed from Him; they have not followed His instruction, and He has come near them in correction; but He has not brought extinction of life. Not one soul has been taken by death. All have been left alive to recognize the Power that no man can gainsay.

Let us praise the Lord that the lives of His children have been so precious in His sight. He might have cut off the workers in their heedlessness and self-sufficiency. But, no! He says: "They shall have another chance. I will let the fire speak to them and will see if they will counterwork the action of My providence. I will try them as by fire to see if they will learn the lesson that I desire to teach them."

When the Battle Creek Sanitarium was destroyed, Christ gave Himself to defend the lives of men and women. In this destruction God was appealing to His people to return to Him. And in the destruction of the Review and Herald office, and the saving of life, He makes a second appeal to them. He desires them to see that the miracle-working power of the Infinite has been exercised to save life, that every worker may have opportunity to repent and be converted. God says: "If they turn to Me, I will restore to them the joy of My salvation. But if they continue to walk in their own way, I will come still closer; and affliction shall come upon the families who claim to believe the truth, but who do not practice the truth, who do not make the Lord God of Israel their fear and their dread."

Let everyone examine himself to see whether he be in the faith. Let the people of God repent and be converted, that their sins may be blotted out when the times of refreshing shall come from the presence of the Lord. Let them ascertain wherein they have failed to walk in the way that God has marked out, wherein they have failed to purify their souls by taking heed to His counsels.

19. What Might Have Been

St. Helena, California
January 5, 1903.
To the Battle Creek Church—

One day at noon I was writing of the work that might have been done at the last General Conference if the men in positions of trust had followed the will and way of God. Those who have had great light have not walked in the light. The meeting was closed, and the break was not made. Men did not humble themselves before the Lord as they should have done, and the Holy Spirit was not imparted.

I had written thus far when I lost consciousness, and I seemed to be witnessing a scene in Battle Creek.

Section 2: Counsels Often Repeated

We were assembled in the auditorium of the Tabernacle. Prayer was offered, a hymn was sung, and prayer was again offered. Most earnest supplication was made to God. The meeting was marked by the presence of the Holy Spirit. The work went deep, and some present were weeping aloud.

One arose from his bowed position and said that in the past he had not been in union with certain ones and had felt no love for them, but that now he saw himself as he was. With great solemnity he repeated the message to the Laodicean church:

"'Because thou sayest, I am rich, and increased with goods, and have need of nothing.' In my self-sufficiency this is just the way I felt," he said. "'And knowest not that thou art wretched, and miserable, and poor, and blind, and naked.' I now see that this is my condition. My eyes are opened. My spirit has been hard and unjust. I thought myself righteous, but my heart is broken, and I see my need of the precious counsel of the One who has searched me through and through. Oh, how gracious and compassionate and loving are the words, 'I counsel thee to buy of Me gold tried in the fire, that thou mayest be rich; and white raiment, that thou mayest be clothed, and that the shame of thy nakedness do not appear; and anoint thine eyes with eyesalve, that thou mayest see.'" Revelation 3:17, 18.

The speaker turned to those who had been praying, and said: "We have something to do. We must confess our sins, and humble our hearts before God." He made heartbroken confessions and then stepped up to several of the brethren, one after another, and extended his hand, asking forgiveness. Those to whom he spoke sprang to their feet, making confession and asking forgiveness, and they fell upon one another's necks, weeping. The spirit of confession spread through the entire congregation. It was a Pentecostal season. God's praises were sung, and far into the night, until nearly morning, the work was carried on.

The following words were often repeated, with clear distinctness: "As many as I love, I rebuke and chasten: be zealous therefore, and repent. Behold, I stand at the door, and knock: if any man hear My voice, and open the door, I will come in to him, and will sup with him, and he with Me." Verses 19, 20.

No one seemed to be too proud to make heartfelt confession, and those who led in this work were the ones who had influence, but had not before had courage to confess their sins.

There was rejoicing such as never before had been heard in the Tabernacle.

Then I aroused from my unconsciousness, and for a while could not think where I was. My pen was still in my hand. The words were spoken to me: "This might have been. All this the Lord was waiting to do for His people. All heaven was waiting to be gracious." I thought of where we might have been had thorough work been done at the last General Conference, and agony of disappointment came over me as I realized that what I had witnessed was not a reality.

God's way is always the right and the prudent way. He always brings honor to His name. Man's only security against rash, ambitious movements is to keep the heart in harmony with Christ Jesus. Man's wisdom is untrustworthy. Man is fickle, filled with self-esteem, pride, and selfishness. Let the workers doing God's service trust wholly in the Lord. Then the leaders will reveal that they are willing to be led, not by human wisdom, which is as useless to lean upon as is a broken reed, but by the wisdom of the Lord, who has said: "If any of you lack wisdom, let him ask of God, that giveth to all men liberally, and upbraideth not; and it shall be given him. But let him ask in faith, nothing wavering." James 1:5, 6.

20. Forgetfulness

All who profess to be children of God I would invite to consider the history of the Israelites, as recorded in the one hundred and fifth, the one hundred and sixth, and the one hundred and seventh psalms. By carefully studying these scriptures, we may be able to appreciate more fully the goodness, mercy, and love of our God.

Section 2: Counsels Often Repeated

- **A Hymn of the Promised Land**

Oh give thanks unto Jehovah, call upon His name;
   Make known among the peoples His doings.
Sing unto Him, sing praises unto Him;
   Talk ye of all His marvelous works.
Glory ye in His holy name:
   Let the heart of them rejoice that seek Jehovah.
Seek ye Jehovah and His strength;
   Seek His face evermore.

Remember His marvelous works that He hath done,
   His wonders, and the judgments of His mouth,
O ye seed of Abraham His servant,
   Ye children of Jacob, His chosen ones.
He is Jehovah our God:
   His judgments are in all the earth.
He hath remembered His covenant forever,
   The word which He commanded to a thousand generations,
The covenant which He made with Abraham,
   And His oath unto Isaac,
And confirmed the same unto Jacob for a statute,
   To Israel for an everlasting covenant,
Saying, Unto thee will I give the land of Canaan,
   The lot of your inheritance;
When they were but a few men in number,
   Yea, very few, and sojourners in it.
And they went about from nation to nation,
   From one kingdom to another people.
He suffered no man to do them wrong;
   Yea, He reproved kings for their sakes,
Saying, Touch not Mine anointed ones,
   And do My prophets no harm.

And He called for a famine upon the land;
  He brake the whole staff of bread.
He sent a man before them;
  Joseph was sold for a servant:
His feet they hurt with fetters:
  He was laid in chains of iron,
Until the time that His word came to pass,
  The word of Jehovah tried him.
The king sent and loosed him;
  Even the ruler of peoples, and let him go free.
He made him lord of his house,
  And ruler of all his substance;
To bind his princes at his pleasure.
  And teach his elders wisdom
Israel also came into Egypt;
  And Jacob sojourned in the land of Ham.
And He increased His people greatly,
  And made them stronger than their adversaries.

He turned their heart to hate His people,
  To deal subtly with His servants.
He sent Moses His servant,
  And Aaron whom He had chosen.
They set among them His signs,
  And wonders in the land of Ham.
He sent darkness, and made it dark;
  And they rebelled not against His words.
He turned their waters into blood,
  And slew their fish.
Their land swarmed with frogs
  In the chambers of their kings.
He spake, and there came swarms of flies,
  And lice in all their borders.
He gave them hail for rain,
  And flaming fire in their land.

He smote their vines also and their fig trees,
  And brake the trees of their borders.
He spake, and the locust came,
  And the grasshopper, and that without number,
And did eat up every herb in their land,
  And did eat up the fruit of their ground.
He smote also all the first-born in their land,
  The chief of all their strength.
And He brought them forth with silver and gold;
  And there was not one feeble person among His tribes.
Egypt was glad when they departed;
  For the fear of them had fallen upon them.

He spread a cloud for a covering,
  And fire to give light in the night.
They asked, and He brought quails,
  And satisfied them with the bread of heaven.
He opened the rock, and waters gushed out;
  They ran in the dry places like a river.

For He remembered His holy word,
  And Abraham His servant.
And He brought forth His people with joy,
  And His chosen with singing.
And He gave them the lands of the nations;
  And they took the labor of the peoples in possession:
That they might keep His statutes,
  And observe His laws.
    Praise ye Jehovah.
Psalm 105, A. R. V.

- **A Hymn of the Captivity**

Praise ye Jehovah.
Oh give thanks unto Jehovah; for He is good;
  For His loving-kindness endureth forever.
Who can utter the mighty acts of Jehovah,
  Or show forth all His praise?
Blessed are they that keep justice,
  And he that doeth righteousness at all times.
Remember me, O Jehovah, with the favor that Thou bearest
  unto Thy people;
Oh visit me with Thy salvation,
That I may see the prosperity of Thy chosen,
That I may rejoice in the gladness of Thy nation,
That I may glory with Thine inheritance.

We have sinned with our fathers,
  We have committed iniquity, we have done wickedly.
  Our fathers understood not Thy wonders in Egypt;
  They remembered not the multitude of Thy loving-kindnesses.
  But were rebellious at the sea, even at the Red Sea.

Nevertheless He saved them for His name's sake,
  That He might make His mighty power to be known.
  He rebuked the Red Sea also, and it was dried up:
  So He led them through the depths, as through a wilderness.
  And He saved them from the hand of him that hated them,
  And redeemed them from the hand of the enemy.
  And the waters covered their adversaries;
  There was not one of them left.
  Then believed they His words;
  They sang His praise.

Section 2: Counsels Often Repeated

II

They soon forgat His works;
They waited not for His counsel,
But lusted exceedingly in the wilderness,
And tempted God in the desert.
And He gave them their request,
But sent leanness into their soul.
They envied Moses also in the camp,
And Aaron the saint of Jehovah.
The earth opened and swallowed up Dathan,
And covered the company of Abiram.
And a fire was kindled in their company
The flame burned up the wicked.
They made a calf in Horeb,
And worshiped a molten image.
Thus they changed their glory
For the likeness of an ox that eateth grass.

They forgot God their Saviour,
Who had done great things in Egypt,
Wondrous works in the land of Ham,
And terrible things by the Red Sea.
Therefore He said that He would destroy them,
Had not Moses His chosen stood before Him in the breach,
To turn away His wrath, lest He should destroy them.

III

Yea, they despised the pleasant land,
They believed not His word,
But murmured in their tents,
And hearkened not unto the voice of Jehovah.
Therefore He sware unto them,

That He would overthrow them in the wilderness,
And that He would overthrow their seed among the nations,
And scatter them in the lands.
They joined themselves also unto Baalpeor,
And ate the sacrifices of the dead.
Thus they provoked Him to anger with their doings;
And the plague brake in upon them.

Then stood up Phinehas, and executed judgment;
  And so the plague was stayed.
  And that was reckoned unto him for righteousness,
  Unto all generations for evermore.

IV

They angered Him also at the waters of Meribah,
So that it went ill with Moses for their sakes;
Because they were rebellious against his spirit,
And he spake unadvisedly with his lips.
They did not destroy the peoples,
As Jehovah commanded them,
But mingled themselves with the nations,
And learned their works,
And served their idols,
Which became a snare unto them.
Yea, they sacrificed their sons and their daughters unto demons,
And shed innocent blood,
Even the blood of their sons and of their daughters,
Whom they sacrificed unto the idols of Canaan;
And the land was polluted with blood.
Thus were they defiled with their works,
And played the harlot in their doings.

Section 2: Counsels Often Repeated

Therefore was the wrath of Jehovah kindled against His people,
And He abhorred His inheritance.
And He gave them into the hand of the nations;
And they that hated them ruled over them.
Their enemies also oppressed them,
And they were brought into subjection under their hand.
Many times did He deliver them;
But they were rebellious in their counsel,
And were brought low in their iniquity.

Nevertheless He regarded their distress,
When He heard their cry:
And He remembered for them His covenant,
And repented according to the multitude of His loving-kindnesses.
He made them also to be pitied
Of all those that carried them captive.

Save us, O Jehovah our God,
   And gather us from among the nations,
To give thanks unto Thy holy name,
   And to triumph in Thy praise.

Blessed be Jehovah, the God of Israel,
From everlasting even to everlasting.
And let all the people say, Amen.
Praise ye Jehovah.
Psalm 106, A. R. V.

- **Song of the Redeemed**

Oh give thanks unto Jehovah; for He is good;
  For His loving-kindness endureth forever.
Let the redeemed of Jehovah say so,
  Whom He hath redeemed from the hand of the adversary,
And gathered out of the lands,
From the east and from the west,
From the north and from the south.

I

They wandered in the wilderness in a desert way;
They found no city of habitation.
Hungry and thirsty,
Their soul fainted in them.
  Then they cried unto Jehovah in their trouble,
  And He delivered them out of their distresses,
  He led them also by a straight way,
  That they might go to a city of habitation.
Oh that men would praise Jehovah for His loving-kindness
And for His wonderful works to the children of men!
For He satisfieth the longing soul,
And the hungry soul He filleth with good.

Such as sat in darkness and in the shadow of death,
Being bound in affliction and iron,

Because they rebelled against the words of God,
And contemned the counsel of the Most High:
Therefore He brought down their heart with labor;
They fell down, and there was none to help.
Then they cried unto Jehovah in their trouble,
And He saved them out of their distresses.

Section 2: Counsels Often Repeated

He brought them out of darkness and the shadow of death,
And brake their bonds in sunder.
Oh that men would praise Jehovah for His loving-kindness,
And for His wonderful works to the children of men!
For He hath broken the gates of brass,
And cut the bars of iron in sunder...

II

He turneth rivers into a wilderness,
And water springs into a thirsty ground;
A fruitful land into a salt desert,
For the wickedness of them that dwell therein.
He turneth a wilderness into a pool of water,
And a dry land into water springs.
And there He maketh the hungry to dwell,
That they may prepare a city of habitation,
And sow fields, and plant vineyards,
And get them fruits of increase.
He blesseth them also, so that they are multiplied greatly;
And He suffereth not their cattle to decrease.

Again, they are diminished and bowed down
Through oppression, trouble, and sorrow.
He poureth contempt upon princes,
And causeth them to wander in the waste, where there is no way.
Yet setteth He the needy on high from affliction,
And maketh him families like a flock.
The upright shall see it, and be glad;
And all iniquity shall stop her mouth.

Whoso is wise will give heed to these things;
And they will consider the loving-kindnesses of Jehovah.
   Psalm 107, A. R. V.

- **"Call to Remembrance the Former Days"**

Why did ancient Israel so easily forget God's dealings? The people did not retain in their memory His works of greatness and power or His words of warning. Had they remembered His wondrous dealings with them they would not have received the reproof:

> Who art thou, that thou art afraid of man that shall die,
> And of the son of man that shall be made as grass;
> And hast forgotten Jehovah thy Maker,
> That stretched forth the heavens,
> And laid the foundations of the earth;
> And fearest continually all the day
> Because of the fury of the oppressor,
> When he maketh ready to destroy?
> And where is the fury of the oppressor?
>   Isaiah 51:12, 13, A. R. V.

But the children of Israel forgot God, whose they were by creation and by redemption. After seeing all His wondrous works, they tempted Him.

To the Israelites were committed the sacred oracles. But God's revealed word was misinterpreted and misapplied. The people despised the word of the Holy One of Israel.

> The vineyard of Jehovah of hosts is the house of Israel,
> And the men of Judah His pleasant plant:
> And He looked for justice, but, behold, oppression;
> For righteousness, but, behold, a cry.
>
> Woe unto them
> That ... regard not the work of Jehovah,
>   Neither have they considered the operation of His hands.
> Therefore My people are gone into captivity
>   For lack of knowledge.

Woe unto them
That call evil good,
 And good evil;
That put darkness for light,
 And light for darkness;
That put bitter for sweet,
 And sweet for bitter!

Woe unto them
That are wise in their own eyes,
And prudent in their own sight!

Therefore as the tongue of fire devoureth the stubble,
And as the dry grass sinketh down in the flame,
So their root shall be as rottenness,
And their blossom shall go up as dust;
Because they have rejected the law of Jehovah of hosts,
And despised the word of the Holy One of Israel.
 Isaiah 5:7, 11-13, 20, 21, 24, A. R. V.

- **"Written for our Admonition"**

"These things ... are written for our admonition, upon whom the ends of the world are come." 1 Corinthians 10:11. The warning comes sounding down along the line to our time:

"Take heed, brethren, lest there be in any of you an evil heart of unbelief, in departing from the living God. But exhort one another daily, while it is called Today; lest any of you be hardened through the deceitfulness of sin. For we are made partakers of Christ, if we hold the beginning of our confidence steadfast unto the end; while it is said,

Today if ye will hear His voice,
Harden not your hearts, as in the provocation.

For some, when they had heard, did provoke: howbeit not all that came out of Egypt by Moses." Hebrews 3:12-16.

Cannot we who are living in the time of the end realize the importance of the apostle's words: "Take heed, brethren, lest there be in any of you an evil heart of unbelief, in departing from the living God"? Verse 12.

Upon us is shining the accumulated light of past ages. The record of Israel's forgetfulness has been preserved for our enlightenment. In this age God has set His hand to gather unto Himself a people from every nation, kindred, and tongue. In the advent movement He has wrought for His heritage, even as He wrought for the Israelites in leading them from Egypt.

In the great disappointment of 1844 the faith of His people was tested as was that of the Hebrews at the Red Sea. Had the Adventists in the early days still trusted to the guiding Hand that had been with them in their past experience, they would have seen of the salvation of God. If all who had labored unitedly in the work of 1844 had received the third angel's message and proclaimed it in the power of the Holy Spirit, the Lord would have wrought mightily with their efforts. A flood of light would have been shed upon the world. Years ago the inhabitants of the earth would have been warned, the closing work would have been completed, and Christ would have come for the redemption of His people.

- ## The Message for this Time

I have been instructed to trace words of warning for our brethren and sisters who are in danger of losing sight of the special work for this time. The Lord has made us depositaries of sacred truth. We are to arise and shine. In every land we are to herald the second coming of Christ, in the language of the revelator proclaiming: "Behold, He cometh with clouds; and every eye shall see Him, and they also which pierced Him: and all kindreds of the earth shall wail because of Him." Revelation 1:7.

What are we doing? Are we giving the message of the third angel? "The third angel followed them [the first and second angels], saying with a loud voice, If any man worship the beast and his image, and receive his mark in his forehead, or in his hand, the same shall drink of the wine of the wrath of God, which is poured out without mixture into the cup of His indignation; and he shall be tormented with fire and brimstone in the presence of the holy angels, and in the presence of the Lamb: and the smoke of their torment ascendeth up for ever and ever: and they have no rest day nor night, who worship the beast and his image, and whosoever receiveth the mark of his name. Here is the patience of the saints: here are they that keep the commandments of God, and the faith of Jesus." Revelation 14:9-12.

The commandments of God and the testimony of Jesus are united. They are to be clearly presented to the world.

• The Opposition of the Enemy

In God's word we are shown the consequences of proclaiming the third angel's message. "The dragon was wroth with the woman, and went to make war with the remnant of her seed, which keep the commandments of God, and have the testimony of Jesus Christ." Revelation 12:17. A refusal to obey the commandments of God, and a determination to cherish hatred against those who proclaim these commandments, leads to the most determined war on the part of the dragon, whose whole energies are brought to bear against the commandment-keeping people of God. "He causeth all, both small and great, rich and poor, free and bond, to receive a mark in their right hand, or in their foreheads: and that no man might buy or sell, save he that had the mark, or the name of the beast, or the number of his name." Revelation 13:16, 17.

The sign, or seal, of God is revealed in the observance of the seventh-day Sabbath, the Lord's memorial of creation. "The Lord spake unto Moses, saying, Speak thou also unto the children of Israel, saying, Verily My Sabbaths ye shall keep: for it is a sign between Me and you throughout your generations; that ye may know that I am the Lord that doth sanctify you." Exodus 31:12, 13. Here the Sabbath is clearly designated as a sign between God and His people.

The mark of the beast is the opposite of this—the observance of the first day of the week. This mark distinguishes those who acknowledge the supremacy of the papal authority from those who acknowledge the authority of God.

- **The Loud Cry**

As foretold in the eighteenth of Revelation, the third angel's message is to be proclaimed with great power by those who give the final warning against the beast and his image:

"I saw another angel come down from heaven, having great power; and the earth was lightened with his glory. And he cried mightily with a strong voice, saying, Babylon the great is fallen, is fallen, and is become the habitation of devils, and the hold of every foul spirit, and a cage of every unclean and hateful bird. For all nations have drunk of the wine of the wrath of her fornication, and the kings of the earth have committed fornication with her, and the merchants of the earth are waxed rich through the abundance of her delicacies. And I heard another voice from heaven, saying, Come out of her, My people, that ye be not partakers of her sins, and that ye receive not of her plagues. For her sins have reached unto heaven, and God hath remembered her iniquities. Reward her even as she rewarded you, and double unto her double according to her works: in the cup which she hath filled fill to her double." Revelation 18:1-6.

This is the message given by God to be sounded forth in the loud cry of the third angel.

Those whose faith and zeal are proportionate to their knowledge of the truth will reveal their loyalty to God by communicating the truth, in all its saving, sanctifying power, to those with whom they associate. Their lives of holiness and unselfish service will be in conformity with the vital principles of the kingdom of heaven.

- **"And Hast Forgotten"**

It is a solemn and terrible truth that many who have been zealous in proclaiming the third angel's message are now becoming listless and indifferent! The line of demarcation between worldlings and many professed Christians is almost indistinguishable. Many who once were earnest Adventists are conforming to the world—to its practices, its customs, its selfishness. Instead of leading the world to render obedience to God's law, the church is uniting more and more closely with the world in transgression. Daily the church is becoming converted to the world. How many professing Christians are slaves of mammon! Their indulgence of appetite, their extravagant expenditure of money for selfish gratification, greatly dishonors God.

And through lack of zeal for the promulgation of the third angel's message, many others, while not apparently living in transgression, are nevertheless as verily lending their influence on the side of Satan as are those who openly sin against God. Multitudes are perishing; but how few are burdened for these souls! There is a stupor, a paralysis, upon many of the people of God, which prevents them from understanding the duty of the hour.

When the Israelites entered Canaan, they did not fulfill God's purpose by taking possession of the whole land. After making a partial conquest, they settled down to enjoy the fruit of their victories. In their unbelief and love of ease they congregated in the portions already conquered, instead of pushing forward to occupy new territory. Thus they began to depart from God. By their failure to carry out His purpose they made it impossible for Him to fulfill to them His promise of blessing.

Is not the church of today doing the same thing? With the whole world before them in need of the gospel, professed Christians congregate where they themselves can enjoy gospel privileges. They do not feel the necessity of occupying new territory, carrying the message of salvation into regions beyond. They refuse to fulfill Christ's commission: "Go ye into all the world, and preach the gospel to every creature." Are they less guilty than was the Jewish church?

- ## "Choose You This Day Whom Ye Will Serve"

There will be a sharp conflict between those who are loyal to God and those who cast scorn upon His law. Reverence for God's law has been subverted. The religious leaders are teaching for doctrine the commandments of men. As it was in the days of ancient Israel, so it is in this age of the world. But because of the prevalence of disloyalty and transgression, will those who have reverenced the law of God now cherish less respect for it? Will they unite with the powers of earth to make it void? The loyal will not be carried away by the current of evil. They will not throw contempt on that which God has set apart as holy. They will not follow Israel's example of forgetfulness; they will call to remembrance

God's dealings with His people in all ages, and will walk in the way of His commandments.

The test comes to everyone. There are only two sides. On which side are you?

• The Shield of Omnipotence

God's commandment-keeping people stand under the broad shield of Omnipotence.

> He that dwelleth in the secret place of the Most High
>   Shall abide under the shadow of the Almighty.
> I will say of Jehovah, He is my refuge and my fortress;
>   My God, in whom I trust.
> For He will deliver thee from the snare of the fowler,
>   And from the deadly pestilence.
> He will cover thee with His pinions,
>   And under His wings shalt thou take refuge:
> His truth is a shield and a buckler.
>   Thou shalt not be afraid for the terror by night,
> Nor for the arrow that flieth by day;
>   For the pestilence that walketh in darkness,
> Nor for the destruction that wasteth at noonday.
>   A thousand shall fall at thy side,
> And ten thousand at thy right hand;
>   But it shall not come nigh thee.
> Only with thine eyes shalt thou behold,
>   And see the reward of the wicked.
>
> For Thou, O Jehovah, art my refuge!
>   Thou hast made the Most High thy habitation;
> There shall no evil befall thee,
>   Neither shall any plague come nigh thy tent.
> For He will give His angels charge over thee,
>   To keep thee in all thy ways.

Section 2: Counsels Often Repeated

They shall bear thee up in their hands,
 Lest thou dash thy foot against a stone.
Thou shalt tread upon the lion and adder:
 The young lion and the serpent shalt thou trample underfoot.
Because he hath set his love upon Me, therefore will I deliver him:
 I will set him on high, because he hath known My name.
He shall call upon Me, and I will answer him;
 I will be with him in trouble:
 I will deliver him, and honor him.
With long life will I satisfy him,
 And show him My salvation.
 Psalm 91, A. R. V.

• Jehovah Reigneth

Oh come, let us sing unto Jehovah;
Let us make a joyful noise to the Rock of our salvation.
Let us come before His presence with thanksgiving;
Let us make a joyful noise unto Him with psalms.

For Jehovah is a great God,
And a great King above all gods.
In His hand are the deep places of the earth;
The heights of the mountains are His also.
The sea is His, and He made it;
And His hands formed the dry land.

Oh come, let us worship and bow down;
Let us kneel before Jehovah our Maker:

For He is our God,
And we are the people of His pasture, and the sheep of His hand.
Today, Oh that ye would hear His voice!
Harden not your heart, as at Meribah,

As in the day of Massah in the wilderness;
When your fathers tempted Me,
Proved Me, and saw My work.

Forty years long was I grieved with that generation,
And said, It is a people that do err in their heart,
And they have not known My ways:
Wherefore I sware in My wrath, that they should not enter into My rest.

Oh sing unto Jehovah a new song:
Sing unto Jehovah, all the earth.
Sing unto Jehovah, bless His name;
Show forth His salvation from day to day.
Declare His glory among the nations,
His marvelous works among all the peoples.

For great is Jehovah, and greatly to be praised:
He is to be feared above all gods.
For all the gods of the peoples are idols;
But Jehovah made the heavens.
Honor and majesty are before Him:
Strength and beauty are in His sanctuary.

Ascribe unto Jehovah, ye kindreds of the peoples,
Ascribe unto Jehovah glory and strength.
Ascribe unto Jehovah the glory due unto His name:
Bring an offering, and come into His courts.
Oh worship Jehovah in holy array:
Tremble before Him, all the earth.

Say among the nations, Jehovah reigneth:
The world also is established that it cannot be moved:
He will judge the peoples with equity.

Let the heavens be glad, and let the earth rejoice;
Let the sea roar, and the fullness thereof;
Let the field exult, and all that is therein;
Then shall all the trees of the wood sing for joy

Before Jehovah; for He cometh,
For He cometh to judge the earth:
He will judge the world with righteousness,
And the peoples with His truth.
Psalm 95; 96, A. R. V.

— Section 3 —

Letters to Physicians

"To write the same things to you, to me indeed is not grievous, but for you it is safe." Philippians 3:1.

21. The Value of Trial

En Route to Copenhagen
July 16, 1886.
To the Medical Superintendent of the Battle Creek Sanitarium—
My Dear Brother: I have the most tender love for you, and I would that those who are pursuing you with reproach would let you alone. But, my brother, you must remember that these perplexities and annoyances are included in the "all things" that work together for good to those who love God. The Lord's eye is upon you, and He beholds those who would misrepresent you and tear you to pieces. But if you will be of good courage, if you will stay your soul upon God, if you will trust your heavenly Father as a child trusts its parent, if you will deal justly and love mercy, God can and will work with you. His promise is sure: "Them that honor Me I will honor." 1 Samuel 2:30.

Remember that your experience is not the first of the kind. You know the history of Joseph and of Daniel. The Lord did not prevent the plottings of wicked men; but He caused their devices to work for good to those who, amidst trial and conflict, preserved their faith and loyalty.

The furnace fires are not to destroy, but to refine, ennoble, sanctify. Without trial we should not feel so much our need of God and His help; and we should become proud and self-sufficient. In the trials that come to you I see evidence

Section 3: Letters to Physicians

that the Lord's eye is upon you and that He means to draw you to Himself. It is not the whole, but the wounded, who need a physician; it is those who are pressed almost beyond the point of endurance who need a helper. Turn to the stronghold. Learn the precious lesson: "Come unto Me, all ye that labor and are heavy-laden, and I will give you rest. Take My yoke upon you, and learn of Me; for I am meek and lowly in heart: and ye shall find rest unto your souls. For My yoke is easy, and My burden is light." Matthew 11:28-30.

Jesus loves you, and I am made glad as I read of the experience through which you are passing, not because you are a sufferer, but because this is an evidence to me that the Lord Jesus is testing and proving you, to see if you will come to Him, to see if you will put your trust in Him and find peace and rest in His love. I am praying for you, that you may come to Him, the Fountain of living water. This is the experience that every one of us must have if we ever dwell with Christ in the mansions that He has gone to prepare for us. You have lessons of the highest value to learn in the school of Christ, lessons that will lead you to work out your own salvation with fear and trembling.

It is when you are prospered, when all men speak well of you, that you are in danger. Be on your guard, for you will be tried. My greatest fear for you has been that you would have too great prosperity, and that you would fail to learn that your dependence is alone upon God. You have been placed in a position of great trust and honor, and there has been danger of your becoming dizzy and forgetting your dependence upon God. You have been placed where you can exert a far-reaching influence for good if you keep your eye single to the glory of God. Your heavenly Father loves you, and He will draw you to Himself by the trials that seem to you severe.

I have a most earnest desire that you shall enter the city of God, not as a culprit barely pardoned, but as a conqueror. My brother, will you think of this? If you are true and humble and faithful in this life, you will be given an abundant entrance. Then the tree of life will be yours, for you will be a victor over sin; the city whose builder and maker is God will be your city. Let your imagination take hold upon things unseen. Let your thoughts be carried away to the evidences of the great love of God for you. In contemplating the object of which you are in pursuit, you will lose the sense of pain brought by the light afflictions that are but for a moment.

- **Paul's Experience**

Copenhagen
July 17, 1886.

Paul was a man who knew what it means to be a partaker of Christ's sufferings. You have no need that I repeat the history of his trials. His life was one of constant activity, notwithstanding he was subject to many infirmities. He was continually followed by the hatred and malice of the Jews. They were exceedingly bitter against him and did all in their power to hinder him in his work. Yet we hear his voice sounding down along the line of our time:

"Our light affliction, which is but for a moment, worketh for us a far more exceeding and eternal weight of glory; while we look not at the things which are seen, but at the things which are not seen: for the things which are seen are temporal; but the things which are not seen are eternal." "I reckon that the sufferings of this present time are not worthy to be compared with the glory which shall be revealed in us." 2 Corinthians 4:17, 18; Romans 8:18. None too highly does Paul estimate the privileges and advantages of the Christian life. I speak with no hesitancy about this matter, for I know for myself that what he says is true.

- **Resting in God's Love**

Paul says further: "As many as are led by the Spirit of God, they are the sons of God. For ye have not received the spirit of bondage again to fear; but ye have received the Spirit of adoption, whereby we cry, Abba, Father." Verses 14, 15. One of the lessons that we are to learn in the school of Christ is that the Lord's love for us is far greater than that of our earthly parents. We are to have unquestioning faith and perfect confidence in Him. "The Spirit itself beareth witness with our spirit, that we are the children of God: and if children, then heirs; heirs of God, and joint heirs with Christ; if so be that we suffer with Him, that we may be also glorified together." Verses 16, 17.

May the Lord help you, as a diligent student in the school of Christ, to learn to lay your burdens on Jesus. And if you are free in His love, you will look above and away from these annoying trials. Think of what Jesus has endured for you, and never forget that it is part of the legacy that we have received as Christians, to be partakers with Him of His sufferings, that we may be partakers with Him of His glory.

• The Danger of Self-Sufficiency

Study Nebuchadnezzar's dream as recorded in the fourth chapter of Daniel. The king saw a lofty tree planted in the earth. Flocks and herds from the mountains and hills enjoyed its shelter, and the birds of the air built their nests in its branches. Thus were represented Nebuchadnezzar's greatness and prosperity. Nations were gathered under his sovereignty. His kingdom was firmly established in the hearts of his loyal subjects.

The king saw his prosperity, and because of it he was lifted up. Notwithstanding the warnings that God had given him, he did the very things which the Lord had told him not to do.

He looked upon his kingdom with pride and exclaimed: "Is not this great Babylon, that I have built for the house of the kingdom by the might of my power, and for the honor of my majesty?" Daniel 4:30. The instant that the words were uttered, the sentence of judgment was pronounced. The king's reason was taken away. The judgment that he had thought so perfect, the wisdom that he had prided himself on possessing, were removed. The jewel of the mind, that which elevates man above the beasts, he no longer retained.

The scepter is no longer held in the hand of a proud and powerful monarch. The mighty ruler is a maniac. He now herds with the cattle to eat as they eat. He is a companion of the beasts of the field. The brow that once wore a coronet is disfigured by the absence of reason and intellect. The mandate has gone forth: "Hew down the tree, and cut off his branches, shake off his leaves, and scatter his fruit." Verse 14.

So the Lord magnifies Himself as the true and living God. Well might David exclaim: "I have seen the wicked in great power, and spreading himself like a green bay tree. Yet he passed away, and, lo, he was not: yea, I sought him, but he could not be found." Psalm 37:35, 36. Let men become lifted up in pride, and the Lord will not sustain them and keep them from falling. Let a church become proud and boastful, not depending on God, not exalting His power, and that church will surely be left by the Lord, to be brought down to the ground. Let a people glory in wealth, intellect, knowledge, or in anything but Christ, and they will soon be brought to confusion.

• Our Burden Bearer

My brother, remember that this earth is not heaven. Christ has declared: "In the world ye shall have tribulation: but be of good cheer; I have overcome the world." "Blessed are they which are persecuted for righteousness' sake: for theirs is the kingdom of heaven. Blessed are ye, when men shall revile you, and persecute you, and shall say all manner of evil against you falsely, for My sake. Rejoice, and be exceeding glad: for great is your reward in heaven: for so persecuted they the prophets which were before you." John 16:33; Matthew 5:10-12.

Jesus has not left you to be amazed at the trials and difficulties you meet. He has told you all about them, and He has told you also not to be cast down and oppressed when trials come. Look to Jesus, your Redeemer, and be cheerful and rejoice. The trials hardest to bear are those that come from our brethren, our own familiar friends; but even these trials may be borne with patience. Jesus is not lying in Joseph's new tomb. He has risen and has ascended to heaven, there to intercede in our behalf. We have a Saviour who so loved us that He died for us, that through Him we might have hope and strength and courage, and a place with Him upon His throne. He is able and willing to help you whenever you call upon Him.

If you try to carry your burdens alone you will be crushed under them. You have heavy responsibilities. Jesus knows about them, and He will not leave you alone if you do not leave Him. He is honored when you commit the keeping of your soul to Him as unto a faithful Creator. He bids you hope in His mercy, believing that He does not desire you to carry these weighty responsibilities in your own strength. Only believe, and you will see the salvation of God.

Do you feel your insufficiency for the position of trust that you occupy? Thank God for this. The more you feel your weakness, the more you will be inclined to seek for a helper. "Draw nigh to God, and He will draw nigh to you." James 4:8.

Jesus wants you to be happy, to be cheerful. He wants you to do your best with the ability that God has given you and then trust the Lord to help you and to raise up those who will be your helpers in carrying burdens.

Let not the unkind speeches of men hurt you. Did not men say unkind things about Jesus? You err, and may sometimes give occasion for unkind remarks; but Jesus never did. He was pure, spotless, undefiled. Do not expect a better portion in this life than the Prince of glory had. When your enemies see that they can make you feel hurt, they will rejoice, and Satan will rejoice. Look to Jesus, and work with an eye single to His glory. Keep your heart in the love of God.

- **Looking Away From Men**

It may be that even the members of the church to which you belong will say and do that which will grieve you. But move right on, calm and peaceful, ever trusting in Jesus, remembering that you are not your own, that you are Christ's property, the purchase of the blood of God's beloved Son, and that you are engaged in His work, seeking to bless humanity. This is a great work. Do not let the perversity of men move you from firm trust and abiding faith in the promises of God.

It hurts you when one for whom you have done much becomes your enemy, having been brought under an influence opposed to you. But do you not do almost the same thing to Jesus when you turn away from Him? He has been your best friend. He has done everything He could to win your love. He has invited your confidence. He has asked you to come to Him with all your burdens and all your griefs, and has pledged His word to give you rest and peace if you will wear His yoke and bear His burdens. He declares that His yoke is easy and His burden is light. Show that you believe this. Take God at His word. You never could have stood where you now stand, bearing the responsibilities that you have borne, unless Jesus had given you special help. Acknowledge this. Praise God for the help that He has been to you, and trust Him still.

Bring Christ into your life. Do not feel that you are answerable for the wrong course of others, even though they are in the church. There are in the church unfaithful ones who treat Jesus far worse than they treat you. Were He on earth, they would insult Him, revile Him, defame Him. "It must needs be that offenses come; but woe to that man by whom the offense cometh." "It were better for him that a millstone were hanged about his neck, and that he were drowned in the depth of the sea." Matthew 18:7, 6.

You are carrying a heavy load. I wish that everyone could feel this as I do. I wish that all your brethren would be true and faithful to you, not hindering you, not extolling or glorifying you, but looking upon you as one whom God is using as His instrument to do a given work, and remembering that they must not block the wheels, but must put their shoulder to the wheel, helping instead of hindering.

- **An Eternal Weight of Glory**

Again I say: Rejoice in the Lord. Rest in Him. You need His power, and this power you may have. Go forward firmly, valiantly, courageously. You may err in judgment, but do not lose your hold on Jesus. He is wisdom, He is light, He is power. He is to you as a great Rock in a weary land. Rest under His shadow. You need wisdom, and Jesus will give it to you. Do not be unbelieving. The more you are jostled, misapprehended, misstated, misrepresented, the more evidence you have that you are doing a work for the Master, and the more closely you must cling to your Saviour. In all your difficulties be calm and undisturbed, patient and forbearing, not rendering evil for evil, but good for evil. Look to the top of the ladder. God is above it. His glory shines on every soul ascending heavenward. Jesus is this ladder. Climb up by Him, cling to Him, and erelong you will step off the ladder into His everlasting kingdom.

I want you to have heaven. I know of no one who would appreciate heaven more than you, who have worked so untiringly to relieve suffering humanity, depriving yourself of sleep, neglecting to take food, bringing but little enjoyment into your life. At times there does not seem to be much sunshine in your path, only one long, continuous shadow. The afflictions you see, the dependent mortals looking and longing for help, your contact with depraved, corrupted human beings —this experience is of a character to undermine your faith in humanity.

You must, indeed, look to Jesus, keeping your eyes fixed on the glory at the top of the ladder. Through Christ alone can you make sure of heaven, where all

Section 3: Letters to Physicians

is purity, holiness, peace, and blessedness, where there are glories that mortal lips cannot describe. The nearest we can come to a description of the reward that awaits the overcomer is to say that it is a far more exceeding and eternal weight of glory. It will be an eternity of bliss, a blessed eternity, unfolding new glories throughout the ceaseless ages.

You must be there. Whatever you lose here, be determined to make sure of eternal life. Never become discouraged. Many times I have seen that the everlasting arms were round about you, when you did not seem to realize or appreciate the great condescension of heaven. Live for Jesus. You can work better as a physician in the sanitarium if you make Christ your physician in chief. Seek earnestly for the crown of life. Make a business of serving God. It will pay, not only in this life, but in the life to come. I feel as deep an interest in you and your wife, whom I love in the Lord, as I do in my own sons and their wives. I want you and your wife to be among the redeemed, to act a part in the coronation of Christ. I greatly desire that you shall come off more than conqueror through Him who gave His life for you. For this reason, my brother, I have spoken plainly to you. I am so desirous that you should have an eternity of bliss. Your position has been most trying. I have feared that you would lose faith and courage. You must grow in grace and in a knowledge of the truth. You must draw close to your brethren. Whatever may come, do not lose faith in them or in Christ; and hold fast to the truth.

Extract from a letter written in 1892 from Adelaide, South Australia.—My brother, you will meet with trials, but hold fast your integrity. Never show anything but a noble spirit. The heavenly universe is watching the conflict. Satan is watching, anxious to catch you off your guard, anxious to see you acting impetuously, that he may obtain the advantage over you. Fight manfully the battle of the Lord. Do just as Christ would do were He in your place. Let there be no inconsistency in your faith or practice. Do not allow yourself to become wrought up over the vexatious troubles that are constantly arising. Keep calm, think of Jesus, and do what you can to please Him. The grace of Christ and the Holy Spirit are God's gifts to you, that you may be strengthened with all might in the inner man.

22. Centering Too Much in Battle Creek

South Lancaster, Massachusetts
October 16, 1890.
To the Managers of the Battle Creek Sanitarium—
Dear Brethren:
While in Petoskey I had some conversation with your physician in chief in regard to establishing a home for orphan children at Battle Creek. I said that this was just what was needed among us as a people, and that in enterprises of this kind we were far behind other denominations.

In my conversation I spoke of my fear that we were centering too many responsibilities in Battle Creek, and I am still of the same opinion. It is perilous to center so much in one locality. A large amount of means is being expended in this one place, while cities are neglected that will become more and more difficult to work.

I have been looking over some of my writings, and I find that warnings on this point were given years ago. It is plainly stated that the buildings in Battle Creek should not be enlarged, that building should not be added to building to increase facilities there. We were instructed not to accumulate interests in that one place, but to enlarge our sphere of labor. There was danger that Battle Creek would become as Jerusalem of old—a powerful center. If we do not heed these warnings, the evils that ruined Jerusalem will come upon us. Pride, self-exaltation, neglect of the poor, and partiality to the wealthy—these were the sins of Jerusalem. Today when large interests are built up in one place, the workers are tempted to become lifted up in selfishness and pride. When they yield to this temptation they are not laborers together with God. Instead of seeking to increase our responsibilities in Battle Creek, we should bravely and willingly divide the responsibilities already there, distributing them to many places.

We are "a spectacle unto the world, and to angels, and to men." 1 Corinthians 4:9. Our mission is the same as that which was announced by Christ, at the beginning of His ministry, to be His mission. "The Spirit of the Lord is upon Me," He said, "because He hath anointed Me to preach the gospel to the poor; He hath sent Me to heal the brokenhearted, to preach deliverance to the captives, and recovering of sight to the blind, to set at liberty them that are bruised, to preach the acceptable year of the Lord." Luke 4:18, 19.

We are to carry forward the work placed in our hands by the Master. He says: "If thou draw out thy soul to the hungry, and satisfy the afflicted soul; then shall thy light rise in obscurity, and thy darkness be as the noonday: and the Lord shall guide thee continually, and satisfy thy soul in drought, and make fat thy bones: and thou shalt be like a watered garden, and like a spring of water, whose waters fail not." "The poor shall never cease out of the land: therefore I command thee, saying, Thou shalt open thine hand wide unto thy brother, to thy poor, and to thy needy, in thy land." "All things whatsoever ye would that men should do to you, do ye even so to them." Isaiah 58:10, 11; Deuteronomy 15:11; Matthew 7:12.

We shall be tempted to be covetous, to be avaricious, to cultivate an insatiable desire for more. If we yield to this temptation, it will bring upon us the same perils that fell upon ancient Jerusalem. We shall fail to know God and to represent Him in character. We need to watch ourselves closely lest we fall because of unbelief, as did the Jews. We are to work unselfishly. We are to feel a deep interest in the establishment and growth of other institutions besides those over which we have supervision. I sincerely wish that the sanitarium were miles away from Battle Creek. From the light given me of God, I know this would be better for its spirituality and usefulness. The college near Lincoln, Nebraska, will take a large number from Battle Creek, and this is as it should be. The light should shine forth from other places, as well as from Battle Creek. God designs that light shall shine forth from different cities and various localities.

To center so much in one place is a mistake; it savors of selfishness. Battle Creek is receiving more than its share of advantages. Were the important interests established there divided and subdivided, strength would be given to other churches. We are to labor unselfishly in the Lord's great vineyard, dividing time, money, educational interests, and ministerial institutes in such a way that as large a number as possible shall reap the benefit. The ambition that leads men to center so many facilities in Battle Creek should be restricted, that other places may be blessed with the benefits that some have planned to center there. In centering so much in one place, a wrong education is given to the people.

To plan largely for Battle Creek is not wise. The world is our field of labor, and the money expended in this one place would go far toward carrying forward successful aggressive work in other places. There are many cities in which the people need the gospel message. Instead of so many of our workers of talent being centered in Battle Creek, men of sanctified ability should be assigned to posts of activity in different localities. These men should have a living interest in many places, studying ways and means by which to advance the work. They are not to move in their own judgment, but are to blend together in the great work. From year to year, as the work strengthens in the place in which they are laboring, they are to educate and train workers, and send help to other places.

• Unselfishness in Service

A limit must be set to the expansion of our institutions in Battle Creek. The field is the world, and God has an interest in other parts of His great vineyard. There are churches and institutions that are straining every nerve to get standing room, that they may live. Let our prosperous institutions see to it that they strengthen the things that remain which are ready to die. How easily might the large church in Battle Creek appropriate some of its means for the aid of the poorer churches, which are nearly crushed under a load of debt! Why is it that these sister churches are left from year to year to struggle with poverty and debt? Selfishness brings spiritual death. What great good our more able churches might accomplish if they would aid their sister churches, bringing them to a condition of prosperity!

• Helping Those Who Need Help

As God's agencies we are to have hearts of flesh, full of the charity that prompts us to be helpful to those more needy than ourselves. If we see our brethren and sisters struggling under poverty and debt, if we see churches that are in need of financial aid, we should manifest an unselfish interest in them and help them in proportion as God has prospered us. If you who have charge of an institution see other institutions bravely struggling for standing room so that they may do a work similar to the work of the institutions with which you are connected, do not be jealous.

Do not seek to push a working force out of existence and to exalt yourselves in conscious superiority. Rather, curtail some of your large plans, and help those who are struggling. Aid them in carrying out some of their plans to increase their facilities. Do not use every dollar in enlarging your facilities and increasing your responsibilities. Reserve part of your means for establishing in other places health institutions and schools. You will need great wisdom to know just where to place these institutions so that the people will be the most benefited. All these matters must receive candid consideration.

Those in positions of responsibility will need wisdom from on high in order to deal justly, to love mercy, and to show mercy, not only to a few, but to everyone with whom they come in contact. Christ identifies His interests with those of His people, no matter how poor and needy they may be. Missions must be opened for the colored people, and everyone should seek to do something and to do it now.

There is need that institutions be established in different places, that men and women may be set at work to do their best in the fear of God. No one should lose sight of his mission and work. Everyone should aim to carry forward to a successful issue the work placed in his hands. All our institutions should keep this in mind and strive for success; but at the same time let them remember that their success will increase in proportion as they exercise disinterested liberality, sharing their abundance with institutions that are struggling for a foothold.

Our prosperous institutions should help those institutions that God has said should live and prosper, but which are still struggling for an existence. There is among us a very limited amount of real, unselfish love. The Lord says: "Everyone that loveth is born of God, and knoweth God. He that loveth not knoweth not God; for God is love." "If we love one another, God dwelleth in us, and His love is perfected in us." 1 John 4:7, 8, 12. It is not pleasing to God to see man looking only upon his own things, closing his eyes to the interests of others.

- **What One Institution Can Do for Another**

In the providence of God the Battle Creek Sanitarium has been greatly prospered, and during this coming year those in charge should restrict their wants. Instead of doing all that they desire to do in enlarging their facilities, they should do unselfish work for God, reaching out the hand of charity to interests centered in other places. What benefit they could confer upon the Rural Health Retreat, at St. Helena, by giving a few thousand dollars to this enterprise! Such a donation would give courage to those in charge, inspiring them to move forward and upward.

Donations were made to the Battle Creek Sanitarium in its earlier history, and should not this sanitarium consider carefully what it can do for its sister institution on the Pacific Coast? My brethren in Battle Creek, does it not seem in accordance with God's order to restrict your wants, to curtail your building operations, not enlarging our institutions in that center? Why should you not feel that it is your privilege and duty to help those who need help?

• A Reformation Needed

I have been instructed that a reformation is needed along these lines, that more liberality should prevail among us. There is constant danger that even Seventh-day Adventists will be overcome with selfish ambition and will desire to center all the means and power in the interests over which they especially preside. There is danger that men will permit a jealous feeling to arise in their hearts and that they will become envious of interests that are as important as those which they are handling. Those who cherish the grace of pure Christianity cannot look with indifference upon any part of the work in the Lord's great vineyard. Those who are truly converted will have an equal interest in the work in all parts of the vineyard and will be ready to help wherever help is needed.

It is selfishness that hinders men from sending help to those places where the work of God is not as prosperous as it is in the institution over which they have supervision. Those who bear responsibilities should carefully seek for the good of every branch of the cause and work of God. They should encourage and sustain the interests in other fields as well as the interests in their own. Thus the bonds of brotherhood would be strengthened between members of God's family on earth, and the door would be closed to the petty jealousies and heartburnings that position and prosperity are sure to arouse unless the grace of God controls the heart.

"This I say," Paul wrote: "He which soweth sparingly shall reap also sparingly; and he which soweth bountifully shall reap also bountifully. Every man according as he purposeth in his heart, so let him give; not grudgingly, or of necessity: for God loveth a cheerful giver. And God is able to make all grace abound toward you; that ye, always having all sufficiency in all things, may abound to every good work; being enriched in everything to all bountifulness, which causeth through us thanksgiving to God. For the administration of this service not only supplieth the want of the saints, but is abundant also by many thanksgivings unto God; whiles by the experiment of this ministration they glorify God for your professed subjection unto the gospel of Christ, and for your liberal distribution unto them, and unto all men; and by their prayer for you, which long after you for the exceeding grace of God in you. Thanks be unto God for His Unspeakable Gift." 2 Corinthians 9:6-8, 11-15.

- **The Living Principle of Brotherhood**

God's law is fulfilled only as men love Him with heart, mind, soul, and strength, and their neighbor as themselves. It is the manifestation of this love that brings glory to God in the highest, and on earth peace and good will to men. The Lord is glorified when the great end of His law is attained. It is the work of the Holy Spirit from age to age to impart love to human hearts, for love is the living principle of brotherhood.

Not one nook or corner of the soul is to be a hiding place for selfishness. God desires that heaven's plan shall be carried out, and heaven's divine order and harmony prevail, in every family, in every church, in every institution. Did this love leaven society, we should see the outworking of noble principles of Christian refinement and courtesy, and in Christian charity toward the purchase of the blood of Christ. Spiritual transformation would be seen in all our families, in our institutions, in our churches. When this transformation takes place, these agencies will become instrumentalities by which God will impart heaven's light to the world and thus, through divine discipline and training, fit men and women for the society of heaven.

Jesus has gone to prepare mansions for those who are preparing themselves, through His love and grace, for the abodes of bliss. In the family of God in heaven there will not be found one who is selfish. The peace and harmony of the heavenly courts will not be marred by the presence of one who is rough or unkind.

He who in this world exalts self in the work given him to do will never see the kingdom of God unless he is changed in spirit, unless he becomes meek and lowly, revealing the simplicity of a little child.

- **The Only Safe Course**

Those who bear responsibilities in our institutions should daily seek the way of the Lord. They should not feel qualified to choose their own way, for in so doing they will walk in the light of the sparks of their own kindling. God alone is to be their guide. Those who seek a wider sphere, those who would have greater freedom than God appoints, those who fail to make Him their counselor, their wisdom, their sanctification, and their righteousness, will never win the crown of life. Day by day the soul needs the religion of Christ. Those who drink deeply of His Spirit will not be ambitious for themselves. They will realize that they cannot go beyond the domain of God, for God reigns everywhere.

He who is fully content to receive his commission from above will be cheered by the promises of God, as he seeks to do justice and judgment. To have unwavering trust in God, to be a doer of His word, is to pursue a safe course. The counsel of God simplifies the perplexities of business transactions and domestic duties. The followers of Christ who work with an eye single to the glory of God will have heavenly wisdom. But it is a painful fact that in our churches and institutions there is a great lack of true Christianity. May the Lord help those who are bearing responsibilities to unite with one another in their work and to become laborers together with God.

Christ said to His disciples: "Ye are the light of the world." Matthew 5:14. Then how important it is that every soul shall keep his light trimmed and burning, that he may give light to all with whom he comes in contact. God has made His people the depositaries of sacred truth. Talents have been committed to them for wise improvement, for God designs that by constant use their talents shall be multiplied.

Section 3: Letters to Physicians

- ### The Danger from Enlargement

My brethren, the enlarging of your facilities, the increasing of your numbers, is not after the order of the Lord. Large buildings call for large patronage, and large patronage calls for men of education and talent, and for men of deep religious experience, to conduct the institution in the ways of God; and to manage it with tact and skill demands that there shall be a general increase in spiritual experience, that the fear of God shall circulate through the sanitarium in order that popular patronage shall not mold and fashion it, and thus cause it to cease to be that which God designed it to be—a refuge for the poor and lowly. Those who are steadfast to the truth should not be set aside in favor of worldlings. Prices should not be set so high to meet current expenses that the poor will, to a large extent, be excluded from the benefits of the sanitarium.

With the present talent and facilities, it is impossible for the physician in chief to do all that is essential to be done in the various branches and departments, much as he may desire to do this. It is not possible for him to give personal supervision to all parts of the work.

This matter has been opened up before me again and again. While there is continual growth in the institution, while the buildings are enlarging and the responsibilities increasing, there is not a corresponding growth in the talent and capability necessary for the management of so large an enterprise. Will our physician in chief and the members of the board consider this? My brother, you are not immortal. I thank the Lord that you are as wise concerning your health as you are. But you cannot always do as you are now doing. Your health may fail. Your life is uncertain, and it has been set before me that there ought to be three times as large a working force in the sanitarium as there is. Even then the workers would all have an abundance to do if they did their work well.

- ### The Question of Wages

The institution is now in a prosperous condition, and its managers should not insist upon the low rate of wages that was necessary in its earlier years. Worthy, efficient workers should receive reasonable wages for their labor, and they should be left to exercise their own judgment as to the use they make of their wages. In no case should they be overworked. The physician in chief himself should have larger wages.

To the physician in chief I wish to say: Although you have not the matter of wages under your personal supervision, it is best for you to look carefully into this matter; for you are responsible, as the head of the institution. Do not call upon the workers to do so much of the sacrificing. Restrict your ambition to enlarge the institution and to accumulate responsibilities. Let some of the means flowing into the sanitarium be given to the institutions needing help. This is certainly right. It is in accordance with God's will and way, and it will bring the blessing of God upon the sanitarium.

I wish to say particularly to the board of directors: "Remember that the workers should be paid according to their faithfulness. God requires us to deal with one another in the strictest faithfulness. Some of you are overburdened with cares and responsibilities, and I have been instructed that there is danger of your becoming selfish and wronging those whom you employ."

Each business transaction, whether it has to do with a worker occupying a position of responsibility or with the lowliest worker connected with the sanitarium, should be such as God can approve. Walk in the light while you have the light, lest darkness come upon you. It would be far better to expend less in buildings and give your workers wages that are in accordance with the value of their work, exercising toward them mercy and justice.

From the light that the Lord has been pleased to give me, I know that He is not pleased with many things which have taken place in reference to the workers. God has not laid every particular open to me, but warnings have come that in many things decided reformation is needed. I have been shown that there is need of fathers and mothers in Israel being united with the institution. Devoted men and women should be employed, who, because they are not continually pressed with cares and responsibilities, can look after the spiritual interests of the employees. It is necessary that such men and women should be constantly at work in missionary lines in this large institution.

Not half is being done that should be done in this respect. It should be the part of these men and women to labor for the employees in spiritual lines, giving them instruction that will teach them how to win souls, showing them that this is to be done, not by much talking, but by a consistent, Christlike life. The workers are exposed to worldly influences; but instead of being molded by these influences, they should be consecrated missionaries, controlled by an influence that elevates and refines. Thus they will learn how to meet unbelievers and how to exert an influence that will win them to Christ.

Extract from a letter written in 1895 from Cooranbong, New South Wales.—God has a work for every believer who labors in the sanitarium. Every nurse is to be a channel of blessing, receiving light from above and letting it shine forth to others. The workers are not to conform to fashionable display of those who come to the sanitarium for treatment, but are to consecrate themselves to God. The atmosphere that surrounds their souls is to be a savor of life unto life. Temptations will beset them on every side, but let them ask God for His presence and guidance. The Lord said to Moses: "Certainly I will be with thee;" and to every faithful, consecrated worker the same assurance is given.

23. Go Forth Into Many Places

Cooranbong, N. S. W.
July 15, 1895.
To a Physician in Battle Creek—

My Dear Brother: I received your letters yesterday and read them with deep interest. I am always glad to hear from you concerning your family and the institution in which you are bearing responsibilities of no ordinary character. Your only safety is in obeying the word of the Lord, in walking in the light of His countenance. The enemy is continually seeking to devise methods by which he may steal a march upon us, and we need to pay strict heed to the cautions given by God.

If those who in the past have been standard-bearers in the work of God had walked in the lines that He has marked out, they would better have honored Him and would have had increased usefulness. Some whose voices are now silent in death might have lived to warn, entreat, and advise. If those who in past years had been entrusted with large responsibilities had heeded the warnings and entreaties of the Spirit of God, they would now be walking before Him in strength and efficiency. When men educate others to rely on them and trust in them, when, by pen or voice, they dictate to others as to what they should do, they are teaching others to make flesh their arm, to give glory to human beings rather than to God.

We are safe only as we exalt Christ, speaking in praise of His excellence. Isaiah says: "Unto us a child is born, unto us a son is given: and the government shall be upon His shoulder: and His name shall be called Wonderful, Counselor, The mighty God, The everlasting Father, The Prince of Peace. Of the increase of His government and peace there shall be no end, upon the throne of David, and upon His kingdom, to order it, and to establish it with judgment and with justice from henceforth even forever. The zeal of the Lord of hosts will perform this." Isaiah 9:6, 7.

There is danger that men will receive the counsel of men, when by so doing they will discard the counsel of God. Oh, what lessons all must learn before they will understand that God seeth not as man seeth. The Lord says: "My thoughts are not your thoughts, neither are your ways My ways... For as the heavens are higher than the earth, so are My ways higher than your ways, and My thoughts than your thoughts." Isaiah 55:8, 9. Unless there is a decided reformation among the people of God, He will turn His face from them.

My brother, there is need of constant watchfulness, lest, in Battle Creek, building shall be piled upon building and advantage heaped upon advantage. The means thus expended will testify against us. You should put wise plans into operation and scatter the influence that is centering in Battle Creek, diffusing the light that God has given you. Blessed are they that sow beside all waters. The more there is invested in Battle Creek, the greater will be the demand for additional investment; but this is not in the order of God, and before a very long period of time shall pass, the mistake of centering interests in Battle Creek will be made evident.

In adding building to building in Battle Creek, we are encouraging neglect of other fields. Superabundant advantages there mean destitution elsewhere. Other parts of the vineyard are robbed of the means they should have. Means should be invested elsewhere in winning souls to the truth and in providing houses of worship for them.

God has pointed out the fact that it is the duty of those in Battle Creek to help His institutions in other places. As a wise steward of means you should scatter your forces, using the power of your influence to help those in darkness to know God as He is.

Section 3: Letters to Physicians

- **The Need of Broader Plans**

How many towns and cities there are that are utterly neglected. Our people are injuring themselves by crowding into one place. When trees in a nursery are crowded thickly together, they cannot grow healthfully and sturdily. Transplant trees from your thickly planted nursery. God is not glorified in the centering of so many advantages in one place. Give room; put your plants in many places, where one will not lean for support upon another. Give them room to grow. This the Lord demands of you.

The means expended in enlarging your advantages in Battle Creek, which are already overgrown and have passed reasonable limits, should be used in establishing missionary stations elsewhere. You should broaden your plans and widen the field of your operations. You should send wise men into the cities and towns that have not yet heard the gospel message. Pick out the best men you can possibly spare, and give them opportunity to become caretakers and burden bearers. Let them have opportunity to develop the talents that in the past have lain idle. Place them where they can use their God-given abilities in calling sinners to repentance. Let men who make it manifest that they love God have a chance to do something for Him.

Let men learn to pray earnestly, and let them make their prayers short and right to the point. Let them learn to speak of the world's Redeemer and to lift up the Man of Calvary higher and still higher.

All the preaching in the world will not make men feel deeply the need of the perishing souls around them. Nothing will so arouse in men and women a self-sacrificing zeal as to send them forth into new fields to work for those in darkness. Prepare workers to go out into the highways and hedges. Do not call men and women to the great center, encouraging them to leave churches that need their aid. Men must learn to bear responsibilities. Not one in a hundred among us is doing anything beyond engaging in common, worldly enterprises. We are not half awake to the worth of the souls for whom Christ died.

We need wise nurserymen, who will transplant trees to different localities and give them advantages that will enable them to grow. It is the positive duty of God's people to go into the regions beyond. Let forces be set at work to clear new ground, to establish new centers of influence wherever an opening can be found. Rally workers who possess true missionary zeal, and let them go forth to diffuse light and knowledge far and near. Let them take the living principles of health reform into the communities that to a large degree are ignorant of these principles. Let classes be formed, and instruction be given regarding the treatment of disease.

It is a fact that through the influence of the sanitarium the truth of heaven has come to the notice of thousands. Yet there is a work to be done that has been neglected. Money has been expended in enlarging facilities in Battle Creek, when the Lord desires the leaven to be introduced into the mass of meal, that the whole may be leavened. Instead of building after building being added to the sanitarium, there should be at this time many institutions fully equipped and in working order in other places.

There are men who have been long connected with the sanitarium who will always be shadows of someone else, if they are retained there, when, if they were permitted to rely upon their own judgment, they would become deep, self-reliant thinkers, capable of giving wise counsel. Let these men have a chance to learn to bear responsibilities in the strength of God. Thus they will gain an experience that will enable them to impart the truth to others.

But instead of men being sent from Battle Creek, as God has directed in the pointed testimonies that have been given, thousands of dollars have been devoted to enlarging the institutions and increasing the facilities in Battle Creek. And the call comes from Battle Creek for more conveniences and more workers. But there must be a change.

We are encouraged as we see the work that is being done in Chicago and a few other places. Years ago the large responsibilities centering in Battle Creek should have been distributed. You may look with satisfaction at the widespreading growth of the sanitarium at Battle Creek, but God does not look upon it with the same approval that you do. If institutions had been built up in other places, if men had been given responsibilities to bear, there would have been far more strength, far more efficiency in our work, and we should have moved more nearly in accordance with the mind and will of God than we have. As it is, a few men are carrying heavy responsibilities. A few wield an influence that has a controlling power in the management of the work far and near, while there are many who carry no burdens.

Many of those carrying heavy responsibilities need to be converted. Christ says to them as He said to Nicodemus: "Ye must be born again." "Except a man be born again, he cannot see the kingdom of God." John 3:7, 3. Many are controlled by an unchristian spirit. They have not yet learned in the school of Christ His meekness and lowliness, and unless they change, they will yield to Satan's temptations. Year after year they carry sacred responsibilities, yet prove themselves incapable of distinguishing between the sacred and the common. How long shall such men continue to wield a controlling influence? How long shall their word be permitted to exalt or to cast down, to condemn or to lift up? How long shall they hold such power that no one dare make a change in their methods?

- ## Build Up New Centers

People are encouraged to settle in Battle Creek, to give their influence to the building up of a modern Jerusalem. This is not after God's order. Thus other places are deprived of facilities that they should have. Enlarge ye; spread ye; yes, but not in one place only. Go out and establish centers of influence in places where nothing, or next to nothing, has been done. Break up your consolidated mass; diffuse the saving beams of light into the darkened corners of the earth. A work similar to that of an eagle stirring up her nest needs to be done.

"Moab hath been at ease from his youth, and he hath settled on his lees, and hath not been emptied from vessel to vessel, neither hath he gone into captivity: therefore his taste remained in him, and his scent is not changed." Jeremiah 48:11. This is true of many of the believers who are coming to Battle Creek. Many have a spasmodic zeal in battle, but their light is like that of a meteor that flashes across the heavens and then goes out.

Let God's workmen who have the interests of His cause at heart do something for the colored people in the Southern field. Let not God's stewards be content merely to touch this field with the tips of their fingers. Let those at the heart of the work plan in earnest for this field. Many have talked about it, but what are they doing as the stewards of God's means? Why do they feel at liberty to bind up God's capital of means in Battle Creek? Why do they do the very things that they have been warned not to do? The matter is becoming serious, for warnings and entreaties have been given in vain. The arms of power in Battle Creek are being extended more and more widely, seeking to control the work far and near, and to crush that which they cannot control. I lift my voice in protest. The spirit that now controls is not the Spirit of the Lord.

The Lord has blessed Battle Creek again and again by pouring out His Spirit upon the church and the workers, but how few have cherished the influence of the Spirit. How few have expended their money as God has directed. Means has been expended in educating those who knew the truth, while fields that are wholly unenlightened have been neglected. Had ministers gone out as Christ has commissioned them, had they used the gifts entrusted them to carry the light to those in darkness, they would have obtained far more knowledge of God and of Christ than they have obtained by seeking additional education in our schools.

• A Failure to Appreciate God-Given Responsibilities

Has not God given us a work to do? Has He not bidden us go among opposing influences and convert men from error to truth? Why have not those who have so frequently gathered in the large assemblies in Battle Creek put into practice the truth that they have heard? If they had imparted the light that they have received, what a transformation of character would have been seen. For every grace imparted, God would have given grace. They have not prized as they should the work that has been done for them, or they would have gone forth into the dark places of the earth, to shed abroad the light. They would have given to the world the message of righteousness by faith, and their own light would have grown clearer and clearer; for God would have worked with them.

Many have gone down into the grave in error because those who know the truth have failed to communicate the precious knowledge they have received. If the light that has shone so freely in Battle Creek had been diffused many would have been raised up to become laborers together with God.

Oh, that our brethren and sisters might value aright the truth! Oh, that they might become sanctified by it! Oh, that they might realize that upon them rests the responsibility of communicating this truth to others! But they do not feel the importance of living the truth, of being doers of the words of Christ. Many are self-sufficient. They are not filled with the missionary spirit that should animate the disciples of Christ. If they knew what it means to have travail of soul for others, angels of God would work through them to communicate a knowledge of the truth. They would know the truth, and the truth would make them free. Money would no longer be expended in adding building to building in one place, but would be used in opening new fields, in planting the standard of truth in cities that have not yet been worked. The elevating, purifying, ennobling principles of heaven would be introduced into society and would work like leaven.

Extract from a letter written in 1899, from Cooranbong, N. S. W., Australia—It is God's design that those fields which have abundant facilities shall share their advantages with more needy fields. The principle is ever to be followed in all our institutions. God requires that there be less planning for buildings in places where the work is already established, and that means be sent to fields where, for lack of facilities, the laborers work at a great disadvantage.

24. God's Purpose for His Institutions

Newtown, Tasmania
December 1, 1895.
To the Medical Superintendent of a Large Sanitarium—
My Dear Brother:
Every institution that bears the name of Seventh-day Adventist is to be to the world as was Joseph in Egypt, and as were Daniel and his fellows in Babylon. In the providence of God these men were taken captive, that they might carry to heathen nations the knowledge of the true God. They were to be representatives of God in our world. They were to make no compromise with the idolatrous nations with which they were brought in contact, but were to stand loyal to their faith, bearing as a special honor the name of worshipers of the God who created the heavens and the earth. These youth stood firm to principle. They lived in close connection with God honoring Him in all their ways, and He honored them. He was their wisdom. He gave them knowledge and understanding.

Today the remnant people of God are to glorify His name by proclaiming the last message of warning, the last invitation to the marriage supper of the Lamb. The only way in which they can fulfill God's expectations is by being representatives of the truth for this time.

The Lord has wrought through human agents to fulfill the prophecies. He has made sacred, eternal truth stand out plainly amidst the heresies and delusions that Christ declared would exist in the last days.

My brother, you are situated where you can be a representative of the truth for this time. Keep close to the Great Teacher. I saw you holding up the banner on which are written the words: "Here is the patience of the saints: here are they that keep the commandments of God, and the faith of Jesus." Revelation 14:12. Several men, some of them those with whom you are connected in the sanitarium, were presenting to you a banner on which was a different inscription. You were letting go the banner of Seventh-day Adventists, and were reaching out to grasp the banner presented to you. One of great dignity approached you and with deep earnestness said:

"Unto you therefore which believe He is precious: but unto them which be disobedient, the stone which the builders disallowed, the same is made the head of the corner, and a stone of stumbling, and a rock of offense, even to them which stumble at the word, being disobedient: whereunto also they were appointed. But ye are a chosen generation, a royal priesthood, an holy nation, a peculiar people; that ye should show forth the praises of Him who hath called you out of darkness into His marvelous light." 1 Peter 2:7-9. Then your hand firmly grasped the true banner, and these encouraging words were spoken: "Let us be glad and rejoice, and give honor to Him: for the marriage of the Lamb is come, and His wife hath made herself ready. And to her, was granted that she should be arrayed in fine linen, clean and white: for the fine linen is the righteousness of saints." Revelation 19:7, 8.

I was instructed that you and your fellow laborers were in danger of hiding the principles of our faith in order to obtain large patronage. Every jot done in this line, instead of extending the influence of the truth, will hinder its advance.

You and your associates in the sanitarium work need a pilot with you constantly, else you will be shipwrecked. You surely must understand your peril. Satan is making every effort to turn you aside into strange paths. God has strengthened you. Your soul must be sanctified through the truth, that your steadfast adherence to principles may be plain to all. The more fully your helpless soul leans upon God, the more fully you make Him your trust, the more hungry you will become for the bread of life.

God is to be recognized and honored by the people calling themselves Seventh-day Adventists. In the past the truth has, to the honor of God, been proclaimed with convincing power by the physicians and helpers in our sanitariums. God will accept no less of you, but will expect far more. You and your associates are to labor on in faith and firmness to prevent decline and to ensure progress. There must be no narrowing down of your work, no concealing of the principles of truth; there must be a widening of the base of operations. Many plants must be made in different places. There is need of more zeal, more faith, more influence, of more active, spirited workers.

Remember that you are working for time and for eternity. Heavenly angels are commissioned to co-operate with your efforts for the conquest of souls. More earnest efforts should be made to establish the truth in various localities. And there must be no covering up of any phase of our message. The truth for this time must be given to the souls ready to perish. Those who in any way hide the truth dishonor God. Upon their garments will be the blood of souls.

- ## God's Purpose for the Sanitarium

The Battle Creek Sanitarium is a broad missionary field. God has been moving upon souls to seek in this institution relief from physical suffering. He requires that everything connected with it shall be such as He can approve.

He is pleased that a chapel should be built in connection with the sanitarium, that those who visit the institution may be given an opportunity to hear for themselves the truth as it is in Jesus. The precious gospel is to be presented to them, not in a weak diluted style but in strong, warm accents. As it is made plain that godliness is necessary to salvation, the peculiarities of our faith will appear, distinguishing us from the world. But no tirade is to be made against the doctrines held by others. In our association with worldlings we are to recommend our faith by living, in all true modesty, the principles of Christianity.

- **The Value of a Study of God's Word**

If the medical students will study the word of God diligently, they will be far better prepared to understand their other studies; for enlightenment always comes with an earnest study of the word of God. Let our medical missionary workers understand that the more they become acquainted with God and with Christ, and the more they become acquainted with Bible history, the better prepared they will be to do their work.

The students in our schools should aspire to higher knowledge. Nothing will so help to give them a retentive memory as a study of the Scriptures. Nothing will so help them in gaining a knowledge of their other studies.

If unbelievers desire to join your classes for the training of medical missionaries, and you think that they would not exert an influence that would draw other students away from the truth, give them a chance. Some of your best missionaries may come from among them. They have never heard the truth, and as they are placed where they are surrounded with an influence that reveals the spirit of the Master, some will be won to the truth. In the studies given, there should be no concealment of one principle of Bible truth. If admitting to your classes those not of our faith will lead to silence on the great themes that concern our present and eternal good,— themes that should ever be kept before the mind,—let them not be admitted. In no case is principle to be sacrificed or the peculiar characteristics of our faith hidden in order to add outside students to our classes.

Faithful teachers should be placed in charge of the Bible classes, teachers who will strive to make the students understand their lessons, not by explaining everything to them, but by requiring them to explain clearly every passage they read. Let these teachers remember that little good will be accomplished by skimming over the surface of the word. Thoughtful investigation and earnest, taxing study are required in order for this word to be understood. There are truths in the word which, like veins of precious ore, are hidden beneath the surface. The hidden treasure is discovered as it is searched for, as a miner searches for gold and silver. The evidence of the truth of God's word is in the word itself. Scripture is the key that unlocks scripture. The deep meaning of the truths of God's word is unfolded to our minds by His Spirit.

The Bible is the great lessonbook for the students in our schools. It teaches the whole will of God concerning the sons and daughters of Adam. It is the rule of life, teaching us of the character that we must form for the future life. We need not the dim light of tradition to make the Scriptures comprehensible. As well might we suppose that the noonday sun needs the glimmering torchlight of earth to increase its glory. The utterances of priest and minister are not needed to save men from error. Those who consult the divine Oracle will have light. In the Bible every duty is made plain. Every lesson given is comprehensible. Every lesson reveals to us the Father and the Son. The word is able to make all wise unto salvation. In the word the science of salvation is plainly revealed. Search the Scriptures, for they are the voice of God speaking to the soul.

25. God's Purpose in Medical Missionary Work

Melbourne, N. S. W.
February 3, 1898.

My Dear Brother: Special light has been given me that you are in danger of losing sight of the work for this time. You are erecting barriers to separate your work, and those you are educating, from the church. This must not be. Those who are receiving instruction in medical missionary lines should be led to realize that their education is to fit them to do better work in connection with the ministers of God. You are to remember, my brother, that the Lord has a people upon the earth whom He respects. But your words, and the way in which they are often spoken, create unbelief in the position that we occupy as a people. You are in danger of failing to hold fast the faith once delivered to the saints, of making shipwreck of your faith. The words were spoken: "A very small leak will sink a ship. One defective link makes a chain worthless."

- **Educate Medical Missionaries**

Remember, my brother, that medical missionary work is not to take men from the ministry, but is to place men in the field, better qualified to minister because of their knowledge of medical missionary work. Young men should receive an education in medical missionary lines and should then go forth to connect with the ministers. They should not be influenced to give themselves exclusively to the work of rescuing the fallen and degraded. That work is found everywhere and is to be combined with the work of preparing a people to make Bible truth their defense against the sophistries of worldlings and of the fallen church. The third angel is to go forth with great power. Let none ignore this work or treat it as of little importance. The truth is to be proclaimed to the world, that men and women may see the light.

• Our Work for Today

What saith the Lord in the fifty-eighth chapter of Isaiah? The whole chapter is of the highest importance. "Is not this the fast that I have chosen?" God asks, "to loose the bands of wickedness, to undo the burdens, and to let the oppressed go free, and that ye break every yoke? Is it not to deal thy bread to the hungry, and that thou bring the poor that are cast out to thy house? when thou seest the naked, that thou cover him; and that thou hide not thyself from thine own flesh? Then shall thy light break forth as the morning, and thine health shall spring forth speedily: and thy righteousness shall go before thee; the glory of the Lord shall be thy rearward. Then shalt thou call, and the Lord shall answer; thou shalt cry, and He shall say, Here I am."

"If thou turn away thy foot from the Sabbath, from doing thy pleasure on My holy day; and call the Sabbath a delight, the holy of the Lord, honorable; and shalt honor Him, not doing thine own ways, nor finding thine own pleasure, nor speaking thine own words: then shalt thou delight thyself in the Lord; and I will cause thee to ride upon the high places of the earth, and feed thee with the heritage of Jacob thy father: for the mouth of the Lord hath spoken it." Verses 6-9, 13, 14.

This is our work. The light that we have upon the third angel's message is the true light. The mark of the beast is exactly what it has been proclaimed to be. Not all in regard to this matter is yet understood, and will not be understood until the unrolling of the scroll; but a most solemn work is to be accomplished in our world. The Lord's command to His servants is: "Cry aloud, spare not, lift up thy voice like a trumpet, and show My people their transgression, and the house of Jacob their sins." Verse 1. A message that will arouse the churches is to be proclaimed. Every effort is to be made to give the light, not only to our people, but to the world. I have been instructed that the prophecies of Daniel and the Revelation should be printed in small books, with the necessary explanations, and should be sent all over the world. Our own people need to have the light placed before them in clearer lines.

- **No Change in God's Cause**

There is to be no change in the general features of God's cause. It is to stand out as clear and distinct as prophecy has made it. We are to enter into no confederacy with the world, supposing that by so doing we could accomplish more. My brother, if you stand in the way to hinder the advancement of the work on the lines that God has appointed, you will greatly displease Him. The warning message is to be given, and after you have faithfully accomplished your part of the work you are not to hinder others of the Lord's servants from going forth to do the work that they should do. Laboring for the degraded and fallen is not to be made the principal and all-important line. This work is to be combined with the work of instructing the churches. Our people are to be taught how to help the needy and the outcast.

No line of our faith that has made us what we are is to be weakened. We have the old landmarks of truth, experience, and duty, and we are to stand firm in defense of our principles, in full view of the world. With hearts filled with interest and solicitude, we are to give the invitation to those in the highways and the byways. Medical missionary work is to be done. But this is only one part of the work that is to be accomplished, and it is not to be made all and in all. It is to be to the work of God as the hand is to the body. There may be unworthy ones connected with the ministry, yet no one can ignore the ministry without ignoring God.

- **Words of Caution**

My brother, you are represented to me as in danger of standing apart from our people, feeling that you are a complete whole. But if you bind yourself up with those of your own mind, apart from the church, which is Christ's body, you will make a confederacy that will be broken to pieces; for no union can stand but that which God has framed. Those who are receiving an education in medical lines hear insinuations from time to time that disparage the church and the ministry. These insinuations are seeds that will spring up and bear fruit. The students might better be educated to realize that the church of Christ on earth is to be respected. They need a clear knowledge of the reasons of our faith. This knowledge they must have, in order to serve God acceptably. Line upon line, precept upon precept, they must receive the Bible evidence of the truth as it is in Jesus.

Do not, I beg of you, instill into the minds of the students ideas that will cause them to lose confidence in God's appointed ministers. But this you are most certainly doing, whether you are aware of it or not. In His providence the Lord has placed you in a position where you may do a good work for Him in connection with the gospel ministry, bringing the truth before many who otherwise would not become acquainted with it. Temptations will come to you to think that in order to carry forward the medical missionary work you must stand aloof from church organization or church discipline. To stand thus would place you on an unsound footing. The work done for those who come to you for instruction is not complete unless they are educated to work in connection with the church.

The medical missionary work is not to be made all and in all. In this point you are carrying things to extremes. There is a large work to be done. Publications teaching the truth are to be circulated everywhere. Medical students should not be encouraged to circulate only the books treating on health reform. Be careful that you are not found working out your own plans, to the disregard of God's plans.

Extract from a letter written in 1898 from Cooranbong, New South Wales.— My brother, the Lord God of Israel must be your counselor. Satan has come down with great power to work with all deceivableness of unrighteousness. Lean hard on Christ. You have worked untiringly to bring about good results. Do not now make mistakes. Never, never seek to remove one landmark that the Lord has given His people. The truth stands firmly established on the eternal Rock—a foundation that storm and tempest can never move.

Remember that just as soon as you allow your influence to lead away from the straight and narrow path that the Lord has cast up for His people, your prosperity will cease; for God will not be your guide. Again and again the record of Nebuchadnezzar's life has been presented to me to present to you, that you may be warned not to trust in your own wisdom or to make flesh your arm. Do not lower the banner of truth or allow it to drop from your hands in order to unite with the solemn message for these last days anything that will tend to hide the peculiar features of our faith.

26. A Word of Caution

Brisbane, Queensland
Australia,
October 26, 1898.
To the Advisers of Medical Students—
There is a burden upon my soul. There are young people who are encouraged to take up a course of study in medical lines who ought to be preparing themselves most decidedly to proclaim the third angel's message. It is not necessary for our medical students to spend all the time that they are spending in medical studies. Their work should be more decidedly combined with a study of God's word. Ideas are inculcated that are not at all necessary, and the necessary things do not receive sufficient attention.

- **A Danger to Be Guarded Against**

While students are being educated in this way, they are being made less able to do acceptable work for the Master. The taxation that they undergo to obtain an extended knowledge in medical lines unfits them to work as they should in ministerial lines. Physical and mental weariness come because of the overstrain of study, and because the students are encouraged to labor unduly for the outcasts and the degraded. Thus some are disqualified for the work that they might have done had they begun missionary work where it was needed and let the medical line come in as an essential part connected with the work of the gospel ministry as a whole, as the hand is connected with the body. Life is not to be imperiled in an effort to obtain a medical education. There is danger, in some cases, that students will ruin their health and unfit themselves to do the service they might have done had they not been unwisely encouraged to take a medical course.

Often erroneous opinions are transcribed on the mind, and these lead to an unwise course of action. Students should have time to talk with God, time to live in hourly, conscious communion with the principles of truth and righteousness and mercy. At this time straightforward investigation of the heart is essential. The student must place himself where he can draw from the Source of spiritual and intellectual power. He must require that every cause which asks his sympathy and co-operation has the approval of the reason which God has given him, and the conscience, which the Holy Spirit is controlling. He is not to perform an action that does not harmonize with the deep, holy principles which minister light to his soul and vigor to his will. Only thus can he do God the highest service. He is not to be taught that medical missionary work will bind him to any man, who shall dictate what his work shall be.

Medical missionary work is not to be drawn apart and made separate from church organization. The medical students are not to receive the idea that they may regard themselves as amenable only to the leaders in the medical work. They are to be left free to receive counsel from God. They are not to pledge themselves and their future to anything that erring human beings may outline for them. No thread of selfishness is to be drawn into the web; no scheme is to be devised that has in it one particle of injustice. Selfishness is not to control any line of the work. Let us remember that individually we are working in full view of the heavenly universe.

- **A High Standard**

"Thou shalt love the Lord thy God with all thy heart, and with all thy soul, and with all thy strength, and with all thy mind; and thy neighbor as thyself." Luke 10:27. Just before He left His disciples to return to heaven, Christ declared: "A new commandment I give unto you, That ye love one another; as I have loved you, that ye also love one another." Here we see the standard lifted higher and still higher. "By this shall all men know that ye are My disciples, if ye have love one to another." John 13:34, 35. The disciples could not then comprehend Christ's words; but after His crucifixion, resurrection, and ascension they understood His love as never before. They had seen it expressed in His suffering in the garden, in the judgment hall, and in His death on the cross of Calvary.

- **Teaching and Healing**

The Lord's people are to be one. There is to be no separation in His work. Christ sent out the twelve apostles, and afterward the seventy disciples, to preach the gospel and to heal the sick. "As ye go," He said, "preach, saying, The kingdom of heaven is at hand. Heal the sick, cleanse the lepers, raise the dead, cast out devils: freely ye have received, freely give." Matthew 10:7, 8. And as they went forth preaching the kingdom of God, power was given them to heal the sick and cast out evil spirits. In God's work, teaching and healing are never to be separated. His commandment-keeping people are to be one. Satan will invent every device to separate those whom God is seeking to make one. But the Lord will reveal Himself as a God of judgment. We are working under the eyes of the heavenly host. There is a divine Watcher among us, inspecting all that is planned and carried on.

27. Uphold the Medical Work

Cooranbong, N. S. W.
February 1, 1899.

I address those in responsible positions in the General Conference and those who are working in medical missionary lines. I am commissioned to speak also to the church in Battle Creek and to all our other churches.

I have been instructed to say, in reference to the medical missionary work, that there is danger of swaying things too heavily in one line. But what I say on this point must not be understood as in any sense justifying those who have held themselves aloof from medical missionary work. There are many who have not been in sympathy with this work. They should now be very careful how they speak in regard to it, for they are not intelligent on the subject because they have not walked in the light. Whatever their position in the work of God, they should be very careful not to give utterance to sentiments that will discourage and hinder our conferences from taking hold of this work. The position that some have occupied in reference to medical missionary work makes it impossible for their words on this subject to have any weight. They are not clear-sighted; their judgment is warped.

Every branch of the work is needed, but every branch of the work is to be under the supervision of God. The medical missionary work is to be to the cause of God as the right hand to the body. It would not be right for all the strength of the body to go into the right hand, and neither would it be right for all the strength of the cause of God to be used in medical missionary work. The ministry of the word must be sustained, and there must be unity, perfect oneness, in God's work. Those who have felt no interest in medical missionary work are treating the right hand of God's cause disrespectfully. Let all such change their attitude toward this work. Let them speak as few words as possible until they stand in a right position. Silence is eloquence when the mind is not sanctified and therefore cannot discern spiritual things.

• The Need of Caution

There is at the present time great need of caution. "Let every man be swift to hear, slow to speak, slow to wrath." James 1:19. Let us heed the warning: "I beseech you, brethren, mark them which cause divisions and offenses contrary to the doctrine which ye have learned; and avoid them. For they that are such serve not our Lord Jesus Christ, ... and by good words and fair speeches deceive the hearts of the simple. For your obedience is come abroad unto all men. I am glad therefore on your behalf: but yet I would have you wise unto that which is good, and simple concerning evil." Romans 16:17-19.

"I beseech you, brethren, by the name of our Lord Jesus Christ, that ye all speak the same thing, and that there be no divisions among you; but that ye be perfectly joined together in the same mind and in the same judgment." 1 Corinthians 1:10. This is the will of God concerning us. Shall we obey it?

"The preaching of the cross is to them that perish foolishness; but unto us which are saved it is the power of God. For it is written, I will destroy the wisdom of the wise, and will bring to nothing the understanding of the prudent. Where is the wise? where is the scribe? where is the disputer of this world? ... For after that in the wisdom of God the world by wisdom knew not God, it pleased God by the foolishness of preaching to save them that believe. For the Jews require a sign, and the Greeks seek after wisdom: but we preach Christ crucified, unto the Jews a stumbling block, and unto the Greeks foolishness; but unto them which are called, both Jews and Greeks, Christ the power of God, and the wisdom of God." Verses 18-24.

What a change would be seen if all who are in responsible positions would realize that they are working under the eye of an all-seeing God. What is needed now is the free working of the Holy Spirit on mind and heart. Without this our efforts will be fruitless. When the Spirit molds and fashions us, our words and acts will reveal heartfelt thanksgiving.

- **The Importance of Medical Missionary Work**

There is great need of an increase of knowledge in every line of health reform. Those who have had the privilege of hearing the truth are to give the trumpet a certain sound as they proclaim the third angel's message. Special lines of work are to be taken up, such as the medical missionary work. This work should be carried forward in connection with the gospel message for this time.

Genuine medical missionary work is the gospel practiced. Those who cannot see the bearing of this work should not feel authorized to control any phase of it until they do understand its bearing. I wish to say decidedly that the Lord has accomplished great good through the medical missionary work, and that He has used our leading physician as His appointed agent. Not everything in the medical work has been without a flaw. With it have been blended many things that have marred its sacredness. But the Lord will take supervision of His cause, and will see that it does not become disproportionate in this one branch. The work will not be marred if the church will arise and shine, making it manifest that her light has come, and that the glory of the Lord is risen upon her.

The medical missionary workers are to be purified, sanctified, ennobled. They are to rise to the highest point of excellence. They are to be molded and fashioned after the divine similitude. Then they will see that health reform and medical missionary work are to be bound up with the preaching of the gospel.

The reason why church members do not understand this branch of the work is that they are not following the light, walking step by step after their great Leader. The medical missionary work is of God and bears His signature. For this reason let man keep his hands off it and not desire to manage it according to his own ideas.

Our message is a world-wide message. And while means is not to be absorbed in one line of work, so that the last gospel message cannot be carried into new fields, the medical missionary work is not in any wise to be disparaged; it is not to be represented as an inferior work. The world is a great lazar house; it is corrupted under the inhabitants thereof, and misery is universal. The Lord has given our leading physician a work in aiding to prepare a people to stand in the great day of God. But he is to work under the supervision of God. There are some things in his labors that will have to be modeled more closely after the principles of the head worker.

• The Cause of Dearth in the Church

He who is appointed to act a part in the work for this time should feel the solemn responsibility resting upon him. We are working for eternity. If we eat of the bread which came from heaven we shall be Christlike in spirit and character. We are living in an age when there is to be no spiritual idleness. Every soul is to be charged with the heavenly current of life. The question is often asked: "What is the cause of the dearth of spiritual power in the church?" The answer comes: "The members allow their minds to be drawn away from the word of God." We are built up physically from that which we eat, and in like manner the character of our spirituality is determined by the food given to the mind. We are to give the mind and heart proper nourishment by eating the flesh and drinking the blood of the Son of God.

Christ declares: "Verily, verily, I say unto you, He that believeth on Me hath everlasting life... I am the living Bread which came down from heaven: if any man eat of this bread, he shall live forever: and the bread that I will give is My flesh, which I will give for the life of the world... Whoso eateth My flesh, and drinketh My blood, hath eternal life; and I will raise him up at the last day. For My flesh is meat indeed, and My blood is drink indeed. He that eateth My flesh, and drinketh My blood, dwelleth in Me, and I in him. As the living Father hath sent Me, and I live by the Father: so he that eateth Me, even he shall live by Me." John 6:47-57.

We must abide in Christ, and Christ must abide in us; "for we are laborers together with God." The work of the Christian is an individual work. Let God's workers cease to find fault, for this is sin. Let them improve themselves as they think that their fellow workers should improve. It is their privilege to live in Christ by eating the bread of life. Those who do this will have a healthy, growing experience, and the righteousness of God will go before them as they do the work specified in the fifty-eighth chapter of Isaiah.

- **To Every Man His Work**

Every branch of the work of God is to have recognition. "He gave some, apostles; and some, prophets; and some, evangelists; and some, pastors and teachers; for the perfecting of the saints, for the work of the ministry, for the edifying of the body of Christ." Ephesians 4:11, 12. This Scripture shows that there are to be different workers, different instrumentalities. Each has a different work. No one is required to lay hold of another's work, and, though untrained, try to do it. God has given to each according to his ability. One man may think that his position gives him authority to dictate to other workers, but this is not so. Ignorant of their work, he would enlarge where he should retrench, and retrench where he should enlarge, because he can see only the part of the vineyard where he is working.

Live for God. Make the Saviour's teaching a part of your life. Your pathway will be brightened by clear, shining light. You will have the heavenly anointing and will be kept from making grave blunders. Do not be so intent upon the work you are doing in one portion of the Lord's vineyard that you cannot appreciate the work that others are doing in other parts of the vineyard. They may be faithfully cultivating their talents so that they can return them, doubled, to their God. Let every man look well to his own work, making sure that it is complete, without spot or wrinkle to mar its perfection. Then leave it with God to say: "Well done, good and faithful servant; thou hast been faithful over a few things, I will make thee ruler over many things: enter thou into the joy of thy Lord." Matthew 25:23.

28. Unity of Effort

Cooranbong, N. S. W.
April 17, 1899.
To a Physician in Perplexity—

My Dear Brother: I have a deep interest in you and your work, and I pray that the Lord will guide my pen as I write to you. The Lord has made you a man of

His appointment, and angels of God have been your helpers. The Lord has placed you in the position that you occupy, not because you are infallible but because He desires to guide your mind by His Holy Spirit. He desires you to impart to those with whom you come in contact a knowledge of present truth.

Grave responsibilities have been entrusted to you, and on no account should you allow yourself to be entangled in work that will weaken your influence with Seventh-day Adventists. The Lord has chosen you to fill a place of His appointment, to stand before the medical profession, not to be molded by worldly influences, but to mold minds. Every day you are to be under the supervision of God. He is your Master, your Redeemer. He has a work for you to do, not separated from Seventh-day Adventists, but united with them. You are to be a great blessing to your brethren by giving them the knowledge that He has given you.

Through you God has worked and desires still to work, honoring you by entrusting to you important responsibilities. "We are laborers together with God." 1 Corinthians 3:9. He will use you and me and each human being who enters His service, if we will submit to His guidance. Each one is to stand in his watchtower, listening attentively to that which the Spirit has to say to him, remembering that his every word and act makes an impression, not only on his own character, but on the characters of those with whom he is connected.

- ## God's Building

"Ye are God's husbandry, ye are God's building." Verse 9. This figure represents human character, which is to be wrought upon, point by point. Each day God works with His building, stroke upon stroke, to perfect the structure, that it may become a holy temple for Him. Man is to co-operate with God. Each worker is to become just what God designs him to be, building his life with pure, noble deeds, that in the end his character may be a symmetrical structure, a fair temple, honored by God and man. There is to be no flaw in the building, for it is the Lord's. Every stone must be perfectly laid, that it may endure the pressure placed upon it. One stone laid wrong will affect the whole building. To you and to every other worker God gives the warning: "Take heed how you build, that your building may stand the test of storm and tempest, because it is founded on the eternal Rock. Place the stone on the sure foundation, that you may make ready for the day of test and trial, when all will be seen just as they are."

• A Temple of Living Stones

This warning God presents to me as especially necessary for your welfare. He loves you with a love that is immeasurable. He loves your brethren in the faith, and He works with them to the same end as that to which He works with you. His church on earth is to assume divine proportions before the world as a temple built of living stones, each one reflecting light. It is to be the light of the world as a city set on a hill, which cannot be hid. It is built of stones laid close together, stone fitting to stone, making a firm, solid building. Not all the stones are of the same form or shape. Some are large, some are small; but each has its own place to fill. And the value of each stone is determined by the light that it reflects. This is God's plan. He desires all His workers to fill their appointed places in the work for this time.

We are living amidst the perils of the last days. We are wisely to cultivate every mental and physical power; for all are needed to make the church a building that will represent the wisdom of the great Designer. The talents given us by God are His gifts, and they are to be used in their right relation to one another so as to make a perfect whole. God gives the talents, the powers of the mind; man forms the character.

• Different Instrumentalities

The Lord has wrought with you, enabling you to act your part as His workman; but there are other workmen also who are to act their part as His instrumentalities. These help to compose the whole body. All are to be united as parts of one great organism. The Lord's church is composed of living, working agencies, who derive their power to act from the Author and Finisher of their faith. They are to carry forward in harmony the great work resting on them. God has given you your work. But He has other instrumentalities, and to them He has given their work, that all may become, through sanctification of the truth, members of Christ's body, of His flesh and of His bones. Representing Christ, we act for time and for eternity; and men, even worldly men, take knowledge of us that we have been with Jesus and have learned of Him.

• Truth a Unit

God's people are not to be in confusion, lacking order and harmony, consistency and beauty. The Lord is greatly dishonored when disunion exists among His people. Truth is a unit. The unity that God requires must be cultivated day by day if we would answer the prayer of Christ. The disunion that is striving for existence among those who profess to believe the last message of mercy to be given to the world, must find no place; for it would be a fearful hindrance to the advancement of God's work. His servants are to be one, as Christ is one with the Father; their powers, illuminated, inspired, and sanctified, must be united to make a complete whole. Those who love God and keep His commandments are not to draw apart; they are to press together.

• Words of Cheer

The Lord does not forsake His faithful workmen. Bear in mind that our life in this world is but a pilgrimage, that heaven is the home to which we are going. Have faith in God. If my words have wounded and bruised your soul, I am sorry; I am wounded and bruised also. Our work, a strange work, a great work, given us by God, links us heart and soul together. You dare not throw off your armor. You must wear it till the end. When the Lord releases you, it will be time for you to lay your armor at His feet. You have enlisted in His army to serve till the close of the battle, and you would not disgrace yourself and dishonor God by deserting.

May the Lord open to you many matters that He has opened to me. Satan is watching his opportunity to dishonor the cause of God. I have been shown your peril, and I have also been shown your guardian angel preserving you again and again from yourself, keeping you from making shipwreck of faith. My brother, lift up the standard, lift it up, and be not fainthearted or discouraged.

I have given the leading men in the General Conference and the Mission Board the light given me by God: that you and they should counsel together; that, instead of holding themselves aloof, they should be your fellow helpers; that you had been ordained by God to stand in a position of trust, and you needed help instead of censure.

In the intensity of my desire that you should make straight paths for your feet, I have written earnest words to you, but never, never, to denounce or condemn you. Oh, that God would make you understand that my deep interest in you has not changed in the least. I have a most earnest desire that you shall stand fast in God, firm, tried, and true. I know that the Lord wants you to have the crown of victory.

"When He ascended up on high, He led captivity captive, and gave gifts unto men... And He gave some, apostles; and some, prophets; and some, evangelists; and some, pastors and teachers; for the perfecting of the saints, for the work of the ministry, for the edifying of the body of Christ: till we all come in the unity of the faith, and of the knowledge of the Son of God, unto a perfect man, unto the measure of the stature of the fullness of Christ: that we henceforth be no more children, tossed to and fro, and carried about with every wind of doctrine, by the sleight of men, and cunning craftiness, whereby they lie in wait to deceive; but speaking the truth in love, may grow up into Him in all things, which is the head, even Christ: from whom the whole body fitly joined together and compacted by that which every joint supplieth, according to the effectual working in the measure of every part, maketh increase of the body unto the edifying of itself in love." Ephesians 4:8-16.

29. Christ the Medium of Prayer and Blessing

Balaclava
Victoria, Australia
March 25, 1898.

To a Sanitarium Physician—

My Dear Brother: I have just received your letters. I see that you are having a close battle financially. I am so glad that you can heed the encouragement in the words: "Let him take hold of My strength, that he may make peace with Me; and he shall make peace with Me." Isaiah 27:5. Let us have faith in God. Let us put our trust in Him. He understands all about the situation in which we are placed, and He will work in our behalf. He is honored when we trust in Him, bringing to Him all our perplexities. "Whatsoever ye shall ask in My name,"

Christ says, "that will I do, that the Father may be glorified in the Son." John 14:13. God's appointments and grants in our behalf are without limit. The throne of grace itself is occupied by One who permits us to call Him Father.

"God so loved the world, that He gave His only-begotten Son, that whosoever believeth in Him should not perish, but have everlasting life." John 3:16. Jehovah did not deem the plan of salvation complete while invested only with His love. He has placed at His altar an Advocate clothed in our nature. As our Intercessor, Christ's office work is to introduce us to God as His sons and daughters. He intercedes in behalf of those who receive Him. With His own blood He has paid their ransom. By virtue of His merits He gives them power to become members of the royal family, children of the heavenly King. And the Father demonstrates His infinite love for Christ by receiving and welcoming Christ's friends as His friends. He is satisfied with the atonement made. He is glorified by the incarnation, the life, death, and mediation of His Son.

In Christ's name our petitions ascend to the Father. He intercedes in our behalf, and the Father lays open all the treasures of His grace for our appropriation, for us to enjoy and impart to others. "Ask in My name," Christ says. "I do not say that I will pray the Father for you; for the Father Himself loveth you. Make use of My name. This will give your prayers efficiency, and the Father will give you the riches of His grace. Wherefore ask, and ye shall receive, that your joy may be full."

Christ is the connecting link between God and man. He has promised His personal intercession. He places the whole virtue of His righteousness on the side of the suppliant. He pleads for man, and man, in need of divine help, pleads for himself in the presence of God, using the influence of the One who gave His life for the life of the world. As we acknowledge before God our appreciation of Christ's merits, fragrance is given to our intercessions. As we approach God through the virtue of the Redeemer's merits, Christ places us close by His side, encircling us with His human arm, while with His divine arm He grasps the throne of the Infinite. He puts His merits, as sweet incense, in the censer in our hands, in order to encourage our petitions. He promises to hear and answer our supplications.

Yes, Christ has become the medium of prayer between man and God. He has also become the medium of blessing between God and man. He has united divinity with humanity. Men are to co-operate with Him for the salvation of their own souls, and then make earnest, persevering efforts to save those who are ready to die.

We must all work now, while the day lasts; for the night cometh, in which no man can work. I am of good courage in the Lord. There are times when I am shown distinctly that there exists in our churches a state of things that will not help but hinder souls. Then I have hours, and sometimes days, of intense anguish. Many of those who have a knowledge of the truth do not obey the words of God. Their influence is no better than the influence of worldlings. They talk like the world and act like the world. Oh, how my heart aches as I think of how the Saviour is put to shame by their un-Christlike behavior! But after the agony is past, I feel like working harder than ever to restore the poor souls, that they may reveal the image of God.

Pray, yes, pray with unshaken faith and trust. The Angel of the covenant, even our Lord Jesus Christ, is the Mediator who secures the acceptance of the prayers of His believing ones.

30. Words of Encouragement

Cooranbong, N. S. W.
December 12, 1899.
To the Medical Superintendent of the Battle Creek Sanitarium—

My Dear Brother: You speak as if you had no friends. But God is your friend, and Sister White is your friend. You have thought that I had lost confidence in you; but, my dear brother, as I have before written you, I know that the Lord has placed you in a very responsible position, standing as you do as a physician to whom the Lord has given knowledge and understanding, that you may do justice and judgment, and reveal a true missionary spirit in the institution established to present truth in contrast with error.

My brother, the Lord has not left you to go on a warfare at your own charges. He has given you wisdom, and favor with God and man. He has been your helper. He has chosen you as His agent to exalt the truth in the Battle Creek Sanitarium as it is not exalted in the medical institutions of the world. It was His purpose that the Battle Creek Sanitarium should be known as an institution where the Lord is daily acknowledged as the Monarch of the universe. "He doeth according to His will in the army of heaven, and among the inhabitants of the earth: and none can stay His hand, or say unto Him, What doest Thou?" Daniel 4:35.

The Lord designs that the proclamation of the third angel's message shall be the highest, greatest work carried on in our world at this time. He has honored you by placing you in a very responsible position in His work. You were not to separate your influence from the ministry of the gospel. Into every line of your work you were to bring an understanding of and obedience to the truth. The place assigned you by the Lord was under Him in the divine theocracy. You were to learn of Jesus, the Great Teacher, planning and working in accordance with His example. You were to make God first, ever obeying His word. In this would be your strength.

You were to be a faithful physician of the souls as well as of the bodies of those under your charge. Had you fulfilled this trust, using aright the talents God gave you, you would not have worked alone. One who never makes a mistake was presiding. Only the Holy Spirit's power can keep the spirit sweet and fragrant, soft and subdued, enabling the worker to speak the right words at the right time.

You have not been faultless. Often you lost control of yourself. Then your words were not what they should have been. At times you were arbitrary and exacting. But when you were striving for the mastery over self, angels of God cooperated with you, because, through you, God was working to exalt His truth and cause it to receive honored recognition in the world. God gave you wisdom, not that your name should be magnified, but that those coming to the sanitarium in Battle Creek should carry away with them favorable impressions regarding the work of Seventh-day Adventists and respect for the principles that are the foundation of their work. The honor given you did not come to you because you were righteous above all men, but because God desired to use you as His Instrument.

- **God's Purpose in Establishing the Sanitarium**

It was God's purpose that in the sanitarium, missionaries, teachers, and physicians should become acquainted with the third angel's message, which embraces so much. Angels of God were to be your strength in the work that was to be done in order that the Battle Creek Sanitarium might be known as an institution under the special supervision of God. The missionary feeling and the sympathy that prevailed in this institution was a result of the work of invisible heavenly agencies there. God said: "I thought it good to show signs and wonders. In My might I wrought to glorify My name." Many have gone from the sanitarium with new hearts. The change has been decided. These, returning to their homes, have been as lights in the world. Their voices have been heard, saying: "Come all ye that fear God, and I will make known to you what He hath done for my soul. I have seen His greatness; I have tasted His goodness."

• A World-Wide Work

The Lord has shown me that if the enemy can by any means divert the work into wrong channels, and thus hinder its advancement, he will do so. Many of our people have made investments without sitting down to count the cost, without finding out whether there was money enough to carry forward the work started. Shortsightedness has been shown. Men have failed to see that the Lord's vineyard embraces the world.

The income of the sanitariums that have been established is not to be drawn upon to sustain numerous lines of work for the lower classes in our wicked cities. Much of the means that has been used to sustain this large and ever-increasing work should, by the Lord's order, have been used in making plants in other countries, where the light of health reform has not shone. Sanitariums, less costly than the large ones erected in America, should have been built in many lands. Thus plants would have been made which, when strong, would have assisted to make plants in other places.

The Lord is not partial. But He has been misrepresented by His workmen. That which should have been done in many different parts of His vineyard has been greatly hindered, because men at the heart of the work have failed to see how the work could be advanced in more distant parts of the vineyard. In some parts of the field the work has been overdone. In this way money has been absorbed that should have been used to enable workers in other parts of the vineyard to move forward without hindrance in planting the standard of truth in new places. Some portions of the vineyard are not to be robbed in order that the means may be used freely in other portions of the field.

Man judges in accordance with his finite judgment. God looks at the character of the fruit borne and then judges the tree. In the name of the Lord I call upon all to think of the work that we are required to do and how this work is to be sustained. The world is the Lord's vineyard, and it is to be worked.

It is not a great number of institutions, large buildings, and outward display that God requires, but the harmonious action of a peculiar people, a people chosen by God and precious, united with one another, their life hid with Christ in God. Every man is to stand in his lot and place, exerting a right influence in thought, word, and deed. When all God's workers do this, and not till then, His work will be a complete, symmetrical whole.

- ## A Word of Caution

God desires His institutions and His chosen, adopted children to honor Him by revealing the attributes of Christian character. The work that the gospel embraces as missionary work is a straightforward, substantial work, which will shine brighter and brighter unto the perfect day. God does not want the faith of His people to take on the features or appearance of the humanitarian work now called medical missionary work. The means and talents of His people are not to be buried in the slums of New York or Chicago. God's work is to be carried on in right lines.

Self-denial and self-sacrifice are to be shown. We are to work as Christ worked, in simplicity and meekness, in lowliness and consecration. Thus we shall be enabled to do a work distinct from all other missionary work in our world.

There are many of those who are supposed to be rescued from the pit into which they have fallen who cannot be relied on as counselors, or trusted to engage in the work in these last days. The enemy is determined to mix error with truth. To do this he uses the opportunity given him by the debased class for whom so much labor and money are expended, the class whose appetites have been perverted through indulgence, whose souls have been abused, whose characters are misshapen and deformed, whose habits and desires are groveling, who think habitually upon evil. Such ones can be transformed in character; but how few there are with whom the work is thorough and lasting!

Some will be sanctified through the truth; but many make a superficial change in their habits and practices, and then suppose that they are Christians. They are received into church fellowship, but they are a great trouble and a great care. Through them Satan tries to sow in the church the seeds of jealousy, dishonesty, criticism, and accusing. Thus he tries to corrupt the other members of the church.

The disposition that has mastered them from childhood, that led them to break away from all restraint and brought them down to degradation, still controls them. They are reported to be rescued, but too often time shows that the work done for them did not make them submissive children of God. At every supposed slight, resentful feelings rise. They cherish bitterness, wrath, malice. By their words and spirit they show that they have not been born again. Their tendencies are downward, tending to sensuality. They are untrustworthy, unthankful, unholy. Thus it is with all who have not been soundly converted. Every one of these marred characters, untransformed, becomes an efficient worker for Satan, creating dissension and strife.

The Lord has marked out our way of working. As a people we are not to imitate and fall in with Salvation Army methods. This is not the work that the Lord has given us to do. Neither is it our work to condemn them and speak harsh words against them. There are precious, self-sacrificing souls in the Salvation Army. We are to treat them kindly. There are in the Army honest souls, who are sincerely serving the Lord and who will see greater light, advancing to the acceptance of all truth. The Salvation Army workers are trying to save the neglected, downtrodden ones. Discourage them not. Let them do that class of work by their own methods and in their own way. But the Lord has plainly pointed out the work that Seventh-day Adventists are to do. Camp meetings and tent meetings are to be held. The truth for this time is to be proclaimed. A decided testimony is to be borne. And the discourses are to be so simple that children can understand them.

- **Helping or Hindering the Lord**

There are those entering the medical missionary work who are in danger of bringing into it the objectionable sentiments received in their former education. They need to practice the principles laid down in the word of God, else the work will be marred by their preconceived ideas. When we work with all the sanctified ability that God has given us, when we put aside our will for the will of God, when self is crucified day by day, then good results are seen. We move forward in faith, knowing that our Lord has promised to undertake the work entrusted to Him and that He will accomplish it; for He never makes a mistake or a failure.

The Lord's servants are merely stewards. The Lord will work through them when they surrender themselves to Him to be worked by the Holy Spirit. When by faith men place themselves in the Lord's hands, saying, "Here am I; send me," He accepts them for service. But men must not hinder His plans by ambitious devisings. For years the Lord has had a controversy with His people because they have followed their own judgment and have not relied on divine wisdom. Let the workers take heed lest they get in the Lord's way, hindering the advancement of His work, thinking that their wisdom is sufficient for the successful planning and carrying forward of the work. If they do this, the Lord will correct their error. By His divine Spirit He enlightens and trains His workers. He shapes His own providences to carry forward His work according to His mind and will.

- **God's Purpose for His Workers**

If men will but humble themselves before God, if they will not exalt their judgment as the all-controlling influence, if they will make room for the Lord to plan and work, God will use the qualifications He has given them in a way that will glorify His name. He will purify His workers from all selfishness, cutting off the branches that would entwine around undesirable objects, pruning the vine so that it will produce fruit. God is the great Husbandman. He will make everything in the lives of those who are laborers together with Christ subservient to His great purpose of growth and fruit bearing. It is His plan, by conforming His servants day by day to the image of Christ, by making them partakers of the divine nature, to cause them to bear fruit abundantly. He desires His people, through actual experience in the truth of the gospel, to become true, solid, trustworthy, experimental missionaries. He would have them show results far higher, holier, and more definite than in our day have yet been revealed.

The potter takes the clay in his hands and molds and fashions it according to his own will. He kneads it and works it. He tears it apart and then presses it together. He wets it and then dries it. He lets it lie for a while without touching it. When it is perfectly pliable, he continues the work of making of it a vessel. He forms it into shape and on the wheel trims and polishes it. He dries it in the sun and bakes it in the oven. Thus it becomes a vessel fit for use. So the great Master Worker desires to mold and fashion us. And as the clay is in the hands of the potter, so are we to be in His hands. We are not to try to do the work of the potter. Our part is to yield ourselves to the molding of the Master Worker.

- ## The Need of Wise Counselors

The Lord has appointed the physicians in the sanitarium to stand as faithful sentinels. Through them God desired to do the work that must be done in the institution. They were to be your helpers. Through them impressions were to be made in regard to the work of relieving suffering humanity.

But you have needed the counsel of others besides your colaborers. Fresh, new ideas were needed in your counsels, for not all your plans bore the divine credentials. You have been swaying the minds of those connected with you in the medical missionary work, until you and they were becoming like men lost in the fog of uncertainty.

I was instructed by the Lord that your temptation would be to make your medical missionary work stand independent of the conference. But this plan was not right. I saw that you could not plan as you had been doing, or carry out your ideas, without injury to yourself and to the cause of God.

- ## A Divine Helper

My brother, as a surgeon you have had the most critical cases to handle, and at times a dread has come upon you. To perform these difficult duties, you knew that rapid work must be done and that no false moves must be made. Again and again you had to pass swiftly from task to task. Who has been by your side as you have performed these critical operations? Who has kept you calm and self-

Section 3: Letters to Physicians

possessed in the crisis, giving you quick, sharp discernment, clear eyesight, steady nerves, and skillful precision? The Lord Jesus has sent His angel to your side to tell you what to do. A hand has been laid upon your hand. Jesus, and not you, has guided the movements of your instrument. At times you have realized this, and a wonderful calmness has come over you. You dared not hurry, and yet you worked rapidly, knowing that there was not a moment to lose.

The Lord has greatly blessed you. You have been under the divine guidance. Others who knew not of the presiding Presence working with you gave you all the glory. Eminent physicians have witnessed your operations and praised your skill. This has been pleasant to you. You have been greatly honored by God, that His name, not yours, should be magnified; but you have not always been able to endure the seeing of the Invisible. You have had a desire to distinguish yourself, and you have not at all times placed your entire dependence upon God. You have not been willing to heed the counsel of the Lord's servants. In your own wisdom you have planned many things. The Lord would have you respect the gospel ministry. At the very time when you needed discernment, that you might see, not only one side of the work, but all sides, you chose for counselors men under the reproof of God. You were willing to link up with them if they would second your propositions.

By prayer and consecration, by seeking the Lord for wisdom and surrendering yourself to His guidance, you would have been prevented from starting many enterprises that have been born, not of the will of God, but of the will of man. You were given your appointed work. But you have neglected things of great importance to take up, with impulsive spirit, unadvised by the Lord or your brethren, things of minor importance. Your brethren could have given you counsel, but you despised any word that interfered with your plans. This has placed you in a difficult position. Had you abode by your appointed work, God would have made you more and more a successful laborer together with Him.

The Lord wants your mind to blend with other minds. Sometimes, when His servants have differed from you, this was the very thing that God required them to do. But you treated their advice in such a way that afterward they remained silent when they should have spoken. God desires those whom He has placed in positions of trust to do justice and judgment in all wisdom.

- **Burdens that the Lord has not Given**

The Lord gave you your work, not to be done in a rush, but in a calm, considerate manner. The Lord never compels hurried, complicated movements. But you have gathered to yourself responsibilities that the Lord, the merciful Father, does not place upon you. Duties He never ordained that you should perform chase one another wildly. Never are His servants to leave one duty marred or incomplete in order to seize hold of another. He who labors in the calmness of the fear of God will not work in a haphazard manner, for fear that something will hinder an anticipated plan.

Not all the burdens that you have been carrying have been laid upon you by the Lord. The result of your carrying these extra burdens is felt all through the field. If you had kept at your appointed work, laboring for the class of people whom the Lord desired, by means of the sanitarium, to reach with present truth, with the message that God has given His people to give to the world, much more would have been accomplished to bring the chosen people of God before men of high standing. Much more would have been accomplished to show forth the ways and works and power of God. The sanitarium was to be His witness in behalf of truth—elevated, sanctifying truth. The Lord made you, my brother, His honored instrument. He never required from you one task that would crowd out your work in connection with the institution that was to stand for the truth, to do a certain work for God, flashing light upon the pathway of thousands.

You have a great and sacred work to do. If you hold faithfully to the part assigned you, through the skill given you will be enabled to work swiftly, though never appearing to be in a hurry. When your eyes are opened, you will see the deep poverty of the mission fields. You will see that the workers there are hampered at every step, while the Lord's money is being used to sustain home enterprises and institutions, so that the message which should be given to the world is lost sight of.

God impresses different men to be laborers together with Him. One man is not authorized to gather too many responsibilities upon himself. The Lord would have the physician upon whom so much depends so closely connected with Him that his spirit will not be irritated by little things. The Lord desires you to be one of the most efficient workers in the medical profession, slighting nothing, marring nothing, knowing that you have a Counselor close by your side, to sustain and strengthen you, to impart quietness and calm to your soul. Feverishness of mind and uncertainty of spirit will make the hand unskillful. The touch of Christ upon the physician's hand brings vitality, restfulness, confidence, and power.

I write to you as a mother would write to her son. I would help you if I could. I would go to see you if I could feel it my duty to leave the work here in Australia, but I dare not do this. You have built up hopes and nurtured plans without due consideration of how the tower is to be completed. As one who knows, as one who has been permitted to see the results of the work that you have taken upon you, I call upon you to stop and consider. God knows your frame. He knows that you are but dust. You will certainly need the counsel, not only of those who have encouraged you to go on in the work which you deem so important, but the counsel of men who, at the present time, are able to see more clearly than you do the results that will follow certain undertakings.

Cast not behind you as of no consequence the warnings that as yet you do not understand. If you receive the messages of warning sent you, you will be saved from great trial.

Extract from a letter written in 1899 from Wellington, New Zealand—We are not to allow our perplexities and disappointments to eat into our souls and make us fretful and impatient. Let there be no strife, no evil thinking or evil-speaking, lest we offend God. My brother, if you open your heart to envy and evil surmising, the Holy Spirit cannot abide with you. Seek for the fullness that is in Christ. Labor in His lines. Let every thought and word and deed reveal Him. You need a daily baptism of the love that in the days of the apostles made them all of one accord. This love will bring health to body, mind, and soul. Surround your soul with an atmosphere that will strengthen spiritual life. Cultivate faith, hope, courage, and love. Let the peace of God rule in your heart. Then you will be enabled to discharge your responsibilities. The Holy Spirit will impart a divine efficiency, a calm, subdued dignity, to all your efforts to relieve suffering. You will testify that you have been with Jesus.

31. The Value of the Word of God

Oakland, California
June 13, 1901.
To a Physician and His Wife—

Dear Brother and Sister: Our homeward journey was a prosperous one. I attended meetings in many places. At Indianapolis I was surprised to meet so large a number of believers. I spoke twice there. The Lord gave me a message for the people similar to the one given in Battle Creek in regard to the errors which have crept in among us. The people were ready to hear and receive the word.

When errors come into our ranks, we are not to enter into controversy over them. We are faithfully to give the message of reproof, and then we are to lead the minds of the people away from fanciful, erroneous ideas, presenting the truth in contrast with error. The presentation of heavenly themes will open up to the mind principles that rest upon a foundation as enduring as eternity.

Those believers whose Christian convictions are consistent and firm, whose characters are of solid worth, are of great service to the Master. Nothing can move them from the faith. Truth is to them a precious treasure.

The truth of God is found in His word. Those who feel that they must seek elsewhere for present truth need to be converted anew. They have wrong habits to mend, evil ways to be abandoned. They need to seek anew the truth as it is in Jesus, that their character building may be in harmony with the lessons of Christ. As they abandon their human ideas and take up their God-given duties, beholding Christ and becoming conformed to His likeness, they say: "Nearer, my God, to Thee; nearer to Thee."

With the word of God in hand we may draw nearer, step by step, in consecrated love to Jesus. As the Spirit of God becomes better known, the Bible will be accepted as the only foundation of faith. God's people will receive the word as the leaves of the tree of life, more precious than fine gold purified in the fire, and more powerful to sanctify than any other agency.

- **The Reward of a Faithful Study of the Word**

Christ and His word are in perfect harmony. Received and obeyed, they open a sure path for the feet of all who are willing to walk in the light as Christ is in the light. If the people of God would appreciate His word, we should have a heaven in the church here below. Christians would be eager, hungry, to search the word. They would be anxious for time to compare scripture with scripture and to meditate upon the word. They would be more eager for the light of the word than for the morning paper, magazines, or novels. Their greatest desire would be to eat the flesh and drink the blood of the Son of God.

And as a result their lives would be conformed to the principles and promises of the word. Its instruction would be to them as the leaves of the tree of life. It would be in them a well of water, springing up into everlasting life. Refreshing showers of grace would refresh and revive the soul, causing them to forget all toil and weariness. They would be strengthened and encouraged by the words of inspiration.

Ministers would be inspired with divine faith. Their prayers would be characterized by earnestness, filled with the divine assurance of truth. Weariness would be forgotten in the sunlight of heaven. Truth would be interwoven with their lives, and its heavenly principles would be as a fresh, running stream, constantly satisfying the soul.

The Lord's philosophy is the rule of the Christian's life. The entire being is imbued with the life-giving principles of heaven. The busy nothings which consume the time of so many shrink into their proper position before a healthy, sanctifying Bible piety.

The Bible, and the Bible alone, can produce this good result. It is the wisdom of God and the power of God, and it works with all power in the receptive heart. Oh, what heights we might reach if we would conform our wills to the will of God! It is the power of God that we need, wherever we are. The frivolity that cumbers the church makes it weak and indifferent. The Father, the Son, and the Holy Spirit are seeking and longing for channels through which to communicate to the world the divine principles of truth.

Artificial lights may appear, claiming to come from heaven, but they cannot shine forth as the star of holiness, the star of heavenly brightness, to guide the feet of the pilgrim and stranger into the city of God. False lights will take the place of the true, and many souls will be for a time deceived. God forbid that it should be so with us. The true light now shineth, and will light up the souls in which the windows are opened heavenward.

32. The Work for this Time

St. Helena, California
June 25, 1903.
To Our Sanitarium Physicians—

My Dear Brethren: Those who stand in responsible positions in the work of the Lord are represented as watchmen on the walls of Zion. God calls upon them to sound an alarm among the people. Let it be heard in all the plain. The day of woe, of wasting and destruction, is upon all who do unrighteousness. With special severity will the Lord's hand fall upon the watchmen who have failed to place before the people in clear lines their obligation to Him who by creation and by redemption is their owner.

My brethren, the Lord calls upon you to examine the heart closely. He calls upon you to adorn the truth in your daily practice and in all your dealings with one another. He requires of you a faith that works by love and purifies the soul. It is dangerous for you to trifle with the sacred demands of conscience, dangerous for you to set an example that leads others in a wrong direction.

Christians should carry with them, wherever they go, the sweet fragrance of Christ's righteousness, showing that they are complying with the invitation: "Learn of Me; for I am meek and lowly in heart: and ye shall find rest unto your souls." Matthew 11:29. Are you learning daily in the school of Christ—learning how to dismiss doubt and evil surmisings, learning how to be fair and noble in your dealings with your brethren, for your own sake, and for Christ's sake?

Present truth leads onward and upward, gathering in the needy, the oppressed, the suffering, the destitute. All that will come are to be brought into the fold. In their lives there is to take place a reformation that will constitute them members of the royal family, children of the heavenly King. By hearing the message of truth, men and women are led to accept the Sabbath and to unite with the church by baptism. They are to bear God's sign by observing the

Sabbath of creation. They are to know for themselves that obedience to God's commandments means eternal life.

Means and earnest labor may be safely invested in such a work as this, for it is a work that will endure. Thus those who have been dead in trespasses and sins are brought into fellowship with the saints and are made to sit in heavenly places with Christ. Their feet are placed on a sure foundation. They are enabled to reach a high standard, even the loftiest heights of faith, because Christians make straight paths for their feet, lest the lame be turned out of the way.

Every church should labor for the perishing within its own borders and for those outside its borders. The members are to shine as living stones in the temple of God, reflecting heavenly light. No random, haphazard, desultory work is to be done. To get fast hold of souls ready to perish means more than praying for a drunkard and then, because he weeps and confesses the pollution of his soul, declaring him saved. Over and over again the battle must be fought.

Let the members of every church feel it their special duty to labor for those in their neighborhood. Let each one who claims to stand under the banner of Christ feel that he has entered into covenant relation with God, to do the work of the Saviour. Let not those who take up this work become weary in well-doing. When the redeemed stand before God, precious souls will respond to their names who are there because of the faithful, patient efforts put forth in their behalf, the entreaties and earnest persuasions to flee to the Stronghold.

Thus those who in this world have been laborers together with God will receive their reward.

The ministers of the popular churches will not allow the truth to be presented to the people from their pulpits. The enemy leads them to resist the truth with bitterness and malice. Falsehoods are manufactured. Christ's experience with the Jewish rulers is repeated. Satan strives to eclipse every ray of light shining from God to His people. He works through the ministers as he worked through the priests and rulers in the days of Christ. Will those who know the truth join his party, to hinder, embarrass, and turn aside those who are trying to work in God's appointed way to advance His work, to plant the standard of truth in the regions of darkness?

- **Our Message**

The third angel's message, embracing the messages of the first and second angels, is the message for this time. We are to raise aloft the banner on which is inscribed: "The commandments of God, and the faith of Jesus." The world is soon to meet the great Lawgiver over His broken law. This is not the time to put out of sight the great issues before us. God calls upon His people to magnify the law and make it honorable.

When the morning stars sang together, and all the sons of God shouted for joy, the Sabbath was given to the world, that man might ever remember that in six days God created the world. He rested upon the seventh day, blessing it as the day of His rest, and gave it to the beings He had created, that they might remember Him as the true and living God. By His mighty power, notwithstanding the opposition of Pharaoh, God delivered His people from Egypt, that they might keep the law which had been given in Eden. He brought them to Sinai to hear the proclamation of this law.

By proclaiming the Ten Commandments to the children of Israel with His own voice, God demonstrated their importance. In awful grandeur He made known His majesty and authority as Ruler of the world. This He did to impress the people with the sacredness of His law and the importance of obeying it. The power and glory with which the law was given reveal its importance. It is the faith once delivered to the saints by Christ our Redeemer speaking from Sinai.

- **The Sign of Our Relationship to God**

By the observance of the Sabbath the children of Israel were to be distinguished from all other nations. "Verily My Sabbaths ye shall keep," Christ said, "for it is a sign between Me and you throughout your generations; that ye may know that I am the Lord that doth sanctify you." "It is a sign between Me and the children of Israel forever: for in six days the Lord made heaven and earth, and on the seventh day He rested, and was refreshed." "Wherefore the children of Israel shall keep the Sabbath, to observe the Sabbath throughout their generations, for a perpetual covenant." Exodus 31:13, 17, 16.

The Sabbath is a sign of the relationship existing between God and His people, a sign that they are His obedient subjects, that they keep holy His law. The observance of the Sabbath is the means ordained by God of preserving a knowledge of Himself and of distinguishing between His loyal subjects and the transgressors of His law. This is the faith once delivered to the saints, who stand in moral power before the world, firmly maintaining this faith.

Opposition we shall have as we voice the message of the third angel. Satan will bring in every possible device to make of no effect the faith once delivered to the saints. "Many shall follow their pernicious ways; by reason of whom the way of truth shall be evil spoken of. And through covetousness shall they with feigned words make merchandise of you: whose judgment now of a long time lingereth not, and their damnation slumbereth not." 2 Peter 2:2, 3. But in spite of opposition, all are to hear the words of truth.

The law of God is the foundation of all enduring reformation. We are to present to the world in clear, distinct lines the need of obeying this law. Obedience to God's law is the greatest incentive to industry, economy, truthfulness, and just dealing between man and man.

The law of God is to be the means of education in the family. Parents are under a most solemn obligation to obey this law, setting their children an example of the strictest integrity. Men in responsible positions, whose influence is far-reaching, are to guard well their ways and works, keeping the fear of the Lord ever before them. "The fear of the Lord is the beginning of wisdom." Psalm 111:10. Those who hearken diligently to the voice of the Lord and cheerfully keep His commandments will be among the number who see God. "The Lord commanded us to do all these statutes, to fear the Lord our God, for our good always, that He might preserve us alive, as it is at this day. And it shall be our righteousness, if we observe to do all these commandments before the Lord our God, as He hath commanded us." Deuteronomy 6:24, 25.

Our work as believers in the truth is to present before the world the immutability of the law of God. Ministers and teachers, physicians and nurses, are bound by covenant with God to present the importance of obeying His law. We are to be distinguished as a people who keep the commandments. The Lord has stated explicitly that He has a work to be done for the world. How shall it be done? Let us seek to find the best way and then perform the will of the Lord.

This world is a training school for the higher school, this life a preparation for the life to come. Here we are to be prepared for entrance into the heavenly courts. Here we are to receive and believe and practice the truth until we are made ready for a home with the saints in light.

Our sanitariums are to be established for one object—the proclamation of the truth for this time. And they are to be so conducted that a decided impression in favor of the truth will be made on the minds of those who come to them for treatment. The conduct of each worker is to tell on the side of right. We have a warning message to bear to the world, and our earnestness, our devotion to God's service, are to bear witness to the truth.

33. A Broader View

St. Helena, California
October 30, 1903.
To Medical Missionaries—

Christ, the great Medical Missionary, came to our world as the ideal of all truth. Truth never languished on His lips, never suffered in His hands. Words of truth fell from His lips with the freshness and power of a new revelation. He unfolded the mysteries of the kingdom of heaven, bringing forth jewel after jewel of truth.

Christ spoke with authority. Every truth essential for the people to know He proclaimed with the unfaltering assurance of certain knowledge. He uttered nothing fanciful or sentimental. He presented no sophistries, no human opinions. No idle tales, no false theories clothed in beautiful language, came from His lips. The statements that He made were truths established by personal knowledge. He foresaw the delusive doctrines that would fill the world, but He did not unfold them. In His teachings He dwelt upon the unchangeable principles of God's word. He magnified the simple, practical truths that the common people could understand and bring into the daily experience.

Christ might have opened to men the deepest truths of science. He might have unlocked mysteries that have required centuries of toil and study to penetrate. He might have made suggestions in scientific lines that would have afforded food for thought and stimulus for invention to the close of time. But He did not do this. He said nothing to gratify curiosity or to satisfy man's ambitions by opening doors to worldly greatness. In all His teaching, Christ brought the minds of men in contact with the Infinite Mind. He did not direct the people to study men's theories about God, His word, or His works. He taught them to behold God as manifested in His works, in His word, and by His providences.

- **Christ's Victory over Unbelief**

While upon this earth, the Son of God was the Son of man; yet there were times when His divinity flashed forth. Thus it was when He said to the paralytic: "Be of good cheer; thy sins be forgiven thee." Matthew 9:2.

"But there were certain of the scribes sitting there," who "began to reason," not openly, "but in their hearts, "saying, "Who is this which speaketh blasphemies? Who can forgive sins, but God alone?" Mark 2:6; Luke 5:21.

"And Jesus knowing their thoughts said, Wherefore think ye evil in your hearts? For whether is easier, to say, Thy sins be forgiven thee; or to say, Arise, and walk? But that ye may know that the Son of man hath power on earth to forgive sins, (then saith He to the sick of the palsy,) Arise, take up thy bed, and go unto thine house." Matthew 9:4-6.

The great Medical Missionary took away the sins of the paralytic and then presented him to God as pardoned. And He gave him also physical healing. God had given His Son power to lay hold of the eternal throne. While Christ stood forth in His own personality, He reflected the luster of the position of honor that He had held within the enriching light of the eternal throne.

On another occasion Christ made the request: "Father, glorify Thy name." And in answer there came "a voice from heaven, saying, I have both glorified it, and will glorify it again." John 12:28.

If this voice did not move the impenitent, if the power that Christ manifested in His mighty miracles did not cause the Jews to believe, we should not be greatly surprised to find that men and women today are in danger, through continual association with those who are incredulous, of manifesting the same unbelief that the Jews manifested, and of developing the same perverted understanding.

I am made unutterably sad as I consider what has been opened before me regarding the condition of things at Battle Creek and other centers of our work, where great light has been shining. In the past, when matters have been shown to be wrong, there has been a realization of the wrong, and this has been followed by confession, repentance, and thorough reformation. But of late there have not been faithful stewards to repress the evils that needed to be repressed. Can we, then, be surprised that there is great spiritual blindness?

Those engaged in the gospel ministry need to learn of Christ His meekness and lowliness, and to be thoroughly converted, that their lives may testify to a world dead in trespasses and sins that they have been born again. Medical missionary workers, also, need to be converted. When they are converted, their influence will be a power for good in the world. They will be willing to receive counsel and help from their brethren, because they have been sanctified through the truth. Daily they will receive rich supplies of grace from heaven to impart to others.

To every one of His appointed agencies the Lord sends the message: "Take your position at your post of duty, and then stand firm for the right." To all I am instructed to say: "Find your place. Receive not the fanciful sentiments of men who are not taught by God. Christ is waiting to give you insight into heavenly things, waiting to quicken your spiritual pulse to renewed activity. No longer subordinate the claims of future, eternal interests to the common affairs of this life. 'Ye cannot serve God and mammon.' Matthew 6:24. Wake up, brethren, wake up."

The breadth of gospel medical missionary work is not understood. The medical missionary work now called for is that outlined in the commission which Christ gave to His disciples just before His ascension. "All power is given unto Me in heaven and in earth," He said. "Go ye therefore, and teach all nations, baptizing them in the name of the Father, and of the Son, and of the Holy Ghost: teaching them to observe all things whatsoever I have commanded you: and, lo, I am with you alway, even unto the end of the world." Matthew 28:18-20.

These words point out our field and our work. Our field is the world; our work the proclamation of the truths which Christ came to our world to proclaim. Men and women are to have opportunity to gain a knowledge of present truth, an opportunity to know that Christ is their Saviour, "that God so loved the world, that He gave His only-begotten Son, that whosoever believeth in Him should not perish, but have everlasting life." John 3:16.

Section 3: Letters to Physicians

- **A Warning against Centralization**

Christ embraced the world in His missionary work, and the Lord has shown me by revelation that it is not His plan for large centers to be made, for large institutions to be established, and for the funds of our people in all parts of the world to be exhausted in the support of a few large institutions, when the necessities of the times call for something to be done, as providence opens the way, in many places. Plants should be established in various places all over the world. First one, and then another, part of the vineyard is to be entered, until all has been cultivated. Efforts are to be put forth wherever the need is greatest. But we cannot carry on this aggressive warfare and at the same time make an extravagant outlay of means in a few places.

The Battle Creek Sanitarium is too large. A great many workers will be required to care for the patients who come. A tenth of the number of patients who come to that institution is as many as can be cared for with the best results in one medical missionary center. Centers should be made in all the cities that are unacquainted with the great work that the Lord would have done to warn the world that the end of all things is at hand. "There is too much," said the Great Teacher, "in one place."

Let those who have fitted themselves to engage in medical missionary work in foreign countries go to the places that they expect to make their field of labor, and begin work right among the people, learning the language as they work. Very soon they will find that they can teach the simple truths of God's word.

- **A Neglected Field Near Us**

There is in this country a great, unworked field. The colored race, numbering thousands upon thousands, appeals to the consideration and sympathy of every true, practical believer in Christ. These people do not live in a foreign country, and they do not bow down to idols of wood and stone. They live among us, and again and again, through the testimonies of His Spirit, God has called our attention to them, telling us that here are human beings neglected. This broad field lies before us unworked, calling for the light that God has given us in trust.

34. Christ Our Example

St. Helena, California, October 30, 1903.

To Medical Missionaries

That which is most needed by medical missionary workers is the guidance of the Spirit of the Lord. Those who labor as Christ, the great Medical Missionary, labored must be spiritually minded. But not all who are doing medical missionary work are exalting God and His truth. Not all are submitting to the guidance of the Holy Spirit. Some are bringing to the foundation wood, hay, and stubble—material that will not bear the test of fire.

I pray that I may have wisdom and power from God to present to you that which constitutes gospel medical missionary work. This is a great and important branch of our denominational work. But many have lost sight of the pure, ennobling principles underlying acceptable medical missionary work.

In my diary I find the following, written one year ago: October 29, 1902. This morning I awoke early. After praying most earnestly for wisdom and clearness of mind, that I might properly express the matters urged upon my attention, I wrote out about ten pages of instruction. I know that the Lord helped me to trace on paper the important matter that should come before His people.

When writing thus, I feel intensely, but after the instruction has been recorded, relief comes to my mind; for I know then that the subject matter presented to me will not be lost, even though the subject may pass from my mind.

Those only who realize that the cross is the center of hope for the human family can understand the gospel that Christ taught. He came to this world for no other purpose than to place man on vantage ground before the world and the heavenly universe. He came to bear testimony that fallen human beings, through faith in His power and efficacy as the Son of God, may become partakers of the divine nature. He alone could make atonement for sinners and open the gates of paradise to the fallen race. He took on Himself, not the nature of angels, but the nature of man, and in this world lived a life untainted by sin. "The Word was made flesh, and dwelt among us, (and we beheld His glory, the glory as of the Only Begotten of the Father,) full of grace and truth." "As many as received Him, to them gave He power to become the sons of God, even to them that believe on His name." John 1:14, 12.

By His life and death Christ taught that only in obedience to God's commandments can man find safety and true greatness "The law of the Lord is perfect, converting the soul." Psalm 19:7. God's law is a transcript of His character. It was given to man in the beginning as the standard of obedience. In succeeding ages this law was lost sight of. Hundreds of years after the Flood Abraham was called, and to him was given the promise that his descendants should exalt God's law. In course of time the Israelites went into Egypt, where for many years they suffered grievous oppression at the hands of the Egyptians. After they had been in slavery for nearly four hundred years, God delivered them by a wonderful manifestation of His power. He revealed Himself to the Egyptians as the Ruler of the universe, One greater than all heathen deities.

At Sinai the law was given a second time. In awful grandeur the Lord spoke His precepts and with His own finger engraved the Decalogue upon tables of stone.

Passing down through the centuries, we find that there came a time when God's law must once more be unmistakably revealed as the standard of obedience. Christ came to vindicate the sacred claims of the law. He came to live a life of obedience to its requirements and thus prove the falsity of the charge made by Satan that it is impossible for man to keep the law of God. As a man He met temptation and overcame in the strength given Him from God. As He went about doing good, healing all who were afflicted by Satan, He made plain to men the character of God's law and the nature of His service. His life testifies that it is possible for us also to obey the law of God.

Never did Christ deviate from loyalty to the principles of God's law. Never did He do anything contrary to the will of His Father. Before angels, men, and demons He could speak words that from any other lips would have been blasphemy: "I do always those things that please Him." John 8:29. Day by day for three years His enemies followed Him, trying to find some stain in His character. Satan, with all his confederacy of evil, sought to overcome Him; but they found nothing in Him by which to gain advantage. Even the devils were forced to confess: "Thou art the Holy One of God."

- **Self-Sacrifice**

What language could so forcibly express God's love for the human family as it is expressed by the gift of His only-begotten Son for our redemption? The Innocent bore the chastisement of the guilty. "God so loved the world, that He gave His only-begotten Son, that whosoever believeth in Him should not perish, but have everlasting life. For God sent not His Son into the world to condemn the world; but that the world through Him might be saved. He that believeth on Him is not condemned: but he that believeth not is condemned already, because he hath not believed in the name of the only-begotten Son of God." John 3:16-18.

Christ gave Himself, an atoning sacrifice, for the saving of a lost world. He was treated as we deserve, in order that we might be treated as He deserves. He was condemned for our sins, in which He had no share, that we might be justified by His righteousness, in which we had no share. He suffered the death which was ours, that we might receive the life which was His. "With His stripes we are healed." Isaiah 53:5.

Christ was tempted in all points like as we are, by the one who once stood in loyalty by His side in the heavenly courts. Behold the Son of God in the wilderness of temptation, in the time of greatest weakness assailed by the fiercest temptation. See Him during the years of His ministry, attacked on every side by the forces of evil. See Him in His agony on the cross. All this He suffered for us.

Christ's earthly life, so full of toil and sacrifice, was cheered by the thought that He would not have all His travail for nought. By giving His life for the life of men, He would win the world back to its loyalty. Although the baptism of blood must first be received, although the sins of the world were to weigh upon His innocent soul, yet, for the joy that was set before Him, He chose to endure the cross and despised the shame.

Study Christ's definition of a true missionary: "Whosoever will come after Me, let him deny himself, and take up his cross, and follow Me." Mark 8:34. Following Christ, as spoken of in these words, is not a pretense, a farce. Jesus expects His disciples to follow closely in His footsteps, enduring what He endured, suffering what He suffered, overcoming as He overcame. He is anxiously waiting to see His professed followers revealing the spirit of self-

Section 3: Letters to Physicians

sacrifice.

Those who receive Christ as a personal saviour, choosing to be partakers of His suffering, to live His life of self-denial, to endure shame for His sake, will understand what it means to be a genuine medical missionary.

When all our medical missionaries live the new life in Christ, when they take His word as their guide, they will have a much clearer understanding of what constitutes genuine medical missionary work. This work will have a deeper meaning to them when they render implicit obedience to the law engraven on tables of stone by the finger of God, including the Sabbath commandment, concerning which Christ Himself spoke through Moses to the children of Israel, saying:

"Speak thou also unto the children of Israel, saying, Verily My Sabbaths ye shall keep: for it is a sign between Me and you throughout your generations; that ye may know that I am the Lord that doth sanctify you... The children of Israel shall keep the Sabbath, to observe the Sabbath throughout their generations, for a perpetual covenant. It is a sign between Me and the children of Israel forever." Exodus 31:13-17.

Let us diligently study God's word, that we may proclaim with power the message that is to be given in these last days. Many of those upon whom the light of the Saviour's self-sacrificing life is shining refuse to live a life in accordance with His will. They are not willing to live a life of sacrifice for the good of others. They desire to exalt themselves. To such ones truth and righteousness have lost their meaning, and their un-Christlike influence leads many to turn away from the Saviour. God calls for true, steadfast workers, whose lives will counteract the influence of those who are working against Him.

To every medical missionary worker I am instructed to say: Follow your Leader. He is the way, the truth, and the life. He is your example. Upon all medical missionary workers rests the responsibility of keeping in view Christ's life of unselfish service. They are to keep their eyes fixed on Jesus, the Author and Finisher of their faith. He is the Source of all light, the fountain of all blessing.

- ## A Firm Stand for the Right

God calls upon His workers, in this age of diseased piety and perverted principle, to reveal a healthy, influential spirituality. My brethren and sisters, this God requires of you. Every jot of your influence is to be used on the side of Christ. You are now to call things by the right name and stand firm in defense of the truth as it is in Jesus.

It behooves every soul whose life is hid with Christ in God to come to the front now and to contend for the faith once delivered to the saints. Truth must be defended and the kingdom of God advanced as it would be were Christ in person on this earth. If He were here He would be drawn out to rebuke many who, though professing to be medical missionaries, have not chosen to learn of the great Medical Missionary His meekness and lowliness. In the lives of some occupying high positions in the medical missionary work, self has been exalted. Until such ones rid themselves of every desire to uplift self, they cannot clearly discern the character of Christ, nor can they do the work that He did.

When the Holy Spirit controls the minds of our church members, there will be seen in our churches a much higher standard in speech, in ministry, in spirituality, than is now seen. The church members will be refreshed by the water of life, and the laborers, working under one Head, even Christ, will reveal their Master in spirit, in word, in deed, and will encourage one another to press forward in the grand, closing work in which we are engaged. There will be a healthy increase of unity and love, which will bear testimony to the world that God sent His Son to die for the redemption of sinners. Divine truth will be exalted; and as it shines forth as a lamp that burneth, we shall understand it more and still more clearly.

The testing truth for this time is not the fabrication of any human mind. It is from God. It is genuine philosophy to those who appropriate it. Christ became incarnate in order that we, through belief of the truth, might be sanctified and redeemed. Let those who hold the truth in righteousness arouse and go forth, shod with the preparation of the gospel of peace, to proclaim the truth to those who know it not. Let them make straight paths for their feet, lest the lame be turned out of the way.

We are now to unify and by true medical missionary work prepare the way for our coming King. But let us remember that Christian unity does not mean that the identity of one person is to be submerged in that of another; nor does it mean that the mind of one is to be led and controlled by the mind of another. God has not given to any man the power that some, by word and act, seek to claim. God requires every man to stand free and to follow the directions of the word.

Let us increase in a knowledge of the truth, giving all praise and glory to Him who is One with the Father. Let us seek most earnestly for the heavenly anointing, the Holy Spirit. Let us have a pure, growing Christianity, that in the heavenly courts we may at last be pronounced complete in Christ.

"Behold, the Bridegroom cometh; go ye out to meet Him." Matthew 25:6. Lose no time now in rising and trimming your lamps. Lose no time in seeking perfect unity with one another. We must expect difficulties. Trials will come. Christ, the Captain of our salvation, was made perfect through suffering. His followers will encounter the enemy many times and will be severely tried, but they need not despair. Christ says to them: "Be of good cheer; I have overcome the world." John 16:33.

The following lines portray the Christian warfare:

> I thought that the course of the Christian to heaven
>   Would be bright as the summer and glad as the morn.
> Thou show'dst me the path; it was dark and rough,
>   All rugged with rocks, all tangled with thorn;
> I dreamed of celestial rewards and renown;
> I asked for the palm branch, the robe, and the crown;
> I asked, and Thou show'dst me a cross and a grave.

— Section 4 —

Be on Guard

"Watch ye, stand fast in the faith, quit you like men, be strong. Let all that ye do be done in love." 1 Corinthians 16:13, 14, A. R. V.

35. Lessons from the Past

- **Centralization**

It was God's design that after the Flood, in fulfillment of the command given to Adam, men should disperse themselves throughout the earth, to replenish and subdue it.

But as Noah's descendants increased in numbers, apostasy manifested itself. Those who desired to cast off the restraint of God's law decided to separate from the worshipers of Jehovah. They determined to keep their community united in one body and to found a monarchy which should eventually embrace the whole earth. In the plain of Shinar they resolved to build a city, and in it a tower that should be the wonder of the world. This tower was to be so high that no flood could rise to the top, so massive that nothing could sweep it away. Thus they hoped to secure their own safety and make themselves independent of God.

This confederacy was born of rebellion against God. The dwellers on the plain of Shinar established their kingdom for self-exaltation, not for the glory of God. Had they succeeded, a mighty power would have borne sway, banishing righteousness and inaugurating a new religion. The world would have been demoralized. Erroneous theories would have diverted minds from allegiance to the divine statutes, and the law of Jehovah would have been ignored and forgotten. But God never leaves the world without witnesses for Him. At this

Section 4: Be on Guard

time there were men who humbled themselves before God and cried unto Him. "O God," they pleaded, "interpose between Thy cause, and the plans and methods of men." "And the Lord came down to see the city and the tower, which the children of men builded." Genesis 11:5. Angels were sent to bring to nought the purposes of the builders.

The tower had reached a lofty height, and it was impossible for the workmen at the top to communicate directly with those at the base; therefore men were stationed at different points, each to receive and report to the one next below him the orders for the needed material, or other directions regarding the work. As messages were thus passing from one to another, the language was confounded, so that material was called for which was not needed, and the directions received were often the reverse of those that had been given.

Confusion and dismay followed. All work came to a standstill. There could be no further harmony or co-operation. The builders were wholly unable to account for the strange misunderstandings among them, and in their rage and disappointment they reproached one another. Their confusion ended in strife and bloodshed. Lightnings from heaven broke off the upper portion of the tower and cast it to the ground. Men were made to feel that there is a God who ruleth in the heavens and that He is able to confuse and to multiply confusion in order to teach men that they are only men.

God bears long with the perversity of men, giving them ample opportunity for repentance; but He marks all their devices to resist the authority of His just and holy law.

Up to this time all had spoken the same language; now those that could understand one another's speech united in companies; some went one way, and some another. "From thence did the Lord scatter them abroad upon the face of all the earth." Verse 9.

In our day the Lord desires that His people shall be dispersed throughout the earth. They are not to colonize. Jesus said: "Go ye into all the world, and preach the gospel to every creature." Mark 16:15. When the disciples followed their inclination to remain in large numbers in Jerusalem, persecution was permitted to come upon them, and they were scattered to all parts of the inhabited world.

For years messages of warning and entreaty have been coming to our people, urging them to go forth into the Master's great harvest field and labor unselfishly for souls.

From testimonies written in 1895 and 1899 I copy the following paragraphs:

"True missionary workers will not colonize. God's people are to be pilgrims and strangers on the earth. The investment of large sums of money in the building up of the work in one place is not in the order of God. Plants are to be made in many places. Schools and sanitariums are to be established in places where there is now nothing to represent the truth. These interests are not to be established for the purpose of making money, but for the purpose of spreading the truth. Land should be secured at a distance from the cities, where schools can be built up in which the youth can be given an education in agricultural and mechanical lines.

The principles of present truth are to become more widespread. There are those who are reasoning from a wrong point of view. Because it is more convenient to have the work centered in one place, they are in favor of crowding everything together in one locality. Great evil is the result. Places that should be helped are left destitute.

What can I say to our people that will lead them to follow the course that will be for their present and future good? Will not those in Battle Creek heed the light given them by God? Will they not deny self, lift the cross, and follow Jesus? Will they not obey the call of their Leader to leave Battle Creek and build up interests in other places? Will they not go to the dark places of the earth to tell the story of the love of Christ, trusting in God to give them success?

It is not God's plan for our people to crowd into Battle Creek. Jesus says: "Go work today in My vineyard. Get away from the places where you are not needed. Plant the standard of truth in towns and cities that have not heard the message. Prepare the way for My coming. Those in the highways and hedges are to hear the call."

The Lord will make the wilderness a sacred place, as His people, filled with the missionary spirit, go forth to make centers for His work, to establish sanitariums, where the sick and afflicted can be cared for; and schools, where the youth can be educated in right lines.

It has been urged that there were great advantages in having so many institutions in close connection; that they would be a strength to one another and could afford help to those seeking education and employment. This is according to human reasoning; it will be admitted that, from a human point of view, many advantages are gained by crowding so many responsibilities in Battle Creek; but the vision needs to be extended."

Notwithstanding frequent counsels to the contrary, men continued to plan for centralization of power, for the binding of many interests under one control. This work was first started in the Review and Herald office. Things were swayed first one way and then another. It was the enemy of our work who prompted the call for the consolidation of the publishing work under one controlling power in Battle Creek.

Then the idea gained favor that the medical missionary work would be greatly advanced if all our medical institutions and other medical missionary interests were bound up under the control of the medical missionary association at Battle Creek.

I was told that I must lift my voice in warning against this. We were not to be under the control of men who could not control themselves and who were not willing to be amenable to God. We were not to be guided by men who wanted their word to be the controlling power. The development of the desire to control has been very marked, and God sent warning after warning, forbidding confederacies and consolidation. He warned us against binding ourselves to fulfill certain agreements that would be presented by men laboring to control the movements of their brethren.

- **An Educational Center**

The Lord is not pleased with some of the arrangements that have been made in Battle Creek. He has declared that other places are being robbed of the light and advantages that have been centered and multiplied in Battle Creek. It is not pleasing to God that our youth from all parts of the country should be called to Battle Creek, to work in the sanitarium, and to receive their education. When we permit this, we are often guilty of robbing needy fields of their most precious treasure.

Through the light given in the testimonies, the Lord has indicated that He does not desire students to leave their home schools and sanitariums to be educated in Battle Creek. He instructed us to remove the college from this place. This was done, but the institutions that remained failed of doing what they should have done to share with other places the advantages still centered in Battle

Creek. The Lord signified His displeasure by permitting the principal buildings of these institutions to be destroyed by fire.

Notwithstanding the plain evidence of the Lord's providence in these destructive fires, some among us have not hesitated to make light of the statement that these buildings were burned because men had been swaying things in directions which the Lord could not approve.

Men have been departing from right principles, for the promulgation of which these institutions were established. They have failed of doing the very work that God ordained should be done to prepare a people to "build the old waste places" and to stand in the breach, as represented in the fifty-eighth chapter of Isaiah. In this scripture the work we are to do is clearly defined as being medical missionary work. This work is to be done in all places. God has a vineyard; and He desires that this vineyard shall be worked unselfishly. No parts are to be neglected. The most neglected portion needs the most wide-awake missionaries to do the work which, through Isaiah, the Holy Spirit has portrayed:

"Is not this the fast that I have chosen? to loose the bands of wickedness, to undo the heavy burdens, and to let the oppressed go free, and that ye break every yoke?" "If thou draw out thy soul to the hungry, and satisfy the afflicted soul; then shall thy light rise in obscurity, and thy darkness be as the noonday: and the Lord shall guide thee continually, and satisfy thy soul in drought, and make fat thy bones: and thou shalt be like a watered garden, and like a spring of water, whose waters fail not. And they that shall be of thee shall build the old waste places: thou shalt raise up the foundations of many generations; and thou shalt be called, The repairer of the breach, The restorer of paths to dwell in." Isaiah 58:6, 10-12.

For His own name's sake, God will not permit the froward and the independent to carry out their unsanctified plans. He will visit them for their perversity of action. "There is no peace, saith my God, to the wicked." Isaiah 57:21. But in His judgments the Lord will remember mercy. He declares:

"I will not contend forever, neither will I be always wroth: for the spirit should fail before Me, and the souls which I have made. For the iniquity of his covetousness was I wroth, and smote him: I hid Me, and was wroth, and he went on frowardly in the way of his heart. I have seen his ways, and will heal him: I will lead him also, and restore comforts unto him and to his mourners. I create the fruit of the lips; Peace, peace to him that is far off, and to him that is near, saith the Lord; and I will heal him." Verses 16-19.

"The spirit of My people should fail before Me," said the Lord, "if I were to deal with them in accordance with their perversity. They could not endure My displeasure and My wrath. I have seen the perverse ways of every sinner. He who repents and does the works of righteousness, I will convert and heal, and restore unto My favor."

Concerning those who have been deceived and led astray by unconsecrated men, the Lord says: "Their course of action has not been in accordance with My will; yet for the righteousness of My own cause, for the truth's sake, I will heal everyone who shall honor My name. All the penitent of Israel shall see of My salvation. I, the Lord, do rule, and I will fill with praise and thanksgiving the hearts of all who are nigh and far off, even all the penitent of Israel who have kept My ways."

"Thus saith the high and lofty One that inhabiteth eternity, whose name is Holy; I dwell in the high and holy place, with him also that is of a contrite and humble spirit, to revive the spirit of the humble, and to revive the heart of the contrite ones." Verse 15.

36. How Shall Our Youth Be Trained?

John the Baptist, the forerunner of Christ, received his early training from his parents. The greater portion of his life was spent in the wilderness, that he might not be influenced by beholding the lax piety of the priests and rabbis or by learning their maxims and traditions, through which right principles were perverted and belittled. The religious teachers of the day had become so blind spiritually that they could hardly recognize the virtues of heavenly origin. So long had they cherished pride, envy, and jealousy that they interpreted the Old Testament Scriptures in such a manner as to destroy their true meaning. It was John's choice to forgo the enjoyments and luxuries of city life for the stern discipline of the wilderness. Here his surroundings were favorable to habits of simplicity and self-denial. Uninterrupted by the clamor of the world, he could here study the lessons of nature, of revelation, and of providence.

The words of the angel to Zacharias had been often repeated to John by his God-fearing parents. From his childhood his mission had been kept before him, and he accepted the holy trust. To him the solitude of the desert was a welcome escape from the society in which suspicion, unbelief, and impurity had become well-nigh all-pervading. He distrusted his own power to withstand temptation and shrank from constant contact with sin lest he should lose the sense of its exceeding sinfulness.

But the life of John was not spent in idleness, in ascetic gloom, or in selfish isolation. From time to time he went forth to mingle with men, and he was ever an interested observer of what was passing in the world. From his quiet retreat he watched the unfolding of events. With vision illuminated by the Divine Spirit, he studied the characters of men, that he might understand how to reach their hearts with the message of heaven.

Christ lived the life of a genuine medical missionary. He desires us to study His life diligently, that we may learn to labor as He labored.

His mother was His first human teacher. From her lips, and from the scrolls of the prophets, He learned of heavenly things. He lived in a peasant's home, and faithfully and cheerfully He acted His part in bearing the household burdens. He had been the Commander of heaven, and angels had delighted to fulfill His word; now He was a willing servant, a loving, obedient son. He learned a trade and with His own hands worked in the carpenter's shop with Joseph. In the simple garb of a common laborer He walked the streets of the little town, going to and returning from His humble work.

With the people of that age the value of things was determined by outward show. As religion had declined in power, it had increased in pomp. The educators of the time sought to command respect by display and ostentation. To all this the life of Jesus presented a marked contrast. His life demonstrated the worthlessness of those things that men regarded as life's great essentials. The schools of His time, with their magnifying of things small and their belittling of things great, He did not seek. His education was gained from heaven-appointed sources, from useful work, from the study of the Scriptures and of nature, and from the experiences of life— God's lessonbooks, full of instruction to all who bring to them the willing heart, the seeing eye, and the understanding heart.

"The Child grew, and waxed strong in spirit, filled with wisdom: and the grace of God was upon Him." Luke 2:40. Thus prepared, He went forth to His mission, in every moment of His contact with men exerting upon them an influence to bless, a power to transform, such as the world had never witnessed.

- **Words of Warning**

We are living in a time of special peril to the youth. Satan knows that the end of the world is soon to come, and he is determined to improve every opportunity for pressing young men and young women into his service. He will devise many specious deceptions to lead them astray. We need to consider carefully the words of warning written by the apostle Paul:

"Be ye not unequally yoked together with unbelievers: for what fellowship hath righteousness with unrighteousness? and what communion hath light with darkness? and what concord hath Christ with Belial? or what part hath he that believeth with an infidel? and what agreement hath the temple of God with idols? for ye are the temple of the living God; as God hath said, I will dwell in them, and walk in them; and I will be their God, and they shall be My people. Wherefore come out from among them, and be ye separate, saith the Lord, and touch not the unclean thing; and I will receive you, and will be a Father unto you, and ye shall be My sons and daughters." 2 Corinthians 6:14-18.

Special light has been given me in regard to why we may accomplish much more for the Master by the establishment of many small sanitariums than by the building up of a few large medical institutions. In large institutions there would be gathered together many who are not very sick, but who, like tourists, are seeking rest and pleasure. These would have to be waited on by nurses and helpers. Young men and young women, who from their earliest years have been shielded from worldly associations, would thus be brought in contact with worldlings of all classes, and to a greater or less degree would be influenced by what they see and hear. They would become like those with whom they associate, losing the simplicity and modesty that Christian fathers and mothers have guarded and cherished by careful instruction and earnest prayer.

We are living amidst the perils of the last days. Something decisive must be said to warn our people against the danger of permitting children who need parental care and instruction, to leave their homes to go to places where they will be brought into contact with pleasure-loving, irreligious worldlings.

In many homes the father and mother have allowed the children to rule. Such children are in far greater danger, when brought into contact with influences opposed to godliness, than are those who have learned to obey. Not having received the necessary disciplinary training, they think that they can do as they please. A knowledge of how to obey would have strengthened them to resist temptation, but this knowledge their parents have not given them. When these undisciplined youth enter an immense institution, where there are many influences opposed to spirituality, they are in grave peril, and often their stay in the institution is an injury to themselves and to the institution.

I am instructed to warn parents whose children have not firmness of principle or a clear Christian experience not to send them away from home to distant places, to be absent for many months and perhaps for years, and, it may be, to have sown in their minds the seeds of unbelief and infidelity. It is safer, and far better, to send such youth to the schools and sanitariums nearest their homes. Let the youth who are forming character be kept away from places where they would have to mingle with a great company of unbelievers, and where the forces of the enemy are strongly entrenched.

Let a decided effort be made by the managers of our large sanitariums to employ older persons as helpers in these institutions. In the visions of the night I was in a large assembly, where this matter was up for consideration. To those who were planning to send their undisciplined children to Battle Creek, One of authority said:

"Dare you make this experiment? The salvation of your children is worth more than the education they will receive in this place, where they are constantly exposed to the influence of unbelievers. Many who come to this institution are unconverted. They are filled with pride and have not through faith a connection with God. Many of the young men and women who wait on these worldlings have had but little Christian experience, and they easily become entangled in the snares that are laid for their feet."

"What can be done to remedy this evil?" someone present asked. The Speaker answered: "Since you have placed yourselves into this position of peril, let Christian men and women of mature years and established character be brought into the institution to exert a counterinfluence for the right. The carrying out of such a plan would increase the running expenses of the sanitarium, but it may be an effective means of guarding the fort and of shielding the youth in the institution from the contaminating influences to which they are now exposed."

"Parents, guardians, place your children in training schools where the influences are similar to those of a rightly conducted home school; schools in which the teachers will carry them forward from point to point and in which the spiritual atmosphere is a savor of life unto life."

The words of warning and instruction that I have written in regard to the sending of our youth to Battle Creek to receive a training for service in the Lord's cause are not idle words. Some God-fearing youth will stand the test, but it is not safe for us to leave even the most conscientious ones without our best care and protection. Whether or not our youth who have received wise instruction and training from godly parents will continue to be sanctified through the truth depends largely upon the influence that, after leaving their homes, they meet among those to whom they look for Christian instruction.

I am instructed to repeat to our brethren and sisters the warning and the exhortation that Paul sent to the church at Thessalonica:

"The mystery of lawlessness doth already work: only there is one that restraineth now, until he be taken out of the way. And then shall be revealed the lawless one, whom the Lord Jesus shall slay with the breath of His mouth, and bring to nought by the manifestation of His coming; even he, whose coming is according to the working of Satan with all power and signs and lying wonders, and with all deceit of unrighteousness for them that perish; because they received not the love of the truth, that they might be saved. And for this cause God sendeth them a working of error, that they should believe a lie: that they all might be judged who believe not the truth, but had pleasure in unrighteousness." 2 Thessalonians 2:7-12, A. R. V.

"But we are bound to give thanks alway to God for you, brethren beloved of the Lord, because God hath from the beginning chosen you to salvation through sanctification of the Spirit and belief of the truth: whereunto He called you by our gospel, to the obtaining of the glory of our Lord Jesus Christ. Therefore, brethren, stand fast, and hold the traditions which ye have been taught, whether by word, or our epistle. Now our Lord Jesus Christ Himself, and God, even our Father, which hath loved us, and hath given us everlasting consolation and good hope through grace, comfort your hearts, and stablish you in every good word and work." 2 Thessalonians 2:13-17.

September, 1903. As I consider the state of things in Battle Creek, I tremble for our youth who go there. The light given me by the Lord, that our youth should not collect in Battle Creek to receive their education, has in no particular changed. The fact that the sanitarium has been rebuilt does not change the light.

That which in the past has made Battle Creek a place unsuitable for the education of our youth makes it unsuitable today so far as influence is concerned.

When the call came to move out of Battle Creek, the plea was: "We are here, and all settled. It would be an impossibility to move without enormous expense."

The Lord permitted fire to consume the principal buildings of the Review and Herald and the sanitarium, and thus removed the greatest objection urged against moving out of Battle Creek. It was His design that instead of rebuilding the one large sanitarium, our people should make plants in several places. These smaller sanitariums should have been established where land could be secured for agricultural purposes.

It is God's plan that agriculture shall be connected with the work of our sanitariums and schools. Our youth need the education to be gained from this line of work. It is well, and more than well,—it is essential,—that efforts be made to carry out the Lord's plan in this respect.

Shall we encourage our most promising young men and women to go to Battle Creek to obtain their training for service where they will be surrounded with so many influences that tend to lead astray? The Lord has revealed to me some of the dangers that the youth connected with so large a sanitarium will have to meet. Many of the wealthy, worldly men and women who patronize this institution will be a source of temptation to the helpers. Some of these helpers will become the favorites of wealthy patients and will be offered strong inducements to enter their employ. Through the influence of the worldly display of some who have been guests at the sanitarium, tares have already been sown in the hearts of young men and women employed as helpers and nurses. This is the way in which Satan is working.

Because the sanitarium is where it ought not to be, shall the word of the Lord regarding the education of our youth be of no account? Shall we allow the most intelligent of our youth in the churches throughout our conferences to be placed where some of them will be robbed of their simplicity through contact with men and women who have not the fear of God in their hearts? Will those in charge of our conferences allow our youth, who, in the schools for Christian workers, could be fitted for the Lord's service, to be drawn to a place from which for years the Lord has been calling upon His people to move?

We desire our youth to be so trained that they will exert a saving influence in our churches, working for greater unity and deeper piety. Men may not see the necessity for the call to families to leave Battle Creek and settle in places where they can do gospel medical missionary work. But the Lord has spoken. Shall we question His word?

- **No Time for Delay**

There are among us many young men and women who, if inducements were held out, would naturally be inclined to take several years' course of study to fit themselves for service. But will it pay? Time is short. Workers for Christ are needed everywhere. There should be a hundred earnest, faithful laborers in home and foreign mission fields where now there is but one. The highways and byways are yet unworked. Urgent inducements should be held out to those who ought now to be engaged in work for the Master.

The signs which show that Christ's coming is near are fast fulfilling. The Lord calls upon our youth to labor as canvassers and evangelists, to do house-to-house work in places that have not yet heard the truth. He speaks to our young men, saying: "Ye are not your own; for ye are bought with a price: therefore glorify God in your body, and in your spirit, which are God's." Those who will go forth to the work under God's direction will be wonderfully blessed. Those who in this life do their best will obtain a fitness for the future, immortal life.

The Lord calls upon those connected with our sanitariums, publishing houses, and schools to teach the youth to do evangelistic work. Our time and energy must not be so largely employed in establishing sanitariums, food stores, and restaurants that other lines of work will be neglected. Young men and young women who should be engaged in the ministry, in Bible work, and in the canvassing work should not be bound down to mechanical employment.

The youth should be encouraged to attend our training schools for Christian workers, which should become more and more like the schools of the prophets. These institutions have been established by the Lord, and if they are conducted in harmony with His purpose, the youth sent to them will quickly be prepared to engage in various lines of missionary work. Some will be trained to enter the field as missionary nurses, some as canvassers, and some as gospel ministers.

- **A Division of Responsibility**

St. Helena, California
August 4, 1903.
To the Leaders in the Medical Work—
Dear Brethren: I have a message for you. I am instructed to say that not all the arrangements connected with the management of the medical missionary work are to originate in Battle Creek. The medical missionary work is God's work, and in every conference and every church we are to take a decided stand against allowing it to be selfishly controlled.

After I received word in regard to the excellent meeting of confession and unity that had been held in Battle Creek I was writing in my diary and was about to record the thankfulness I felt because a change had come, when my hand was arrested, and there came to me the words: "Write it not. No change for the better has taken place. Teachings that are turning souls from the truth are being presented as of great worth. Doctrines are being taught that lead into bypaths and forbidden paths; doctrines that lead men to act in harmony with their own inclinations and to work out their unsanctified purposes; doctrines that, if received, would destroy the dignity and power of God's people, obscuring the light that would otherwise come to them through God's appointed agencies."

The leaders in our medical work at Battle Creek have endeavored to bind our medical institutions fast, in accordance with their plans. Notwithstanding the many warnings given them that this should not be done, they have desired to bind up these institutions in some way so that all our medical work shall be under their control.

In the past I have written much upon this subject, and I must now repeat the admonitions given, for it seems difficult for my brethren to understand their perilous position.

"The Lord forbids that every sanitarium and bathhouse established should be brought under one control—bound up with the medical institution at Battle Creek. The managers of the Battle Creek Sanitarium have their hands full now. They should devote their strength to the work of making this sanitarium what it should be."

"One man is not to think that he can be conscience for all the medical workers. Human beings are to look to the Lord God of heaven alone for wisdom and guidance."

"In establishing and developing medical institutions, our brethren must not be asked to work in accordance with the plans of a kingly, ruling power. A change must be brought about. The plan to fasten every medical institution to the central organization at Battle Creek must be relinquished. This plan God forbids."

"For years I have been instructed that there is danger, constant danger, that our brethren will look to their fellow men for permission to do this or that, instead of looking to God. Thus they become weaklings, and permit themselves to be bound with man-made restrictions disapproved by God. The Lord can impress minds and consciences to do His work under bonds to Him, and in a spirit of fraternity that is in accordance with the principles of His law..."

"God knows the future. He is the One to whom we are to look for guidance. Let us trust Him to direct us in the development of the various branches of His work. Let none attempt to labor in accordance with unsanctified impulses..."

"The division of the General Conference into District Union Conferences was God's arrangement. In the work of the Lord for these last days there should be no Jerusalem centers, no kingly power. And the work in the different countries is not to be bound by contracts to the work centering in Battle Creek, for this is not God's plan. Brethren are to counsel together, for we are just as much under the control of God in one part of His vineyard as in another. Brethren are to be one in heart and soul, even as Christ and the Father are one. Teach this, practice this, that we may be one with Christ in God, all working to build up one another."

"The kingly power formerly revealed in the General Conference at Battle Creek is not to be perpetuated. The publishing institution is not to be a kingdom of itself. It is essential that the principles that govern in General Conference affairs should be maintained in the management of the publishing work and the sanitarium work. One is not to think that the branch of the work with which he is connected is of vastly more importance than other branches."

"Educational work must be done in every sanitarium that shall be established. God has control of the work, and no one is to feel that everything done in the sanitariums established must first be submitted to one group of men. This course God forbids. The same God who has instructed the physicians at Battle Creek will instruct the men and women who are called to do service for the Master in various parts of His vineyard."

"Human laws and human arrangements are being framed that are not acceptable to God. They will not prove a savor of life unto life. I am under the necessity of lifting the danger signal. The managers of every one of our institutions need to become more intelligent in regard to their individual work, not by depending upon another institution, but, while preserving the identity of their work, by looking to God as their instructor and by revealing their faith in Him through whole-hearted service. Then they will develop talents and capabilities."

"Christ calls for service of a higher order than that which has been given Him. Men in positions of responsibility should, through receiving the power of the Holy Spirit, reveal the Redeemer much more clearly than they have revealed Him. The infinite God so loved the world that He gave His only-begotten Son as a sacrifice for us, in order that we, by receiving Him in faith and practicing His virtues, might not perish, but have everlasting life. My brethren, how do you suppose He regards that great lack of spiritual enthusiasm manifested over the record of the infinite sacrificial offering made for our salvation?"

"All human ambition, all boasting, is to be laid in the dust. Self, sinful self, is to be abased, not exalted. By holiness in the daily life we are to reveal Christ to those around us. Corrupt human nature is to be subdued, not exalted. Thus only can we become pure and undefiled. We are to be humble, faithful men and women. Never are we to sit upon the judgment seat. God demands that His representatives shall be pure and holy, revealing the beauty of sanctification. The channel is always to remain unobstructed, that the Holy Spirit may have free course; otherwise some will gloss over the work that must be done in the natural heart in order to perfect Christian character; and they will present their own imperfections in such a way as to make of no effect God's truth, which is as steadfast as the eternal throne. And while God calls upon His watchmen to lift the danger signal, at the same time He presents before them the life of the Saviour as an example of what they must be and do in order to be saved."

For His disciples Christ prayed: "Sanctify them through Thy truth: Thy word is truth." A pleasant, self-satisfied feeling is not an evidence of sanctification. A faithful record is kept of all the acts of the children of men. Nothing can be concealed from the eye of the high and holy One that inhabiteth eternity. Some make Christ ashamed of them by their devising and planning and scheming. God does not approve of their conduct, for the Lord Jesus is dishonored by their spirit and their works. They forget the words of the apostle: "We are made a spectacle unto the world, and to angels, and to men." 1 Corinthians 4:9.

The instruction that the Lord has given concerning His work points out the right way. God's plans and God's thoughts are as much higher than man's plans and man's thoughts as the heavens are higher than the earth. God's voice is to be heard, His wisdom is to guide. He has outlined His plan in His word and in the testimonies that He has sent to His people. That work only which is carried on in accordance with the principles of His word will stand fast forever.

37. Leadership

St. Helena, California
November 17, 1903.

In the daily papers of various cities there have appeared articles which represent that there is a strife between Dr. Kellogg and Mrs. Ellen G. White as to which of them shall be leader of the Seventh-day Adventist people. As I read these articles I felt distressed beyond measure that anyone should so misunderstand my work and the work of Dr. Kellogg as to publish such misrepresentations. There has been no controversy between Dr. Kellogg and myself as to the question of leadership. No one has ever heard me claim the position of leader of the denomination.

I have a work of great responsibility to do—to impart by pen and voice the instruction given me, not alone to Seventh-day Adventists, but to the world. I have published many books, large and small, and some of these have been translated into several languages. This is my work—to open the Scriptures to others as God has opened them to me.

God has not set any kingly power in the Seventh-day Adventist Church to control the whole body or to control any branch of the work. He has not provided that the burden of leadership shall rest upon a few men. Responsibilities are distributed among a large number of competent men.

Every member of the church has a voice in choosing officers of the church. The church chooses the officers of the state conferences. Delegates chosen by the state conferences choose the officers of the union conferences, and delegates chosen by the union conferences choose the officers of the General Conference. By this arrangement every conference, every institution, every church, and every individual, either directly or through representatives, has a voice in the election of the men who bear the chief responsibilities in the General Conference.

• Early Experiences

In the early days of our denominational work the Lord did designate Elder James White as one who, in connection with his wife, and under the Lord's special guidance, was to take a leading part in the advancement of this work.

The history of how the work grew is well known. The printing plant was first established at Rochester, New York, and was afterward moved to Battle Creek, Michigan. And in afteryears a publishing house was established on the Pacific Coast.

I thank the Lord that He gave us the privilege of acting a part in the work from the beginning. But neither then nor since the work has grown to large proportions, during which time responsibilities have been widely distributed, has anyone heard me claiming the leadership of this people.

From the year 1844 till the present time I have received messages from the Lord and have given them to His people. This is my work—to give to the people the light that the Lord gives me. I am commissioned to receive and communicate His messages. I am not to appear before the people as holding any other position than that of a messenger with a message.

For many years Dr. J. H. Kellogg has occupied the position of leading physician in the medical work carried on by the Seventh-day Adventists. It would be impossible for him to act as leader of the general work. This has never been his part, and it never can be.

• God Our Leader

I write this that all may know that there is no controversy among Seventh-day Adventists over the question of leadership. The Lord God of heaven is our King. He is a leader whom we can safely follow, for He never makes a mistake.

Let us honor God and His Son, through whom He communicates with the world.

God would work mightily for His people today if they would place themselves wholly under His guidance. They need the constant abiding of the Holy Spirit. If there were more prayer in the councils of those bearing responsibilities, more humbling of the heart before God, we should see abundant evidence of divine leadership, and our work would make rapid progress.

38. One with Christ in God

The Lord calls for men of genuine faith and sound minds, men who recognize the distinction between the true and the false. Each one should be on his guard, studying and practicing the lessons given in the seventeenth chapter of John, and preserving a living faith in the truth for this time. We need that self-control which will enable us to bring our habits into harmony with the prayer of Christ.

The instruction given me by One of authority is that we are to learn to answer the prayer recorded in the seventeenth chapter of John. We are to make this prayer our first study. Every gospel minister, every medical missionary, is to learn the science of this prayer. My brethren and sisters, I ask you to heed these words and to bring to your study a calm, humble, contrite spirit, and the healthy energies of a mind under the control of God. Those who fail to learn the lessons contained in this prayer are in danger of making one-sided developments, which no future training will ever fully correct.

"Neither pray I for these alone," Christ said, "but for them also which shall believe on Me through their word; that they all may be one; as Thou, Father, art in Me, and I in Thee, that they also may be one in Us: that the world may believe that Thou hast sent Me. And the glory which Thou gavest Me I have given them; that they may be one, even as We are one: I in them, and Thou in Me, that they may be made perfect in one; and that the world may know that Thou hast sent Me, and hast loved them, as Thou hast loved Me."

"Father, I will that they also, whom Thou hast given Me, be with Me where I am; that they may behold My glory, which Thou hast given Me: for Thou lovedst Me before the foundation of the world. O righteous Father, the world hath not known Thee: but I have known Thee, and these have known that Thou hast sent Me. And I have declared unto them Thy name, and will declare it: that the love wherewith Thou hast loved Me may be in them, and I in them." John 17:20-26.

It is the purpose of God that His children shall blend in unity. Do they not expect to live together in the same heaven? Is Christ divided against Himself? Will He give His people success before they sweep away the rubbish of evil surmising and discord, before the laborers, with unity of purpose, devote heart and mind and strength to the work so holy in God's sight? Union brings strength; disunion, weakness. United with one another, working together in harmony for the salvation of men, we shall indeed be "laborers together with God." Those who refuse to work in harmony greatly dishonor God. The enemy of souls delights to see them working at cross purposes with one another. Such ones need to cultivate brotherly love and tenderness of heart. If they could draw aside the curtain veiling the future and see the result of their disunion they would surely be led to repent.

The world is looking with gratification at the disunion amongst Christians. Infidelity is well pleased. God calls for a change among His people. Union with Christ and with one another is our only safety in these last days. Let us not make it possible for Satan to point to our church members, saying: "Behold how these people, standing under the banner of Christ, hate one another. We have nothing to fear from them while they spend more strength fighting one another than in warfare with my forces."

After the descent of the Holy Spirit the disciples went forth to proclaim a risen Saviour, their one desire the salvation of souls. They rejoiced in the sweetness of the communion with saints. They were tender, thoughtful, self-denying, willing to make any sacrifice for the truth's sake. In their daily association with one another they revealed the love that Christ had commanded them to reveal. By unselfish words and deeds they strove to kindle this love in other hearts.

The believers were ever to cherish the love that filled the hearts of the apostles after the descent of the Holy Spirit. They were to go forward in willing obedience to the new commandment: "As I have loved you, that ye also love one another." John 13:34. So closely were they to be united to Christ that they would be enabled to fulfill His requirements. The power of a Saviour who could justify them by His righteousness was to be magnified.

But the early Christians began to look for defects in one another. Dwelling upon mistakes, giving place to unkind criticism, they lost sight of the Saviour and of the great love He had revealed for sinners. They became more strict in regard to outward ceremonies, more particular about the theory of the faith, more severe in their criticisms. In their zeal to condemn others they forgot their own errors. They forgot the lesson of brotherly love that Christ had taught. And, saddest of all, they were unconscious of their loss. They did not realize that happiness and joy were going out of their lives, and that soon they would walk in darkness, having shut the love of God out of their hearts.

The apostle John realized that brotherly love was waning in the church, and he dwelt particularly upon this point. Up to the day of his death he urged upon believers the constant exercise of love for one another. His letters to the churches are filled with this thought. "Beloved, let us love one another," he writes; "for love is of God... God sent His only-begotten Son into the world, that we might live through Him... Beloved, if God so loved us, we ought also to love one another." 1 John 4:7-11.

In the church of God today brotherly love is greatly lacking. Many of those who profess to love the Saviour neglect to love those who are united with them in Christian fellowship. We are of the same faith, members of one family, all children of the same heavenly Father, with the same blessed hope of immortality. How close and tender should be the tie that binds us together. The people of the world are watching us to see if our faith is exerting a sanctifying influence upon our hearts. They are quick to discern every defect in our lives, every inconsistency in our actions. Let us give them no occasion to reproach our faith.

It is not the opposition of the world that endangers us the most; it is the evil cherished in the hearts of professed believers that works our most grievous disaster and most retards the progress of God's cause. There is no surer way of weakening our spirituality than by being envious, suspicious of one an other, full of faultfinding and evil surmising. "This wisdom descendeth not from above, but is earthly, sensual, devilish. For where envying and strife is, there is confusion and every evil work. But the wisdom that is from above is first pure, then peaceable, gentle, and easy to be entreated, full of mercy and good fruits, without partiality, and without hypocrisy. And the fruit of righteousness is sown in peace of them that make peace." James 3:15-18.

Harmony and union existing among men of varied dispositions is the strongest witness that can be borne that God has sent His Son into the world to save sinners. It is our privilege to bear this witness. But, in order to do this, we must place ourselves under Christ's command. Our characters must be molded in harmony with His character, our wills must be surrendered to His will. Then we shall work together without a thought of collision.

Little differences dwelt upon lead to actions that destroy Christian fellowship. Let us not allow the enemy thus to gain the advantage over us. Let us keep drawing nearer to God and to one another. Then we shall be as trees of righteousness, planted by the Lord, and watered by the river of life. And how fruitful we shall be! Did not Christ say: "Herein is My Father glorified, that ye bear much fruit"? John 15:8.

The heart of the Saviour is set upon His followers' fulfilling God's purpose in all its height and depth. They are to be one in Him, even though they are scattered the world over. But God cannot make them one in Christ unless they are willing to give up their own way for His way.

When Christ's prayer is fully believed, when its instruction is brought into the daily life of God's people, unity of action will be seen in our ranks. Brother will be bound to brother by the golden bonds of the love of Christ. The Spirit of God alone can bring about this oneness. He who sanctified Himself can sanctify His disciples. United with Him, they will be united with one another in the most holy faith. When we strive for this unity as God desires us to strive for it, it will come to us.

39. Lay Members to Go Forth

There is a much greater work devolving upon the individual members of the church than they realize. They are not awake to the claims of God. The time has come when every means should be devised that can aid in preparing a people to stand in the day of God. We must be wide awake, refusing to let precious opportunities pass unimproved. We must do all that we possibly can to win souls to love God and keep His commandments. Jesus requires this of those who know the truth. Is His demand unreasonable? Have we not the life of Christ as our example? Do we not owe the Saviour a debt of love, of earnest, unselfish labor for the salvation of those for whom He gave His life?

Section 4: Be on Guard

Many of the members of our large churches are doing comparatively nothing. They might accomplish a good work if, instead of crowding together, they would scatter into places that have not yet been entered by the truth. Trees that are planted too thickly do not flourish. They are transplanted by the gardener, that they may have room to grow and not become dwarfed and sickly. The same rule would work well for our large churches. Many of the members are dying spiritually for want of this very work. They are becoming sickly and inefficient. Transplanted, they would have room to grow strong and vigorous.

It is not the purpose of God that His people should colonize or settle together in large communities. The disciples of Christ are His representatives upon the earth, and God designs that they shall be scattered all over the country, in the towns, cities, and villages, as lights amidst the darkness of the world. They are to be missionaries for God, by their faith and works testifying to the near approach of the coming Saviour.

The lay members of our churches can accomplish a work which, as yet, they have scarcely begun. None should move into new places merely for the sake of worldly advantage; but where there is an opening to obtain a livelihood, let families that are well grounded in the truth enter, one or two families in a place, to work as missionaries. They should feel a love for souls, a burden of labor for them, and should make it a study how to bring them into the truth. They can distribute our publications, hold meetings in their homes, become acquainted with their neighbors, and invite them to come to these meetings. Thus they can let their light shine in good works.

Let the workers stand alone in God, weeping, praying, laboring for the salvation of their fellow men. Remember that you are running a race, striving for a crown of immortality. While so many love the praise of men more than the favor of God, let it be yours to labor in humility. Learn to exercise faith in presenting your neighbors before the throne of grace and pleading with God to touch their hearts. In this way effectual missionary work may be done. Some may be reached who would not listen to a minister or a colporteur. And those who thus labor in new places will learn the best ways of approaching the people and can prepare the way for other laborers.

A precious experience may be gained by one who engages in this work. He has upon his heart the burden of the souls of his neighbors. He must have the help of Jesus. How careful he will be to walk circumspectly, that his prayers may not be hindered, that no cherished sin may separate him from God. While helping others, such a worker is himself obtaining spiritual strength and understanding, and in this humble school he may become qualified to enter a wider field.

Christ declares: "Herein is My Father glorified, that ye bear much fruit." John 15:8. God has endowed us with faculties and has entrusted us with talents in order that we may use them for Him. To every man is given his work—not merely work in his fields of corn and wheat, but earnest, persevering work for the salvation of souls. Every stone in God's temple must be a living stone, a stone that shines, reflecting light to the world. Let the laymen do all that they can; and as they use the talents they already have, God will give them more grace and increased ability. Many of our missionary enterprises are crippled because there are so many who refuse to enter the doors of usefulness that are opened before them. Let all who believe the truth begin to work. Do the work that lies nearest you; do anything, however humble, rather than be, like the men of Meroz, do-nothings.

We shall not be stinted for means if we will only go forward trusting in God. The Lord is willing to do a great work for all who truly believe in Him. If the lay members of the church will arouse to do the work that they can do, going on a warfare at their own charges, each seeing how much he can accomplish in winning souls to Jesus, we shall see many leaving the ranks of Satan to stand under the banner of Christ. If our people will act upon the light that is given in these few words of instruction, we shall surely see of the salvation of God. Wonderful revivals will follow. Sinners will be converted, and many souls will be added to the church. When we bring our hearts into unity with Christ, and our lives into harmony with His work, the Spirit that fell on the disciples on the Day of Pentecost will fall on us.

40. Shall We Be Found Wanting?

St. Helena, California
April 21, 1903.

Our position in the world is not what it should be. We are far from where we should have been had our Christian experience been in harmony with the light and the opportunities given us, had we from the beginning constantly pressed onward and upward. Had we walked in the light that has been given us, had we followed on to know the Lord, our path would have grown brighter and brighter. But many of those who have had special light are so conformed to the world that they can scarcely be distinguished from worldlings. They do not stand forth as God's peculiar people, chosen and precious. It is difficult to discern between him that serveth God and him that serveth Him not.

In the balances of the sanctuary the Seventh-day Adventist church is to be weighed. She will be judged by the privileges and advantages that she has had. If her spiritual experience does not correspond to the advantages that Christ, at infinite cost, has bestowed on her, if the blessings conferred have not qualified her to do the work entrusted to her, on her will be pronounced the sentence: "Found wanting." By the light bestowed, the opportunities given, will she be judged.

- **God's Purpose for His People**

God has in store love, joy, peace, and glorious triumph for all who serve Him in spirit and in truth. His commandment-keeping people are to stand constantly in readiness for service. They are to receive increased grace and power, and increased knowledge of the Holy Spirit's working. But many are not ready to receive the precious gifts of the Spirit which God is waiting to bestow on them. They are not reaching higher and still higher for power from above that through the gifts bestowed, they may be recognized as God's peculiar people, zealous of good works.

- **"Repent, and Do the First Works"**

Solemn admonitions of warning, manifest in the destruction of dearly cherished facilities for service, say to us: "Remember therefore from whence thou art fallen, and repent, and do the first works." Revelation 2:5. Why is there so dim a perception of the true spiritual condition of the church? Has not blindness fallen upon the watchmen standing on the walls of Zion? Are not many of God's servants unconcerned and well satisfied, as if the pillar of cloud by day and the pillar of fire by night rested upon the sanctuary? Are there not those in positions of responsibility, professing to know God, who in life and character deny Him? Are not many of those who count themselves as His chosen, peculiar people satisfied to live without the evidence that of a truth God is among them to save them from Satan's snares and attacks?

Would we not now have much greater light if, in the past, we had received the Lord's admonitions, acknowledged His presence, and turned away from all practices contrary to His will? Had we done this, the light of heaven would have shone into the soul-temple, enabling us to comprehend the truth and to love God supremely and our neighbors as ourselves. Oh, how greatly Christ is dishonored by those who, professing to be Christians, disgrace the name they bear by failing to make their lives correspond to their profession, by failing to treat one another with the love and respect that God expects them to reveal in kind words and courteous acts!

The powers from beneath are stirred with deep intensity. War and bloodshed are the result. The moral atmosphere is poisoned with cruel, horrible doings. The spirit of strife is spreading; it abounds in every place. Many souls are being taken possession of by the spirit of fraud, or underhand dealing. Many will depart from the faith, giving heed to seducing spirits and doctrines of devils. They do not discern what spirit has taken possession of them.

- **A Failure to Honor God**

One who sees beneath the surface, who reads the hearts of all men, says of those who have had great light: "They are not afflicted and astonished because of their moral and spiritual condition. Yea, they have chosen their own ways, and their soul delighteth in their abominations. I also will choose their delusions, and will bring their fears upon them; because when I called, none did answer; when I spake, they did not hear: but they did evil before Mine eyes, and chose that in which I delighted not." "God shall send them strong delusion, that they should believe a lie," because they received not the love of the truth, that they might be saved," "but had pleasure in unrighteousness." Isaiah 66:3, 4; 2 Thessalonians 2:11, 10, 12.

The heavenly Teacher inquired: "What stronger delusion can beguile the mind than the pretense that you are building on the right foundation and that God accepts your works, when in reality you are working out many things according to worldly policy and are sinning against Jehovah? Oh, it is a great deception, a fascinating delusion, that takes possession of minds when men who have once known the truth, mistake the form of godliness for the spirit and power thereof; when they suppose that they are rich and increased with goods and in need of nothing, while in reality they are in need of everything."

God has not changed toward His faithful servants who are keeping their garments spotless. But many are crying, "Peace and safety," while sudden destruction is coming upon them. Unless there is thorough repentance, unless men humble their hearts by confession and receive the truth as it is in Jesus, they will never enter heaven. When purification shall take place in our ranks, we shall no longer rest at ease, boasting of being rich and increased with goods, in need of nothing.

Who can truthfully say: "Our gold is tried in the fire; our garments are unspotted by the world"? I saw our Instructor pointing to the garments of so-called righteousness. Stripping them off, He laid bare the defilement beneath. Then He said to me: "Can you not see how they have pretentiously covered up their defilement and rottenness of character? 'How is the faithful city become an harlot!' My Father's house is made a house of merchandise, a place whence the divine presence and glory have departed! For this cause there is weakness, and strength is lacking."

- **A Call for Reformation**

Unless the church, which is now being leavened with her own backsliding, shall repent and be converted, she will eat of the fruit of her own doing, until she shall abhor herself. When she resists the evil and chooses the good, when she seeks God with all humility and reaches her high calling in Christ, standing on the platform of eternal truth and by faith laying hold upon the attainments prepared for her, she will be healed. She will appear in her God-given simplicity and purity, separate from earthly entanglements, showing that the truth has made her free indeed. Then her members will indeed be the chosen of God, His representatives.

The time has come for a thorough reformation to take place. When this reformation begins, the spirit of prayer will actuate every believer and will banish from the church the spirit of discord and strife. Those who have not been living in Christian fellowship will draw close to one another. One member working in right lines will lead other members to unite with him in making intercession for the revelation of the Holy Spirit. There will be no confusion, because all will be in harmony with the mind of the Spirit. The barriers separating believer from believer will be broken down, and God's servants will speak the same things. The Lord will co-operate with His servants. All will pray understandingly the prayer that Christ taught His servants: "Thy kingdom come. Thy will be done in earth, as it is in heaven." Matthew 6:10.

41. Homeward Bound

As I hear of the terrible calamities that from week to week are taking place, I ask myself: What do these things mean? The most awful disasters are following one another in quick succession. How frequently we hear of earthquakes and tornadoes, of destruction by fire and flood, with great loss of life and property! Apparently these calamities are capricious outbreaks of seemingly disorganized, unregulated forces, but in them God's purpose may be read. They are one of the means by which He seeks to arouse men and women to a sense of their danger.

The coming of Christ is nearer than when we first believed. The great controversy is nearing its end. The judgments of God are in the land. They speak

Section 4: Be on Guard

in solemn warning, saying: "Be ye also ready: for in such an hour as ye think not the Son of man cometh." Matthew 24:44.

But there are many, many in our churches who know little of the real meaning of the truth for this time. I appeal to them not to disregard the fulfilling of the signs of the times, which says so plainly that the end is near. Oh, how many who have not sought their souls' salvation will soon make the bitter lamentation: "The harvest is past, the summer is ended, and we are not saved"!

We are living in the closing scenes of this earth's history. Prophecy is fast fulfilling. The hours of probation are fast passing. We have no time—not a moment—to lose. Let us not be found sleeping on guard. Let no one say in his heart or by his works: "My Lord delayeth His coming." Let the message of Christ's soon return sound forth in earnest words of warning. Let us persuade men and women everywhere to repent and flee from the wrath to come. Let us arouse them to immediate preparation, for we little know what is before us. Let ministers and lay members go forth into the ripening fields to tell the unconcerned and indifferent to seek the Lord while He may be found. The workers will find their harvest wherever they proclaim the forgotten truths of the Bible. They will find those who will accept the truth and will devote their lives to winning souls to Christ.

The Lord is soon to come, and we must be prepared to meet Him in peace. Let us be determined to do all in our power to impart light to those around us. We are not to be sad, but cheerful, and we are to keep the Lord Jesus ever before us. He is soon coming, and we must be ready and waiting for His appearing. Oh, how glorious it will be to see Him and be welcomed as His redeemed ones! Long have we waited, but our hope is not to grow dim. If we can but see the King in His beauty we shall be forever blessed. I feel as if I must cry aloud: "Homeward bound!" We are nearing the time when Christ will come in power and great glory to take His ransomed ones to their eternal home.

"And it shall be said in that day, Lo, this is our God; we have waited for Him, and He will save us: this is the Lord; we have waited for Him, we will be glad and rejoice in His salvation." Isaiah 25:9.

"Go through, go through the gates; prepare ye the way of the people; cast up, cast up the highway; gather out the stones; lift up a standard for the people. Behold, the Lord hath proclaimed unto the end of the world, Say ye to the daughter of Zion, Behold, thy salvation cometh; behold, His reward is with Him, and His work before Him. And they shall call them, The holy people, The redeemed of the Lord: and thou shalt be called, Sought out, A city not forsaken." Isaiah 62:10-12.

In the great closing work we shall meet with perplexities that we know not how to deal with; but let us not forget that the three great powers of heaven are working, that a divine hand is on the wheel, and that God will bring His promises to pass. He will gather from the world a people who will serve Him in righteousness.

"Let not your heart be troubled: ye believe in God, believe also in Me. In My Father's house are many mansions: if it were not so, I would have told you. I go to prepare a place for you. And if I go and prepare a place for you, I will come again, and receive you unto Myself; that where I am, there ye may be also." John 14:1-3.

Long have we waited for our Saviour's return. But nonetheless sure is the promise. Soon we shall be in our promised home. There Jesus will lead us beside the living stream flowing from the throne of God and will explain to us the dark providences through which on this earth He brought us in order to perfect our characters. There we shall behold with undimmed vision the beauties of Eden restored. Casting at the feet of the Redeemer the crowns that He has placed on our heads, and touching our golden harps, we shall fill all heaven with praise to Him that sitteth on the throne.

— Section 5 —
The Essential Knowledge

"The light of the knowledge of the glory of God in the face of Jesus Christ." 2 Corinthians 4:6.

42. God in Nature

Before the entrance of sin not a cloud rested upon the minds of our first parents to obscure their perception of the character of God. They were perfectly conformed to the will of God. For a covering a beautiful light, the light of God, surrounded them. This clear and perfect light illuminated everything which they approached.

Nature was their lessonbook. In the Garden of Eden the existence of God was demonstrated, His attributes were revealed, in the objects of nature that surrounded them. Everything upon which their eyes rested spoke to them. The invisible things of God, "even His everlasting power and divinity," were clearly seen, being understood by the things that were made.

Results of Sin

But while it is true that in the beginning God could be discerned in nature, it does not follow that after the Fall a perfect knowledge of God was revealed in the natural world to Adam and his posterity. Nature could convey her lessons to man in his innocence. But transgression brought a blight upon the earth and intervened between nature and nature's God. Had Adam and Eve never disobeyed their Creator, had they remained in the path of perfect rectitude, they would have continued to learn of God through His works. But when they listened to the tempter and sinned against God, the light of the garments of heavenly innocence departed from them. Deprived of the heavenly light, they could no longer discern the character of God in the works of His hand.

And through man's disobedience a change was wrought in nature itself. Marred by the curse of sin, nature can bear but an imperfect testimony regarding the Creator. It cannot reveal His character in its perfection.

A Divine Teacher

We need a divine Teacher. In order that the world might not remain in darkness, in eternal spiritual night, God met us in Jesus Christ. Christ is "the true Light, which lighteth every man that cometh into the world." John 1:9. "The light of the knowledge of the glory of God" is revealed "in the face of Jesus Christ." 2 Corinthians 4:6. The light of Christ, illuminating our understanding, and shining upon the face of nature, enables us still to read the lesson of God's love in His created works.

Nature Testifies of God

The things of nature upon which we look today give us but a faint conception of Eden's beauty and glory. Yet much that is beautiful remains. Nature testifies that One infinite in power, great in goodness, mercy, and love, created the earth and filled it with life and gladness. Even in their blighted state all things reveal the handiwork of the great Master Artist. Though sin has marred the form and beauty of the things of nature, though on them may be seen traces of the work of the prince of the power of the air, yet they still speak of God. In the briers, the thistles, the thorns, the tares, we may read the law of condemnation; but from the beauty of natural things, and from their wonderful adaptation to our needs and our happiness, we may learn that God still loves us, that His mercy is yet manifested to the world.

"The heavens declare the glory of God;
And the firmament showeth His handiwork.
Day unto day uttereth speech,
And night unto night showeth knowledge.
There is no speech nor language,
Where their voice is not heard."
Psalm 19:1-3.

Man's Failure to Interpret Nature

Apart from Christ we are still incapable of interpreting rightly the language of nature. The most difficult and humiliating lesson that man has to learn is his own inefficiency in depending upon human wisdom, and the sure failure of his efforts to read nature correctly. Of himself he cannot interpret nature without placing it above God. He is in a condition similar to that of the Athenians, who, amidst their altars dedicated to the worship of nature, had one inscribed: "To the unknown God." God was indeed unknown to them. He is unknown to all who, without the guidance of the divine Teacher, take up the study of nature. They will assuredly come to wrong conclusions.

In its human wisdom the world knows not God. Its wise men gather an imperfect knowledge of Him from His created works; but this knowledge, so far from giving them exalted conceptions of God, so far from elevating the mind and the soul, and bringing the whole being into conformity with His will, tends to make men idolaters. In their blindness they exalt nature and the laws of nature above nature's God.

God has permitted a flood of light to be poured upon the world in the discoveries of science and art; but when professedly scientific men reason upon these subjects from a merely human point of view, they are sure to err. The greatest minds, if not guided by the word of God, become bewildered in their attempts to investigate the relations of science and revelation. The Creator and His works are beyond their comprehension; and because these cannot be explained by natural laws, Bible history is pronounced unreliable.

Those who question the reliability of the Scripture records have let go their anchor and are left to beat about upon the rocks of infidelity. When they find themselves incapable of measuring the Creator and His works by their own imperfect knowledge of science, they question the existence of God and attribute infinite power to nature.

In true science there can be nothing contrary to the teaching of the word of God, for both have the same Author. A correct understanding of both will always prove them to be in harmony. Truth, whether in nature or in revelation, is harmonious with itself in all its manifestations. But the mind not enlightened by God's Spirit will ever be in darkness in regard to His power. This is why human ideas in regard to science so often contradict the teaching of God's word.

The Work of Creation

The work of creation can never be explained by science. What science can explain the mystery of life?

The theory that God did not create matter when He brought the world into existence is without foundation. In the formation of our world, God was not indebted to pre-existing matter. On the contrary, all things, material or spiritual, stood up before the Lord Jehovah at His voice and were created for His own purpose. The heavens and all the host of them, the earth and all things therein, are not only the work of His hand; they came into existence by the breath of His mouth.

"Through faith we understand that the worlds were framed by the word of God, so that things which are seen were not made of things which do appear." Hebrews 11:3.

"By the word of the Lord were the heavens made;
And all the host of them by the breath of His mouth...
He spake, and it was done;
He commanded, and it stood fast."
   Psalm 33:6-9.

Laws of Nature

In dwelling upon the laws of matter and the laws of nature, many lose sight of, if they do not deny, the continual and direct agency of God. They convey the idea that nature acts independently of God, having in and of itself its own limits and its own powers wherewith to work. In their minds there is a marked distinction between the natural and the supernatural. The natural is ascribed to ordinary causes, unconnected with the power of God. Vital power is attributed to matter, and nature is made a deity. It is supposed that matter is placed in certain relations and left to act from fixed laws with which God Himself cannot interfere; that nature is endowed with certain properties and placed subject to laws, and is then left to itself to obey these laws and perform the work originally commanded.

This is false science; there is nothing in the word of God to sustain it. God does not annul His laws, but He is continually working through them, using them as His instruments. They are not self-working. God is perpetually at work in nature. She is His servant, directed as He pleases. Nature in her work testifies of the intelligent presence and active agency of a being who moves in all His works according to His will. It is not by an original power inherent in nature that year by year the earth yields its bounties and continues its march around the sun. The hand of infinite power is perpetually at work guiding this planet. It is God's power momentarily exercised that keeps it in position in its rotation.

The God of heaven is constantly at work. It is by His power that vegetation is caused to flourish, that every leaf appears and every flower blooms. Every drop of rain or flake of snow, every spire of grass, every leaf and flower and shrub, testifies of God. These little things so common around us teach the lesson that nothing is beneath the notice of the infinite God, nothing is too small for His attention.

The mechanism of the human body cannot be fully understood; it presents mysteries that baffle the most intelligent. It is not as the result of a mechanism, which, once set in motion, continues its work, that the pulse beats and breath follows breath. In God we live and move and have our being. Every breath, every throb of the heart, is a continual evidence of the power of an ever-present God.

It is God that causes the sun to rise in the heavens. He opens the windows of heaven and gives rain. He causes the grass to grow upon the mountains. "He giveth snow like wool: He scattereth the hoarfrost like ashes." "When He uttereth His voice, there is a multitude of waters in the heavens; ... He maketh lightnings with rain, and bringeth forth the wind out of His treasures." Psalm 147:16; Jeremiah 10:13.

The Lord is constantly employed in upholding and using as His servants the things that He has made. Said Christ: "My Father worketh hitherto, and I work." John 5:17.

Mysteries of Divine Power

Men of the greatest intellect cannot understand the mysteries of Jehovah as revealed in nature. Divine inspiration asks many questions which the most profound scholar cannot answer. These questions were not asked that we might answer them, but to call our attention to the deep mysteries of God and to teach us that our wisdom is limited; that in the surroundings of our daily life there are many things beyond the comprehension of finite minds; that the judgment and purposes of God are past finding out. His wisdom is unsearchable.

Skeptics refuse to believe in God because with their finite minds they cannot comprehend the infinite power by which He reveals Himself to men. But God is to be acknowledged more from what He does not reveal of Himself than from that which is open to our limited comprehension. Both in divine revelation and in nature, God has given to men mysteries to command their faith. This must be so. We may be ever searching, ever inquiring, ever learning, and yet there is an infinity beyond.

> Who hath measured the waters in the hollow of His hand,
> And meted out heaven with the span,
> And comprehended the dust of the earth in a measure,
> And weighed the mountains in scales,
> And the hills in a balance?
> Who hath directed the Spirit of Jehovah,
> Or being His counselor hath taught Him? ...

Section 5: The Essential Knowledge

Behold, the nations are as a drop of a bucket,
And are accounted as the small dust of the balance:
Behold, He taketh up the isles as a very little thing.

And Lebanon is not sufficient to burn,
Nor the beasts thereof sufficient for a burnt offering.
All the nations are as nothing before Him;
They are accounted by Him as less than nothing, and vanity.

To whom then will ye liken God?
Or what likeness will ye compare unto Him? ...
Have ye not known? Have ye not heard?
Hath it not been told you from the beginning?
Have ye not understood from the foundations of the earth?
It is He that sitteth above the circle of the earth,
And the inhabitants thereof are as grasshoppers;
That stretcheth out the heavens as a curtain,
And spreadeth them out as a tent to dwell in...
To whom then will ye liken Me,
That I should be equal to him?
Saith the Holy One.
Lift up your eyes on high,
And see who hath created these,
That bringeth out their host by number;
He calleth them all by name;
By the greatness of His might, and for that He is strong in power,
Not one is lacking.
Why sayest thou, O Jacob, and speakest, O Israel,
My way is hid from Jehovah,
And the justice due to me is passed away from my God?
Hast thou not known?
Hast thou not heard?
The everlasting God, Jehovah,
The Creator of the ends of the earth,
Fainteth not, neither is weary,

There is no searching of His understanding.
He giveth power to the faint;
And to him that hath no might He increaseth strength.
Even the youths shall faint and be weary,
And the young men shall utterly fall:
But they that wait for Jehovah shall renew their strength;
They shall mount up with wings as eagles;
They shall run, and not be weary;
They shall walk, and not faint.
  Isaiah 40:12-31, A. R. V.

43. A Personal God

The mighty power that works through all nature and sustains all things is not, as some men of science represent, merely an all-pervading principle, an actuating energy. God is a spirit; yet He is a personal being, for man was made in His image.

Nature is not God

God's handiwork in nature is not God Himself in nature. The things of nature are an expression of God's character; by them we may understand His love, His power, and His glory; but we are not to regard nature as God. The artistic skill of human beings produces very beautiful workmanship, things that delight the eye and these things give us something of the idea of the designer; but the thing made is not the man. It is not the work, but the workman, that is counted worthy of honor. So, while nature is an expression of God's thought, it is not nature but the God of nature that is to be exalted.

The gods that have not made the heavens and the earth,
These shall perish from the earth, and from under the heavens.
The portion of Jacob is not like these;
For He is the former of all things.
"He hath made the earth by His power,
He hath established the world by His wisdom,
And by His understanding hath He stretched out the heavens."
Jeremiah 10:11, 16, 12, A.R.V.

"Seek Him that maketh the Pleiades and Orion,
And turneth the shadow of death into the morning,
And maketh the day dark with night;
That calleth for the waters of the sea,
And poureth them out upon the face of the earth
(Jehovah is His name)." Amos 5:8, A.R.V.

A Personal God Created Man

In the creation of man was manifest the agency of a personal God. When God had made man in His image, the human form was perfect in all its arrangements, but it was without life. Then a personal, self-existing God breathed into that form the breath of life, and man became a living, breathing, intelligent being. All parts of the human organism were put in action. The heart, the arteries, the veins, the tongue, the hands, the feet, the senses, the perceptions of the mind—all began their work, and all were placed under law. Man became a living soul. Through Jesus Christ a personal God created man and endowed him with intelligence and power.

Our substance was not hid from Him when we were made in secret. His eyes saw our substance, yet being imperfect; and in His book all our members were written, when as yet there were none of them. Above all lower orders of being, God designed that man, the crowning work of His creation, should express His thought and reveal His glory. But man is not to exalt himself as God.

Make a joyful noise unto Jehovah...
Serve Jehovah with gladness:
Come before His presence with singing.

Know ye that Jehovah, He is God:
It is He that hath made us, and we are His;
We are His people, and the sheep of His pasture.

Enter into His gates with thanksgiving,
And into His courts with praise:
Give thanks unto Him, and bless His name.

Exalt ye Jehovah our God,
And worship at His holy hill;
For Jehovah our God is holy.
   Psalm 100:1-4; 99:9, A.R.V.

God Revealed in Christ

As a personal being, God has revealed Himself in His Son. Jesus, the outshining of the Father's glory, "and the express image of His person" (Hebrews 1:3), was on earth found in fashion as a man. As a personal Saviour He came to the world. As a personal Saviour He ascended on high. As a personal Saviour He intercedes in the heavenly courts. Before the throne of God in our behalf ministers "One like unto the Son of man." Revelation 1:13.

Christ, the Light of the world, veiled the dazzling splendor of His divinity and came to live as a man among men, that they might, without being consumed, become acquainted with their Creator. No man has seen God at any time except as He is revealed through Christ.

"I and My Father are one," Christ declared. "No man knoweth the Son, but the Father; neither knoweth any man the Father, save the Son, and he to whomsoever the Son will reveal Him." John 10:30; Matthew 11:27.

Section 5: The Essential Knowledge

Christ came to teach human beings what God desires them to know. In the heavens above, in the earth, in the broad waters of the ocean, we see the handiwork of God. All created things testify to His power, His wisdom, His love. But not from the stars or the ocean or the cataract can we learn of the personality of God as it is revealed in Christ.

God saw that a clearer revelation than nature was needed to portray both His personality and His character. He sent His Son into the world to reveal, so far as could be endured by human sight, the nature and the attributes of the invisible God.

Had God desired to be represented as dwelling personally in the things of nature,—in the flower, the tree, the spire of grass,—would not Christ have spoken of this to His disciples when He was on the earth? But never in the teaching of Christ is God thus spoken of. Christ and the apostles taught clearly the truth of the existence of a personal God.

Christ revealed all of God that sinful human beings could bear without being destroyed. He is the divine Teacher, the Enlightener. Had God thought us in need of revelations other than those made through Christ and in His written word, He would have given them.

Christ's Revelation of God to the Disciples

Let us study the words that Christ spoke in the upper chamber on the night before His crucifixion. He was nearing His hour of trial, and He sought to comfort His disciples, who were to be so severely tempted and tried.

"Let not your heart be troubled, He said; ye believe in God, believe also in Me. In My Father's house are many mansions: if it were not so, I would have told you. I go to prepare a place for you…

Thomas saith unto Him, Lord, we know not whither Thou goest; and how can we know the way? Jesus saith unto him, I am the way, the truth, and the life: no man cometh unto the Father, but by Me. If ye had known Me, ye should have known My Father also: and from henceforth ye know Him, and have seen Him… Lord, show us the Father, said Philip, and it sufficeth us. Jesus saith unto him, Have I been so long time with you, and yet hast thou not known Me, Philip? he that hath seen Me hath seen the Father; and how sayest thou then, Show us the Father? Believest thou not that I am in the Father, and the Father in Me? the words that I speak unto you I speak not of Myself: but the Father that dwelleth in Me, He doeth the works." John 14:1-10. The disciples did not yet understand Christ's words concerning His relation to God. Much of His teaching was still dark to them.

They had asked many questions that revealed their ignorance of God's relation to them and to their present and future interests. Christ desired them to have a clearer, more distinct knowledge of God.

"These things have I spoken unto you in parables," He said; "but the time cometh, when I shall no more speak unto you in parables, but I shall show you plainly of the Father." John 16:25, margin.

When on the Day of Pentecost the Holy Spirit was poured out upon the disciples, they understood the truths that Christ had spoken in parables. The teachings that had been mysteries to them were made clear. The understanding that came to them with the outpouring of the Spirit made them ashamed of their fanciful theories. Their suppositions and interpretations were foolishness when compared with the knowledge of heavenly things which they now received. They were led by the Spirit, and light shone into their once darkened understanding.

But the disciples had not yet received the complete fulfillment of Christ's promise. They received all the knowledge of God that they could bear, but the complete fulfillment of the promise that Christ would show them plainly of the Father was yet to come. Thus it is today. Our knowledge of God is partial and imperfect. When the conflict is ended and the Man Christ Jesus acknowledges before the Father His faithful workers, who, in a world of sin, have borne true witness for Him, they will understand clearly what now are mysteries to them.

Christ took with Him to the heavenly courts His glorified humanity. To those who receive Him, He gives power to become the sons of God, that at last God may receive them as His, to dwell with Him throughout eternity. If, during this life, they are loyal to God, they will at last "see His face; and His name shall be in their foreheads." Revelation 22:4. And what is the happiness of heaven but to see God? What greater joy could come to the sinner saved by the grace of Christ than to look upon the face of God and know Him as Father?

Testimony of Scripture

The Scriptures clearly indicate the relation between God and Christ, and they bring to view as clearly the personality and individuality of each.

"God, who at sundry times and in divers manners spake in time past unto the fathers by the prophets, hath in these last days spoken unto us by His Son, whom He hath appointed heir of all things, by whom also He made the worlds; who being the brightness of His glory, and the express image of His person, and upholding all things by the word of His power, when He had by Himself purged our sins, sat down on the right hand of the Majesty on high; being made so much better than the angels, as He hath by inheritance obtained a more excellent name than they. For unto which of the angels said He at any time, Thou art My Son, this day have I begotten Thee? And again, I will be to Him a Father, and He shall be to Me a Son?" Hebrews 1:1-5.

God is the Father of Christ; Christ is the Son of God. To Christ has been given an exalted position. He has been made equal with the Father. All the counsels of God are opened to His Son.

Jesus said to the Jews: "My Father worketh hitherto, and I work... The Son can do nothing of Himself, but what He seeth the Father do: for what things soever He doeth, these also doeth the Son likewise. For the Father loveth the Son, and showeth Him all things that Himself doeth." John 5:17-20.

Here again is brought to view the personality of the Father and the Son, showing the unity that exists between them. This unity is expressed also in the seventeenth chapter of John, in the prayer of Christ for His disciples:

"Neither pray I for these alone, but for them also which shall believe on Me through their word; that they all may be one; as Thou, Father, art in Me, and I in Thee, that they also may be one in Us: that the world may believe that Thou hast sent Me. And the glory which Thou gavest Me I have given them; that they may be one, even as We are one: I in them, and Thou in Me, that they may be made perfect in one; and that the world may know that Thou hast sent Me, and hast loved them, as Thou hast loved Me." John 17:20-23.

Wonderful statement! The unity that exists between Christ and His disciples does not destroy the personality of either. They are one in purpose, in mind, in character, but not in person. It is thus that God and Christ are one. The relation between the Father and the Son, and the personality of both, are made plain in this scripture also:

> Thus speaketh Jehovah of hosts, saying,
> Behold, the man whose name is the Branch:
> And He shall grow up out of His place;
> And He shall build the temple of Jehovah; ...
> And He shall bear the glory,
> And shall sit and rule upon His throne;
> And He shall be a priest upon His throne;
> And the counsel of peace shall be between Them both.
> Zechariah 6:12, 13, A. R. V.

"The Everlasting God"

In the word, God is spoken of as "the everlasting God." This name embraces past, present, and future. God is from everlasting to everlasting. He is the Eternal One.

> The eternal God is Thy dwelling place,
>   And underneath are the everlasting arms:
> And He thrust out the enemy from before thee,
>   And said, Destroy.
> And Israel dwelleth in safety,
>   The fountain of Jacob alone,
> In a land of corn and wine;
>   Yea, His heavens drop down dew.
> Happy art thou, O Israel:
> Who is like unto thee,
>   A people saved by the Lord,

Section 5: The Essential Knowledge

The shield of thy help,
  And that is the sword of thy excellency.
Deuteronomy 33:27-29, R. V.

Before the mountains were brought forth,
Or ever Thou hadst formed the earth and the world,
  Even from everlasting to everlasting, Thou art God.
Thou turnest man to dust,
  And sayest, Return, ye children of men.
For a thousand years in Thy sight
  Are but as yesterday when it is past,
  And as a watch in the night.
Thou carriest them away as with a flood;
  They are as a sleep:
In the morning they are like grass which groweth up.
  In the morning it flourisheth, and groweth up;
  In the evening it is cut down, and withereth.
  Psalm 90:2-6, A. R. V., margin.

So teach us to number our days,
That we may apply our hearts unto wisdom.

O satisfy us early with Thy mercy;
  That we may rejoice and be glad all our days.

Make us glad according to the days wherein Thou hast afflicted us,
  And the years wherein we have seen evil.
Let Thy work appear unto Thy servants,
  And Thy glory unto their children.

And let the beauty of the Lord our God be upon us:
  And establish Thou the work of our hands upon us;
  Yea, the work of our hands establish Thou it.
  Psalm 90:12, 14-17.

"The Lord reigneth, He is clothed with majesty;
The Lord is clothed with strength, wherewith He hath girded Himself:
The world also is stablished, that it cannot be moved.
Thy throne is established of old:
Thou art from everlasting."
Psalm 93:1, 2.

His Loving-Kindness

All His work is done in faithfulness.
He loveth righteousness and justice:
The earth is full of the loving-kindness of Jehovah.

Blessed is the nation whose God is Jehovah,
The people whom He hath chosen for His own inheritance.

Behold, the eye of Jehovah is upon them that fear Him,
Upon them that hope in His loving-kindness;
To deliver their soul from death,
And to keep them alive in famine.

Our soul hath waited for Jehovah:
He is our help and our shield.

For our heart shall rejoice in Him,
Because we have trusted in His holy name.
Psalm 33:4, 5, 12, 18-21, A. R. V.

I sought Jehovah, and He answered me,
 And delivered me from all my fears.
They looked unto Him, and were radiant;
 And their faces shall never be confounded.

This poor man cried, and Jehovah heard him,
  And saved him out of all his troubles.

The angel of Jehovah encampeth round about them that fear Him,
  And delivereth them.
O taste and see that Jehovah is good:
  Blessed is the man that taketh refuge in Him.

O fear Jehovah, ye His saints;
  For there is no want to them that fear Him.
The young lions do lack, and suffer hunger;
  But they that seek Jehovah shall not want any good thing.

The righteous cried, and Jehovah heard,
  And delivered them out of all their troubles.
Jehovah is nigh unto them that are of a broken heart,
  And saveth such as are of a contrite spirit.
  Psalm 34:4-10, 17, 18, A. R. V.

The Lord redeemeth the soul of His servants:
  And none of them that trust in Him shall be desolate.
  Verse 22

Jehovah is merciful and gracious,
  Slow to anger, and abundant in loving-kindness.
He will not always chide;
  Neither will He keep His anger forever.
He hath not dealt with us after our sins,
  Nor rewarded us after our iniquities.

For as the heavens are high above the earth,
  So great is His loving-kindness toward them that fear Him.
As far as the east is from the west,
  So far hath He removed our transgressions from us.
Like as a father pitieth his children,

So Jehovah pitieth them that fear Him.
For He knoweth our frame;
  He remembereth that we are dust.

As for man, his days are as grass;
  As a flower of the field, so he flourisheth.
For the wind passeth over it, and it is gone;
  And the place thereof shall know it no more.
But the loving-kindness of Jehovah is from everlasting to
  everlasting upon them that fear Him,
  And His righteousness unto children's children;
To such as keep His covenant,
And to those that remember His precepts to do them.
Psalm 103:8-18, A. R. V.

His Providential Care

Our God has heaven and earth at His command, and He knows just what we need. We can see only a little way before us; "but all things are naked and opened unto the eyes of Him with whom we have to do." Hebrews 4:13.

Above the distractions of the earth He sits enthroned; all things are open to His divine survey; and from His great and calm eternity He orders that which His providence sees best.

Not even a sparrow falls to the ground without the Father's notice. Satan's hatred against God leads him to delight in destroying even the dumb creatures. It is only through God's protecting care that the birds are preserved to gladden us with their songs of joy. But He does not forget even the sparrows. "Fear ye not therefore, ye are of more value than many sparrows." Matthew 10:31.

Bless Jehovah, O my soul.
  O Jehovah my God, Thou art very great;
  Thou art clothed with honor and majesty:

Section 5: The Essential Knowledge

    Who coverest Thyself with light as with a garment;
Who stretchest out the heavens like a curtain;
    Who layeth the beams of His chambers in the waters;
Who maketh the clouds His chariot;
    Who walketh upon the wings of the wind;
Who maketh winds His messengers;
    Flames of fire His ministers;
"Who laid the foundations of the earth,
    That it should not be moved forever.
Thou coveredst it with the deep as with a vesture;
    The waters stood above the mountains.
At Thy rebuke they fled;
    At the voice of Thy thunder they hasted away
(The mountains rose, the valleys sank down)
    Unto the place which Thou hadst founded for them.
Thou hast set a bound that they may not pass over;
    That they turn not again to cover the earth.

He sendeth forth springs into the valleys;
    They run among the mountains;
They give drink to every beast of the field;
    The wild asses quench their thirst.
By them the birds of the heavens have their habitation;
    They sing among the branches.
He watereth the mountains from His chambers:
    The earth is filled with the fruit of Thy works.
He causeth the grass to grow for the cattle,
    And herb for the service of man;

That He may bring forth food out of the earth,
    And wine that maketh glad the heart of man,
And oil to make his face to shine
    And bread that strengtheneth man's heart.
The trees of Jehovah are filled with moisture,
    The cedars of Lebanon, which He hath planted;

Where the birds make their nests:
  As for the stork, the fir trees are her house.
The high mountains are for the wild goats;
  The rocks are a refuge for the conies.

He appointed the moon for seasons:
  The sun knoweth his going down.
Thou makest darkness, and it is night,
  Wherein all the beasts of the forest creep forth.
The young lions roar after their prey,
  And seek their food from God.
The sun ariseth, they get them away,
  And lay them down in their dens.
Man goeth forth unto his work
  And to his labor until the evening.

O Jehovah, how manifold are Thy works!
In wisdom hast Thou made them all:
  The earth is full of Thy riches.
Yonder is the sea, great and wide,
Wherein are things creeping innumerable,
  Both small and great beasts.
There go the ships;
  There is leviathan, whom Thou hast formed to play therein.
These wait all for Thee,
That Thou mayest give them their food in due season.
  Thou givest unto them, they gather;
Thou openest Thy hand,
  They are satisfied with good.
Thou hidest Thy face,
  They are troubled;
Thou takest away their breath,
  They die,

And return to their dust.
Thou sendest forth Thy Spirit,
  They are created;
  And Thou renewest the face of the ground.

"Let the glory of Jehovah endure forever;
  Let Jehovah rejoice in His works:
Who looketh on the earth, and it trembleth;
  He toucheth the mountains, and they smoke.

I will sing unto Jehovah as long as I live:
  I will sing praise to my God while I have any being.
Let my meditation be sweet unto Him:
  I will rejoice in Jehovah.
Psalm 104:1-34, A. R. V.

Thou that art the confidence of all the ends of the earth,
  And of them that are afar off upon the sea:
Who by His strength setteth fast the mountains,
  Being girded about with might:
Who stilleth the roaring of the seas, ...
  And the tumult of the peoples...
Thou makest the outgoings of the morning and evening to rejoice...
Thou crownest the year with Thy goodness;
  And Thy paths drop fatness.
  Psalm 65:5-11, A. R. V.

Jehovah upholdeth all that fall,
  And raiseth up all those that are bowed down.
The eyes of all wait for Thee;
  And Thou givest them their food in due season.
Thou openest Thy hand,
  And satisfiest the desire of every living thing.
  Psalm 145:14-16, A. R. V.

His Long-Suffering Mercy

No earthly parent ever pleaded so earnestly with an erring child as He who made us pleads with the transgressor. No human, loving interest ever followed the impenitent with invitations so tender:

Thou hast not called upon Me, O Jacob; but
Thou hast been weary of Me, O Israel.
Isaiah 43:22

O My people, what have I done unto thee?
And wherein have I wearied thee?
Micah 6:3

When Israel was a child, then I loved him,
And called My son out of Egypt.
Hosea 11:1

Jehovah's portion is His people;
Jacob is the lot of His inheritance.
He found him in a desert land,
   And in the waste howling wilderness;
He compassed him about, He cared for him,
   He kept him as the apple of His eye.
As an eagle that stirreth up her nest,
   That fluttereth over her young,
He spread abroad His wings, He took them,
   He bare them on His pinions.
Deuteronomy 32:9-11, A. R. V.

They kept not the covenant of God,
And refused to walk in His law.
Psalm 78:10

Section 5: The Essential Knowledge

> The more the prophets called them, the more they went from them...
> Yet I taught Ephraim to walk;
> I took them on My arms;
> But they knew not that I healed them.
> I drew them with cords of a man, with bands of love...
> My people are bent on backsliding from Me:
> Though they call them to Him that is on high,
> None at all will exalt Him.
> Hosea 11:2-7, A. R. V.

> But He, being full of compassion, forgave their iniquity,
> And destroyed them not:
> Yea, many a time turned He His anger away,
> And did not stir up all His wrath.
> For He remembered that they were but flesh;
> A wind that passeth away, and cometh not again.
> Psalm 78:38, 39

Though He "delivered His strength into captivity, and His glory into the enemy's hand," yet He said, "My lovingkindness will I not utterly take from him, nor suffer My faithfulness to fail." Psalm 78:61; 89:33.

"Is Ephraim My dear son? is he a pleasant [Authorized Version] child? for as often as I speak against him, I do earnestly remember him still: therefore My heart yearneth for him." Jeremiah 31:20, A. R. V.

> How shall I give thee up, Ephraim?
> How shall I cast thee off, Israel?
>
> How shall I make thee as Admah?
> How shall I set thee as Zeboiim?
> My heart is turned within Me,

My compassions are kindled together.
I will not execute the fierceness of Mine anger,
I will not return to destroy Ephraim:
For I am God, and not man;
The Holy One in the midst of thee;
And I will not come in wrath.
Hosea 11:8, 9, A. R. V.

O Israel, return unto Jehovah thy God;
For thou hast fallen by thine iniquity.
Take with you words,
And return unto Jehovah: say unto Him,
Take away all iniquity, and accept that which is good...
Assyria shall not save us;
We will not ride upon horses;
Neither will we say any more to the work of our hands,
Ye are our gods;
For in Thee the fatherless findeth mercy.
   Hosea 14:1-3, A. R. V.

They shall walk after Jehovah...
The children shall come trembling from the west.
They shall come trembling as a bird out of Egypt,
And as a dove out of the land of Assyria;
And I will make them to dwell in their houses, saith Jehovah.
Hosea 11:10, 11, A. R. V.

I will heal their backsliding, I will love them freely;
For Mine anger is turned away from him.
I will be as the dew unto Israel;
He shall blossom as the lily,
And cast forth his roots as Lebanon.
His branches shall spread,

And his beauty shall be as the olive tree,
And his smell as Lebanon.
They that dwell under his shadow shall return;
They shall revive as the grain,
And blossom as the vine...
Ephraim shall say, What have I to do any more with idols?
I have answered, and will regard him:
I am like a green fir tree; From Me is thy fruit found.
Who is wise, that he may understand these things?
Prudent, that he may know them?
For the ways of Jehovah are right,
And the just shall walk in them.
Hosea 14:4-9, A. R. V.

Who is a God like unto Thee, that pardoneth iniquity,
 and passeth over the transgression
Of the remnant of His heritage?
He retaineth not His anger forever,
Because He delighteth in loving-kindness.
He will again have compassion upon us;
He will tread our iniquities underfoot;
And Thou wilt cast all their sins into the depths of the sea.
Micah 7:18, 19, A. R. V.

"Jehovah appeared of old unto me, saying, Yea, I have loved thee with an everlasting love: therefore with lovingkindness have I drawn thee." "The Lord hath redeemed Jacob, and ransomed him from the hand of him that was stronger than he." "I will turn their mourning into joy, and will comfort them, and make them rejoice from their sorrow." "My people shall be satisfied with My goodness, saith Jehovah." Jeremiah 31:3, A.R.V., 11, 13, A.V., 14, A.R.V.

Sing, O daughter of Zion;
Shout, O Israel; Be glad and rejoice with all the heart,
O daughter of Jerusalem.

Jehovah hath taken away thy judgments,
He hath cast out thine enemy:
The King of Israel, even Jehovah, is in the midst of thee;
Thou shalt not fear evil any more.
In that day it shall be said to Jerusalem, Fear thou not;
O Zion, let not thy hands be slack.
Jehovah thy God is in the midst of thee,
A Mighty One who will save;
He will rejoice over thee with joy;
He will rest in His love;
He will joy over thee with singing.
   Zephaniah 3:14-17, A. R. V.

This God is our God for ever and ever:
He will be our guide even unto death.
Psalm 48:14

44. A False and a True Knowledge of God

• Speculative Theories

"Those things which are revealed belong unto us and to our children forever; but the secret things belong unto the Lord our God." Deuteronomy 29:29. The revelation of Himself that God has given in His word is for our study. This we may seek to understand. But beyond this we are not to penetrate. The highest intellect may tax itself until it is wearied out in conjectures regarding the nature of God; but the effort will be fruitless. This problem has not been given us to solve. No human mind can comprehend God. Let not finite man attempt to interpret Him. Let none indulge in speculation regarding His nature. Here silence is eloquence. The Omniscient One is above discussion.

Even the angels were not permitted to share the counsels between the Father and the Son when the plan of salvation was laid. Those human beings who seek to intrude into the secrets of the Most High show their ignorance of spiritual and eternal things. Far better might they, while mercy's voice is still heard, humble themselves in the dust and plead with God to teach them His ways.

We are as ignorant of God as little children, but as little children we may love and obey Him. Instead of speculating in regard to His nature or His prerogatives, let us give heed to the word He has spoken: "Be still, and know that I am God." Psalm 46:10.

> Canst thou by searching find out God?
> Canst thou find out the Almighty unto perfection?
> It is as high as heaven; what canst thou do?
> Deeper than hell; what canst thou know?
> The measure thereof is longer than the earth,
> And broader than the sea.
> Job 11:7-9

> Where shall wisdom be found?
> And where is the place of understanding?
> Man knoweth not the price thereof;
> Neither is it found in the land of the living.
> The depth saith, It is not in me:
> And the sea saith, It is not with me.
> It cannot be gotten for gold,
> Neither shall silver be weighed for the price thereof.
> It cannot be valued with the gold of Ophir,
> With the precious onyx or the sapphire.
>   The gold and the crystal cannot equal it,
> And the exchange of it shall not be for jewels of fine gold.
>   No mention shall be made of coral, or of pearls:
>   For the price of wisdom is above rubies.
> The topaz of Ethiopia shall not equal it,
>   Neither shall it be valued with pure gold.
>   Whence then cometh wisdom?
>   And where is the place of understanding? ...

Destruction and death say,
We have heard the fame thereof with our ears.
God understandeth the way thereof,
And He knoweth the place thereof.

For He looketh to the ends of the earth,
And seeth under the whole heaven...
When He made a decree for the rain,
And a way for the lightning of the thunder:
Then did He see it, and declare it;
He prepared it, yea, and searched it out.
 And unto man He said,
Behold, the fear of the Lord, that is wisdom;
And to depart from evil is understanding.
Job 28:12-28

Neither by searching the recesses of the earth nor in vain endeavors to penetrate the mysteries of God's being is wisdom found. It is found, rather, in humbly receiving the revelation that He has been pleased to give, and in conforming the life to His will.

- ## The Greatness of Our God

From the representations given by the Holy Spirit to His prophets, let us learn the greatness of our God. The prophet Isaiah writes:

"In the year that King Uzziah died I saw the Lord sitting upon a throne, high and lifted up; and His train filled the temple. Above Him stood the seraphim: each one had six wings; with twain he covered his face, and with twain he covered his feet, and with twain he did fly. And one cried unto another, and said, Holy, holy, holy, is Jehovah of hosts: the whole earth is full of His glory. And the foundations of the thresholds shook at the voice of him that cried, and the house was filled with smoke."

Section 5: The Essential Knowledge

"Then said I, Woe is me! for I am undone; because I am a man of unclean lips, and I dwell in the midst of a people of unclean lips: for mine eyes have seen the King, Jehovah of hosts."

"Then flew one of the seraphim unto me, having a live coal in his hand, which he had taken with the tongs from off the altar: and he touched my mouth with it, and said, Lo, this hath touched thy lips; and thine iniquity is taken away, and thy sin expiated." Isaiah 6:1-7, A. R. V., margin.

There is none like unto Thee, O Jehovah; Thou art great,
And Thy name is great in might.
Who should not fear Thee, O King of the nations?
Jeremiah 10:6, 7, A. R. V.

O Jehovah, Thou hast searched me, and known me.
  Thou knowest my downsitting and mine uprising;
  Thou understandest my thought afar off.
Thou searchest out my path and my lying down,
  And art acquainted with all my ways.

For there is not a word in my tongue,
  But, lo, O Jehovah, Thou knowest it altogether.
Thou hast beset me behind and before,
  And laid Thy hand upon me.
Such knowledge is too wonderful for me;
  It is high, I cannot attain unto it.
Psalm 139:1-6, A. R. V.

Great is our Lord, and of great power:
  His understanding is infinite.
Psalm 147:5

"He revealeth the deep and secret things: He knoweth what is in the darkness, and the light dwelleth with Him." Daniel 2:22.

"Known unto God are all His works from the beginning of the world."
"Who hath known the mind of the Lord? or who hath been His counselor?

or who hath first given to Him, and it shall be recompensed unto him again? For of Him, and through Him, and to Him, are all things: to whom be glory forever." Acts 15:18; Romans 11:34-36.

"Unto the King eternal, incorruptible, invisible," "who only hath immortality, dwelling in light unapproachable; whom no man hath seen, nor can see," —to Him "be honor and power eternal." 1 Timothy 1:17, margin; 6:16, A. R. V.

> He stretcheth out the north over the empty place,
> And hangeth the earth upon nothing.
> He bindeth up the waters in His thick clouds;
> And the cloud is not rent under them...
> He hath compassed the waters with bounds,
> Until the day and night come to an end.
> Job 26:7-10

> The pillars of heaven tremble
> And are astonished at His rebuke.
> He stilleth the sea with His power...
> By His Spirit the heavens are beauty;
> His hand hath pierced the gliding serpent.
> Lo, these are but the outskirts of His ways:
> And how small a whisper do we hear of Him!
> But the thunder of His power who can understand?
> Job 26:11-14, A. R. V., margin.

> The Lord hath His way in the whirlwind and in the storm,
> And the clouds are the dust of His feet.
> Nahum 1:3

> Who is like unto the Lord our God, who dwelleth on high,
> Who humbleth Himself to behold the things that are in heaven, and in the earth! Psalm 113:5, 6

Great is Jehovah, and greatly to be praised;
  And His greatness is unsearchable.
One generation shall laud Thy works to another,
  And shall declare Thy mighty acts.
Of the glorious majesty of Thine honor,
  And of Thy wondrous works, will I meditate.
And men shall speak of the might of Thy terrible acts;
  And I will declare Thy greatness.
They shall utter the memory of Thy great goodness,
  And shall sing of Thy righteousness...

All Thy works shall give thanks unto Thee, O Jehovah;
  And Thy saints shall bless Thee.
They shall speak of the glory of Thy kingdom,
  And talk of Thy power;
To make known to the sons of men His mighty acts,
  And the glory of the majesty of His kingdom.
Thy kingdom is an everlasting kingdom,
  And Thy dominion endureth throughout all generations...

My mouth shall speak the praise of Jehovah;
  And let all flesh bless His holy name for ever and ever.
Psalm 145:3-21, A. R. V.

- **Warnings against Presumption**

As we learn more and more of what God is, and of what we ourselves are in His sight, we shall fear and tremble before Him.

Let men of today take warning from the fate of those who in ancient times presumed to make free with that which God had declared sacred. When the Israelites ventured to open the ark on its return from the land of the Philistines, their irreverent daring was signally punished. "He smote of the men of Beth-shemesh, because they had looked into the ark of Jehovah, He smote of the people seventy men, and fifty thousand men; and the people mourned, because Jehovah had smitten the people with a great slaughter. And the men of Beth-shemesh said, Who is able to stand before Jehovah, this holy God?" 1 Samuel 6:19, 20, A. R. V.

Again, consider the judgment that fell upon Uzzah. As in David's reign, the ark was being carried to Jerusalem, Uzzah put forth his hand to keep it steady. For presuming to touch the symbol of God's presence, he was smitten with instant death.

At the burning bush, when Moses, not recognizing God's presence, turned aside to behold the wonderful sight, the command was given:

"Draw not nigh hither: put off thy shoes from off thy feet, for the place whereon thou standest is holy ground... And Moses hid his face; for he was afraid to look upon God." Exodus 3:5, 6.

"And it came to pass, when Joshua was by Jericho, that he lifted up his eyes and looked, and, behold, there stood a Man over against him with His sword drawn in His hand: and Joshua went unto Him, and said unto Him, Art Thou for us, or for our adversaries? And He said, Nay; but as Captain of the host of the Lord am I now come. And Joshua fell on his face to the earth, and did worship, and said unto Him, What saith my Lord unto His servant? And the Captain of the Lord's host said unto Joshua, Loose thy shoe from off thy foot; for the place whereon thou standest is holy. And Joshua did so." Joshua 5:13-15.

In the sanctuary and the temple, that were the earthly symbols of God's dwelling place, one apartment was sacred to His presence. The veil inwrought with cherubim at its entrance was not to be lifted by any hand save one. To lift that veil and intrude unbidden into the sacred mystery of the most holy place was death. For above the mercy seat and the bowed, worshiping angels dwelt the glory of the Holiest, glory upon which no man might look and live. On the one day of the year appointed for ministry in the most holy place, the high priest with trembling entered God's presence, while clouds of incense veiled the glory from his sight. Throughout the courts of the temple every sound was hushed. No priests ministered at the altars. The hosts of worshipers, bowed in silent awe, sent up their petitions for God's mercy.

Section 5: The Essential Knowledge

"These things happened unto them by way of example; and they were written for our admonition, upon whom the ends of the ages are come." 1 Corinthians 10:11, A. R. V.

The Lord is in His holy temple:
Let all the earth keep silence before Him.
Habakkuk 2:20

Jehovah reigneth; let the peoples tremble:
He sitteth above the cherubim; let the earth be moved.
Jehovah is great in Zion;
And He is high above all the peoples.
Let them praise Thy great and terrible name:
Holy is He.
Psalm 99:1-3, A. R. V.

The Lord's throne is in heaven:
His eyes behold, His eyelids try, the children of men.
From the height of His sanctuary He hath looked down.
Psalm 11:4; 102:19

From the place of His habitation He looketh forth
Upon all the inhabitants of the earth,
He that fashioneth the hearts of them all,
That considereth all their works.
Let all the earth fear Jehovah:
Let all the inhabitants of the world stand in awe of Him.
Psalm 33:14, 15, 8, A. R.V.

Man cannot by searching find out God. Let none seek with presumptuous hand to lift the veil that conceals His glory. "Unsearchable are His judgments, and His ways past finding out!" Romans 11:33. It is a proof of His mercy that there is the hiding of His power; for to lift the veil that conceals the divine presence is death. No mortal mind can penetrate the secrecy in which the Mighty One dwells and works.

Only that which He sees fit to reveal can we comprehend of Him. Reason must acknowledge an authority superior to itself. Heart and intellect must bow to the great I AM.

- **Christ's Revelation of God**

All that man needs to know or can know of God has been revealed in the life and character of His Son.

"No man hath seen God at any time; the only-begotten Son, which is in the bosom of the Father, He hath declared Him." John 1:18.

Taking humanity upon Him, Christ came to be one with humanity and at the same time to reveal our heavenly Father to sinful human beings. He was in all things made like unto His brethren. He became flesh, even as we are. He was hungry and thirsty and weary. He was sustained by food and refreshed by sleep. He shared the lot of men, and yet He was the blameless Son of God. He was a stranger and sojourner on the earth—in the world, but not of the world; tempted and tried as men and women today are tempted and tried, yet living a life free from sin.

Tender, compassionate, sympathetic, ever considerate of others, He represented the character of God, and was constantly engaged in service for God and man. "The Word was made flesh, and dwelt among us, ... full of grace and truth." Verse 14.

"Unto the men whom Thou gavest Me out of the world," He said, "I manifested Thy name," "that the love wherewith Thou hast loved Me may be in them." John 17:6, A. R. V., 26.

"Love your enemies," He bade them; "bless them that curse you, do good to them that hate you, and pray for them which despitefully use you, and persecute you; that ye may be the children of your Father which is in heaven;" "for He is kind unto the unthankful and to the evil." "He maketh His sun to rise on the evil and on the good, and sendeth rain on the just and on the unjust." "Be ye therefore merciful, as your Father also is merciful." Matthew 5:44, 45; Luke 6:35, 36.

Section 5: The Essential Knowledge

- **The Glory of the Cross**

The revelation of God's love to men centers in the cross. Its full significance tongue cannot utter; pen cannot portray; the mind of man cannot comprehend. Looking upon the cross of Calvary we can only say: "God so loved the world, that He gave His only-begotten Son, that whosoever believeth in Him should not perish, but have everlasting life." John 3:16.

Christ crucified for our sins, Christ risen from the dead, Christ ascended on high, is the science of salvation that we are to learn and to teach.

"Who, being in the form of God, counted it not a thing to be grasped to be on an equality with God, but emptied Himself, taking the form of a servant, being made in the likeness of men; and being found in fashion as a man, He humbled Himself, becoming obedient even unto death, yea, the death of the cross." Philippians 2:6-8, R. V., margin.

"It is Christ that died, yea rather, that is risen again, who is even at the right hand of God." "Wherefore He is able also to save them to the uttermost that come unto God by Him, seeing He ever liveth to make intercession for them." Romans 8:34; Hebrews 7:25.

"We have not a high priest that cannot be touched with the feeling of our infirmities; but One that hath been in all points tempted like as we are, yet without sin." Hebrews 4:15, A. R. V. Here are infinite wisdom, infinite love, infinite justice, infinite mercy—"the depth of the riches both of the wisdom and knowledge of God." Romans 11:33.

It is through the gift of Christ that we receive every blessing.

Through that gift there comes to us day by day the unfailing flow of Jehovah's goodness. Every flower, with its delicate tints and sweet fragrance, is given for our enjoyment through that one Gift. The sun and moon were made by Him; there is not a star that beautifies the heavens which He did not make. There is not an article of food upon our tables that He has not provided for our sustenance. The superscription of Christ is upon it all. Everything is supplied to man through the one unspeakable Gift, the only-begotten Son of God. He was nailed to the cross that all these bounties might flow to God's workmanship.

The fruit of the tree of life in the Garden of Eden possessed supernatural virtue. To eat of it was to live forever. Its fruit was the antidote of death. Its leaves were for the sustaining of life and immortality. But through man's disobedience death entered the world. Adam ate of the tree of the knowledge of good and evil, the fruit of which he had been forbidden to touch. His transgression opened the floodgates of woe upon our race.

After the entrance of sin the heavenly Husbandman transplanted the tree of life to the Paradise above; but its branches hang over the wall to the lower world. Through the redemption purchased by the blood of Christ, we may still eat of its life-giving fruit.

Of Christ it is written: "In Him was life; and the life was the light of men." John 1:4. He is the Fountain of life. Obedience to Him is the life-giving power that gladdens the soul.

Christ declares: "I am the Bread of Life: he that cometh to Me shall never hunger; and he that believeth on Me shall never thirst." "As the living Father hath sent Me, and I live by the Father: so he that eateth Me, even he shall live by Me... It is the Spirit that quickeneth; the flesh profiteth nothing: the words that I speak unto you, they are spirit, and they are life." "To him that overcometh will I give to eat of the tree of life, which is in the midst of the Paradise of God." John 6:35, 57-63; Revelation 2:7.

"Behold, what manner of love the Father hath bestowed upon us, that we should be called the sons of God!" 1 John 3:1.

• The Knowledge that Works Transformation

The knowledge of God as revealed in Christ is the knowledge that all who are saved must have. It is the knowledge that works transformation of character. This knowledge, received, will re-create the soul in the image of God. It will impart to the whole being a spiritual power that is divine.

"We all, with unveiled face beholding as in a mirror the glory of the Lord, are transformed into the same image from glory to glory." 2 Corinthians 3:18, A. R. V. Of His own life the Saviour said: "I have kept My Father's commandments." "The Father hath not left Me alone; for I do always those things that please Him." John 15:10; 8:29. As Jesus was in human nature, so God means His followers to be. In His strength we are to live the life of purity and nobility which the Saviour lived.

"For this cause," Paul says, "I bow my knees unto the Father of our Lord Jesus Christ, of whom the whole family in heaven and earth is named, that He would grant you, according to the riches of His glory, to be strengthened with might by His Spirit in the inner man; that Christ may dwell in your hearts by faith; that ye, being rooted and grounded in love, may be able to comprehend with all saints what is the breadth, and length, and depth, and height; and to know the love of Christ, which passeth knowledge, that ye might be filled with all the fullness of God." Ephesians 3:14-19.

45. Danger in Speculative Knowledge

False science is one of the agencies that Satan used in the heavenly courts, and it is used by him today. The false assertions that he made to the angels, his subtle scientific theories, seduced many of them from their loyalty.

Having lost his place in heaven, Satan presented his temptations to our first parents. Adam and Eve yielded to the enemy, and by their disobedience humanity was estranged from God, and the earth was separated from heaven.

If Adam and Eve had never touched the forbidden tree, the Lord would have imparted to them knowledge, knowledge upon which rested no curse of sin, knowledge that would have brought them everlasting joy. All that they gained by their disobedience was an acquaintance with sin and its results.

- **Last-Day Deceptions**

The field into which Satan led our first parents is the same to which he is leading men today. He is flooding the world with pleasing fables. By every device at his command he seeks to prevent men from obtaining that knowledge of God which is salvation.

We are living in an age of great light; but much that is called light is opening the way for the wisdom and arts of Satan. Many things will be presented that appear to be true, and yet they need to be carefully considered with much prayer; for they may be specious devices of the enemy. The path of error often appears to lie close to the path of truth. It is hardly distinguishable from the path that leads to holiness and heaven. But the mind enlightened by the Holy Spirit may discern that it is diverging from the right way. After a while the two are seen to be widely separated.

- **Pantheistic Theories**

Already there are coming in among our people spiritualistic teachings that will undermine the faith of those who give heed to them. The theory that God is an essence pervading all nature is one of Satan's most subtle devices. It misrepresents God and is a dishonor to His greatness and majesty.

Pantheistic theories are not sustained by the word of God. The light of His truth shows that these theories are soul-destroying agencies. Darkness is their element, sensuality their sphere. They gratify the natural heart and give license to inclination. Separation from God is the result of accepting them.

Our condition through sin has become preternatural, and the power that restores us must be supernatural, else it has no value. There is but one power that can break the hold of evil from the hearts of men, and that is the power of God in Jesus Christ. Only through the blood of the Crucified One is there cleansing from sin. His grace alone can enable us to resist and subdue the tendencies of our fallen nature. This power the spiritualistic theories concerning God make of no effect. If God is an essence pervading all nature, then He dwells in all men; and in order to attain holiness, man has only to develop the power that is within him.

These theories, followed to their logical conclusion, sweep away the whole Christian economy. They do away with the necessity for the atonement and make man his own savior. These theories regarding God make His word of no effect, and those who accept them are in great danger of being led finally to look upon the whole Bible as a fiction. They may regard virtue as better than vice; but God being removed from His position of sovereignty, they place their dependence upon human power, which, without God, is worthless. The unaided human will has no real power to resist and overcome evil. The defenses of the soul are broken down. Man has no barrier against sin. When once the restraints of God's word and His Spirit are rejected, we know not to what depths one may sink.

Those who continue to hold these spiritualistic theories will surely spoil their Christian experience, sever their connection with God, and lose eternal life.

The sophistries regarding God and nature that are flooding the world with skepticism are the inspiration of the fallen foe, who is himself a Bible student, who knows the truth that it is essential for the people to receive, and whose study it is to divert minds from the great truths given to prepare them for what is coming upon the world.

I have seen the results of these fanciful views of God, in apostasy, spiritualism, and free-lovism. The free love tendency of these teachings was so concealed that at first it was difficult to make plain its real character. Until the Lord presented it to me, I knew not what to call it, but I was instructed to call it unholy spiritual love.

- **Fanaticism After 1844**

After the passing of the time in 1844, we had fanaticism of every kind to meet. Testimonies of reproof were given me to bear to some holding spiritualistic theories.

There were those who were active in disseminating false ideas in regard to God. Light was given me that these men were making the truth of no effect by their false teachings.

I was instructed that they were misleading souls by presenting speculative theories regarding God.

I went to the place where they were and opened before them the nature of their work. The Lord gave me strength to lay plainly before them their danger. Among other views they held that those who were once sanctified could not sin. Their false teaching was working great harm to themselves and to others. They were gaining a spiritualistic power over those who could not see the evil of these beautifully clothed theories. The doctrine that all were holy had led to the belief that the affections of the sanctified would never lead astray. The result of this belief was the fulfillment of the evil desires of hearts that, though professedly sanctified, were far from purity of thought and life.

Ungodly teaching is followed by sinful practice. It is the seducing bait of the father of lies, and results in the impenitence of self-satisfied impurity.

This is only one of the instances in which I was called upon to rebuke those who were presenting the doctrine of an impersonal God pervading all nature, and similar errors.

- ## Past Experiences to be Repeated

The experience of the past will be repeated. In the future, Satan's superstitions will assume new forms. Errors will be presented in a pleasing and flattering manner. False theories, clothed with garments of light, will be presented to God's people. Thus Satan will try to deceive, if possible, the very elect. Most seducing influences will be exerted; minds will be hypnotized.

Corruptions of every type, similar to those existing among the antediluvians, will be brought in to take minds captive.

The exaltation of nature as God, the unrestrained license of the human will, the counsel of the ungodly—these Satan uses as agencies to bring about certain ends. He will employ the power of mind over mind to carry out his designs. The most sorrowful thought of all is that under his deceptive influence men will have a form of godliness, without having a real connection with God. Like Adam and Eve, who ate the fruit from the tree of the knowledge of good and evil, many are even now feeding upon the deceptive morsels of error.

Satanic agencies are clothing false theories in an attractive garb, even as Satan in the Garden of Eden concealed his identity from our first parents by speaking through the serpent. These agencies are instilling into human minds that which in reality is deadly error. The hypnotic influence of Satan will rest upon those who turn from the plain word of God to pleasing fables.

Section 5: The Essential Knowledge

It is those who have had the most light that Satan most assiduously seeks to ensnare. He knows that if he can deceive them, they will, under his control, clothe sin with garments of righteousness, and lead many astray.

I say to all: Be on your guard; for as an angel of light Satan is walking in every assembly of Christian workers, and in every church, trying to win the members to his side. I am bidden to give to the people of God the warning: "Be not deceived; God is not mocked." Galatians 6:7.

• Beware of a Sensational Religion

At this time we need in the cause of God spiritually minded men, men who are firm in principle and who have a clear understanding of the truth.

I have been instructed that it is not new and fanciful doctrines which the people need. They do not need human suppositions. They need the testimony of men who know and practice the truth, men who understand and obey the charge given to Timothy: "Preach the word; be instant in season, out of season; reprove, rebuke, exhort with all long-suffering and doctrine. For the time will come when they will not endure sound doctrine; but after their own lusts shall they heap to themselves teachers, having itching ears; and they shall turn away their ears from the truth, and shall be turned unto fables. But watch thou in all things, endure afflictions, do the work of an evangelist, make full proof of thy ministry." 2 Timothy 4:2-5.

Walk firmly, decidedly, your feet shod with the preparation of the gospel of peace. You may be sure that pure and undefiled religion is not a sensational religion. God has not laid upon anyone the burden of encouraging an appetite for speculative doctrines and theories. My brethren, keep these things out of your teaching. Do not allow them to enter into your experience. Let not your lifework be marred by them.

• A Warning against False Teaching

A warning against false teaching is found in Paul's letter to the Colossians. The apostle declares that the hearts of the believers are to be "knit together in love, and unto all riches of the full assurance of understanding, to the acknowledgment of the mystery of God, and of the Father, and of Christ; in whom are hid all the treasures of wisdom and knowledge."

"And this I say," he continues, "lest any man should beguile you with enticing words... As ye have therefore received Christ Jesus the Lord, so walk ye in Him: rooted and built up in Him, and stablished in the faith, as ye have been taught, abounding therein with thanksgiving. Beware lest any man spoil you through philosophy and vain deceit, after the tradition of men, after the rudiments of the world, and not after Christ. For in Him dwelleth all the fullness of the Godhead bodily. And ye are complete in Him, which is the head of all principality and power." Colossians 2:2-10.

I am instructed to say to our people: Let us follow Christ. Do not forget that He is to be our pattern in all things. We may safely discard those ideas that are not found in His teaching. I appeal to our ministers to be sure that their feet are placed on the platform of eternal truth. Beware how you follow impulse, calling it the Holy Spirit. Some are in danger in this respect. I call upon them to be sound in the faith, able to give to everyone who asks a reason of the hope that is in them.

- **Diverting Minds from Present Duty**

The enemy is seeking to divert the minds of our brethren and sisters from the work of preparing a people to stand in these last days. His sophistries are designed to lead minds away from the perils and duties of the hour. They estimate as nothing the light that Christ came from heaven to give to John for His people. They teach that the scenes just before us are not of sufficient importance to receive special attention. They make of no effect the truth of heavenly origin and rob the people of God of their past experience, giving them instead a false science.

"Thus saith the Lord, Stand ye in the ways, and see, and ask for the old paths, where is the good way, and walk therein." Jeremiah 6:16.

Let none seek to tear away the foundations of our faith—the foundations that were laid at the beginning of our work by prayerful study of the word and by revelation. Upon these foundations we have been building for the last fifty years. Men may suppose that they have found a new way and that they can lay a stronger foundation than that which has been laid. But this is a great deception. Other foundation can no man lay than that which has been laid.

In the past many have undertaken the building of a new faith, the establishment of new principles. But how long did their building stand? It soon fell, for it was not founded upon the Rock.

Did not the first disciples have to meet the sayings of men? Did they not have to listen to false theories, and then, having done all, to stand firm, saying: "Other foundation can no man lay than that is laid"? 1 Corinthians 3:11.

So we are to hold the beginning of our confidence steadfast unto the end. Words of power have been sent by God and by Christ to this people, bringing them out from the world, point by point, into the clear light of present truth. With lips touched with holy fire, God's servants have proclaimed the message. The divine utterance has set its seal to the genuineness of the truth proclaimed.

- **A Renewal of the Straight Testimony**

The Lord calls for a renewal of the straight testimony borne in years past. He calls for a renewal of spiritual life. The spiritual energies of His people have long been torpid, but there is to be a resurrection from apparent death.

By prayer and confession of sin we must clear the King's highway. As we do this, the power of the Spirit will come to us. We need the Pentecostal energy. This will come, for the Lord has promised to send His Spirit as the all-conquering power.

Perilous times are before us. Everyone who has a knowledge of the truth should awake and place himself, body, soul, and spirit, under the discipline of God. The enemy is on our track. We must be wide awake, on our guard against him. We must put on the whole armor of God. We must follow the directions given through the spirit of prophecy. We must love and obey the truth for this time. This will save us from accepting strong delusions. God has spoken to us through His word. He has spoken to us through the testimonies to the church and through the books that have helped to make plain our present duty and the position that we should now occupy. The warnings that have been given, line upon line, precept upon precept, should be heeded. If we disregard them, what excuse can we offer?

I beseech those who are laboring for God not to accept the spurious for the genuine. Let not human reason be placed where divine, sanctifying truth should be. Christ is waiting to kindle faith and love in the hearts of His people. Let not erroneous theories receive countenance from the people who ought to be standing firm on the platform of eternal truth. God calls upon us to hold firmly to the fundamental principles that are based upon unquestionable authority.

- **Seek the First Love**

Into the hearts of many who have been long in the truth there has entered a hard, judicial spirit. They are sharp, critical, faultfinding. They have climbed upon the judgment seat to pronounce sentence upon those who do not conform to their ideas. God calls upon them to come down and bow before Him in repentance, confessing their sins. He says to them: "I have somewhat against thee, because thou hast left thy first love. Remember therefore from whence thou art fallen, and repent, and do the first works; or else I will come unto thee quickly, and will remove thy candlestick out of his place, except thou repent." Revelation 2:4, 5. They are striving for the first place, and by their words and acts they make many hearts sore.

Against this spirit, and against the false religion of sentimentalism, which is equally dangerous, I bear my warning. Take heed, brethren and sisters. Who is your leader—Christ or the angel that fell from heaven? Examine yourselves and know whether you are sound in the faith.

- **The Word of God our Safeguard**

Our watchword is to be: "To the law and to the testimony: if they speak not according to this word, it is because there is no light in them." Isaiah 8:20.

Section 5: The Essential Knowledge

We have a Bible full of the most precious truth. It contains the alpha and omega of knowledge. The Scriptures, given by inspiration of God, are "profitable for doctrine, for reproof, for correction, for instruction in righteousness: that the man of God may be perfect, throughly furnished unto all good works." 2 Timothy 3:16, 17. Take the Bible as your study book. All can understand its instruction.

I call upon our ministers, physicians, and all church members to study the lessons that Christ gave His disciples just before His ascension. These lessons contain instruction that the people need.

Eternal life is obtained only by eating the flesh and drinking the blood of the Son of God. "Verily, verily, I say unto you," Christ declared, "he that believeth on Me hath everlasting life... I am the living Bread which came down from heaven: if any man eat of this bread, he shall live for ever: and the bread that I will give is My flesh, which I will give for the life of the world... Whoso eateth My flesh, and drinketh My blood, hath eternal life; and I will raise him up at the last day. For My flesh is meat indeed, and My blood is drink indeed. He that eateth My flesh, and drinketh My blood, dwelleth in Me, and I in him... It is the Spirit that quickeneth; the flesh profiteth nothing: the words that I speak unto you, they are spirit, and they are life." John 6:47-63.

Christ calls upon His people to believe and practice His word. Those who receive and assimilate this word, making it a part of every action, of every attribute of character, will grow strong in the strength of God. It will be seen that their faith is of heavenly origin. They will not wander into strange paths. Their minds will not turn to a religion of sentimentalism and excitement. Before angels and before men, they will stand as those who have strong, consistent Christian characters.

In the golden censer of truth, as presented in Christ's teachings, we have that which will convict and convert souls. Present, in the simplicity of Christ, the truths that He came to this world to proclaim, and the power of your message will make itself felt. Do not present theories or tests that Christ has never mentioned and that have no foundation in the Bible. We have grand, solemn truths to present."It is written" is the test that must be brought home to every soul.

Men may still learn the things that belong to their peace. Mercy's voice may still be heard calling: "Come unto Me, all ye that labor and are heavy-laden, and I will give you rest. Take My yoke upon you, and learn of Me; for I am meek and lowly in heart: and ye shall find rest unto your souls. For My yoke is easy, and My burden is light." Matthew 11:28-30. It is only when spiritual life is given that rest is found and lasting good secured. We must be able to say, in storm and tempest: "My anchor holds."

Let us go to the word of God for guidance. Let us seek for a "Thus saith the Lord." We have had enough of human methods. A mind trained only in worldly science fails to understand the things of God; but the same mind, converted and sanctified, will see the divine power in the word. Only the mind and heart cleansed by the sanctification of the Spirit can discern heavenly things.

Brethren, in the name of the Lord I call upon you to awake to your duty. Let your hearts be yielded to the power of the Holy Spirit, and they will be made susceptible to the teaching of the word. Then you will be able to discern the deep things of God.

May God bring His people under the deep movings of His Spirit! May He lead them to arouse, to see their peril, and to prepare for what is coming upon the earth!

- **Study the Revelation**

To John the Lord opened the subjects that He saw would be needed by His people in the last days. The instruction that He gave is found in the book of Revelation. Those who would be co-workers with our Lord and Saviour Jesus Christ will show a deep interest in the truths found in this book. With pen and voice they will strive to make plain the wonderful things that Christ came from heaven to reveal.

"The revelation of Jesus Christ, which God gave unto Him, to show unto His servants things which must shortly come to pass; and He sent and signified it by His angel unto His servant John: who bare record of the word of God, and of the testimony of Jesus Christ, and of all things that he saw.

Blessed is he that readeth, and they that hear the words of this prophecy, and keep those things which are written therein: for the time is at hand." Revelation 1:1-3.

The solemn messages that have been given in their order in the Revelation are to occupy the first place in the minds of God's people. Nothing else is to be allowed to engross our attention.

Precious time is rapidly passing, and there is danger that many will be robbed of the time which should be given to the proclamation of the messages that God has sent to a fallen world. Satan is pleased to see the diversion of minds that should be engaged in a study of the truths which have to do with eternal realities.

The testimony of Christ, a testimony of the most solemn character, is to be borne to the world. All through the book of Revelation there are the most precious, elevating promises, and there are also warnings of the most fearfully solemn import. Will not those who profess to have a knowledge of the truth read the testimony given to John by Christ? Here is no guesswork, no scientific deception. Here are the truths that concern our present and future welfare. What is the chaff to the wheat?

- **To the Church in Sardis**

"Unto the angel of the church in Sardis write; These things saith He that hath the seven Spirits of God, and the seven stars; I know thy works, that thou hast a name that thou livest, and art dead. Be watchful, and strengthen the things which remain, that are ready to die: for I have not found thy works perfect before God. Remember therefore how thou hast received and heard, and hold fast, and repent.

If therefore thou shalt not watch, I will come on thee as a thief, and thou shalt not know what hour I will come upon thee.

Thou hast a few names even in Sardis which have not defiled their garments; and they shall walk with Me in white: for they are worthy. He that overcometh, the same shall be clothed in white raiment; and I will not blot out his name out of the book of life, but I will confess his name before My

Father, and before His angels. He that hath an ear, let him hear what the Spirit saith unto the churches." Revelation 3:1-6.

- **Message to the Philadelphia Church**

"And to the angel of the church in Philadelphia write; These things saith He that is holy, He that is true, He that hath the key of David, He that openeth, and no man shutteth; and shutteth, and no man openeth; I know thy works: behold, I have set before thee an open door, and no man can shut it: for thou hast a little strength, and hast kept My word, and hast not denied My name. Behold, I will make them of the synagogue of Satan, which say they are Jews, and are not, but do lie; behold, I will make them to come and worship before thy feet, and to know that I have loved thee. Because thou hast kept the word of My patience, I also will keep thee from the hour of temptation, which shall come upon all the world, to try them that dwell upon the earth. Behold, I come quickly: hold that fast which thou hast, that no man take thy crown. Him that overcometh will I make a pillar in the temple of My God, and he shall go no more out: and I will write upon him the name of My God, and the name of the city of My God, which is New Jerusalem, which cometh down out of heaven from My God: and I will write upon him My new name." Verses 7-12.

- **The Laodicean Message**

"Unto the angel of the church of the Laodiceans write; These things saith the Amen, the faithful and true Witness, the Beginning of the creation of God; I know thy works, that thou art neither cold nor hot: I would thou wert cold or hot. So then because thou art lukewarm, and neither cold nor hot, I will spew thee out of My mouth. Because thou sayest, I am rich, and increased with goods, and have need of nothing; and knowest not that thou art wretched, and miserable, and poor, and blind, and naked: I counsel thee to buy of Me gold tried in the fire, that thou mayest be rich; and white raiment, that thou mayest be clothed, and that the shame of thy nakedness do not appear; and anoint thine eyes with eyesalve, that thou mayest see."

"As many as I love, I rebuke and chasten: be zealous therefore, and repent. Behold, I stand at the door, and knock: if any man hear My voice, and open the door, I will come in to him, and will sup with him, and he with Me. To him that overcometh will I grant to sit with Me in My throne, even as I also overcame, and am set down with My Father in His throne. He that hath an ear, let him hear what the Spirit saith unto the churches." Verses 14-22.

The Lord is soon coming. The watchmen on the walls of Zion are called upon to awake to their God-given responsibilities. God calls for watchmen who, in the power of the Spirit, will give to the world the last warning message; who will proclaim the time of night. He calls for watchmen who will arouse men and women from their lethargy, lest they sleep the sleep of death.

46. The False and the True in Education

The master mind in the confederacy of evil is ever working to keep out of sight the words of God and to bring into full view the opinions of men. He means that we shall not hear the voice of God saying: "This is the way, walk ye in it." Through educational processes he is doing all in his power to obscure heaven's light.

- **Philosophical Speculation**

Philosophical speculation and scientific research in which God is not acknowledged are making skeptics of thousands of the youth. In the schools of today the conclusions that learned men have reached as the result of their scientific investigations are carefully taught and fully explained; while the impression is distinctly given that if these learned men are correct, the Bible cannot be. Skepticism is attractive to the human mind. The youth see in it an independence that captivates the imagination, and they are deceived. Satan triumphs; it is altogether as he meant it should be. He nourishes every seed of doubt that is sown in young hearts. He causes it to grow and bear fruit, and soon a plentiful harvest of infidelity is reaped.

It is because the human heart is inclined to evil that there is so great danger in sowing the seeds of skepticism in young minds. Whatever weakens faith in God, robs the soul of power to resist temptation. It removes the only real safeguard against sin.

We are not to institute schools of scholastic philosophy or for the so-called "higher education." Our greatness consists in honoring God by simple, practical experience in everyday life. We need to walk with God, to bring Him into our hearts and our homes.

- **Infidel Authors**

Many think that in order to obtain an education it is necessary to study the productions of writers who teach infidelity, because their works contain some bright gems of thought. But who was the originator of these gems of thought? It was God, and God alone. He is the source of all light. Why should we wade through the mass of error contained in the works of pagans and infidels, for the sake of a few intellectual truths, when all truth is at our command?

There is a reason why these men sometimes display remarkable wisdom. Satan himself was educated in the heavenly courts, and he has a knowledge of good as well as of evil. He mingles the precious with the vile, and this is what gives him power to deceive. But because Satan has robed himself in garments of heavenly brightness, shall we receive him as an angel of light? The tempter has his agents, educated according to his methods, inspired by his spirit, and adapted to his work. Shall we co-operate with them? Shall we receive the works of his agents as essential to the acquirement of an education?

"Who can bring a clean thing out of an unclean? not one." Job 14:4. Can we then expect the youth to maintain Christian principles and to develop Christian character while their education is largely influenced by the teachings of pagans, atheists, and infidels?

Section 5: The Essential Knowledge

If the time and effort spent in seeking to grasp the bright ideas of infidels were given to studying the precious things in the word of God, thousands who now sit in darkness and in the shadow of death would be rejoicing in the glory of the Light of life.

- **Historical and Theological Lore**

Many who are seeking a preparation for the Lord's work think it essential to accumulate large volumes of historical and theological writings. They suppose that the study of these works will be a great advantage to them in learning how to reach the people. This is an error. As I see shelves piled with these books, some of them rarely looked into, I think: Why spend money for that which is not bread? The sixth chapter of John tells us more than can be found in such works. Christ says: "I am the Bread of Life." "The words that I speak unto you, they are spirit, and they are life." John 6:35, 63.

There is a study of history that is not to be condemned. Sacred history was one of the studies in the schools of the prophets. In the record of His dealings with the nations were traced the footsteps of Jehovah. So today we are to consider the dealings of God with the nations of the earth. We are to see in history the fulfillment of prophecy, to study the workings of Providence in the great reformatory movements, and to understand the progress of events in the marshalling of the nations for the final conflict of the great controversy.

But too often the motive of those who study these many books is not so much to obtain food for mind or soul. It is an ambition to become acquainted with philosophers and theologians, a desire to present Christianity to the people in learned terms and propositions.

"Learn of Me," said the greatest Teacher the world ever knew. "Take My yoke upon you, learn My meekness and lowliness." Your intellectual pride will not aid in the work of communicating with souls that are perishing for want of the bread of life. In your study of these books you are allowing them to take the place, in mind and heart, of the practical lessons you should be learning from the Great Teacher. With the results of this study the people are not fed. Very little of the study and research which is so wearying to the mind furnishes anything that will make one a successful laborer for souls.

Men and women who spend their lives in humble, commonplace work need words as simple as Christ gave in His lessons, words that are easily understood. The Saviour came "to preach the gospel to the poor." And it is written that "the common people heard Him gladly." Those who are teaching the truth for this time need a deeper insight into the lessons He has given.

The words of the living God are the highest of all education. The studied phrases designed to please the taste of the supposed-to-be refined fall short of the mark. Those who minister to the people need to eat the bread of life. This will give them spiritual strength; then they will be prepared to minister to all classes of people. The piety, the spiritual energy of the church is sustained by feeding on the bread that came down from heaven. At the feet of Jesus we are to learn the simplicity of true Godliness.

- **Myths and Fairy Tales**

In the education of children and youth, fairy tales, myths, and fictitious stories are now given a large place. Books of this character are used in the schools, and they are to be found in many homes. How can Christian parents permit their children to use books so filled with falsehood? When the children ask the meaning of stories so contrary to the teaching of their parents, the answer is that the stories are not true; but this does not do away with the evil results of their use. The ideas presented in these books mislead the children. They impart false views of life and beget and foster a desire for the unreal.

The widespread use of such books at this time is one of the cunning devices of Satan. He is seeking to divert the minds of old and young from the great work of preparation for the things that are coming upon the earth. He means that our children and youth shall be swept away by the soul-destroying deceptions with which he is flooding the world. Therefore he seeks to divert their minds from the word of God, and thus prevent them from gaining a knowledge of those truths that would be their safeguard.

Section 5: The Essential Knowledge

Never should books containing a perversion of truth be placed before children or youth. And if those with mature minds had nothing to do with such books, they would be far safer.

- **A Purer Fountain**

We have an abundance of that which is real, that which is divine. Those who thirst for knowledge need not go to polluted fountains.

Christ presented the principles of truth in the gospel. In His teaching we may drink of the pure streams that flow from the throne of God.

Christ could have imparted to men knowledge that would have surpassed any previous disclosures and put in the background every other discovery. He could have unlocked mystery after mystery, and could have concentrated around these wonderful revelations the active, earnest thought of successive generations till the close of time. But He would not spare a moment from teaching the knowledge of the science of salvation. His time, His faculties, His life itself, was appreciated and used only as the means for working out the salvation of the souls of men. He had come to seek and to save that which was lost, and He would not be turned from His one object. He allowed nothing to divert Him.

Christ imparted only that knowledge which could be utilized. His instruction of the people was confined to the needs of their own condition in practical life. The curiosity that led them to come to Him with prying questions, He did not gratify. All such questionings He made the occasion for solemn, earnest, vital appeals. To those who were so eager to pluck from the tree of knowledge, He offered the fruit of the tree of life. They found every avenue closed, except the narrow way that leads to God. Every fountain was sealed, save the fountain of eternal life.

Our Saviour did not encourage any to attend the rabbinical schools of His day for the reason that their minds would be corrupted with the continually repeated, "They say," or, "It has been said." Why, then, should we accept the unstable words of men as exalted wisdom, when a greater, a certain wisdom is at our command?

That which I have seen of eternal things, and that which I have seen of the weakness of men, as God has presented it before me, has deeply impressed my mind and influenced my life and character. I see nothing wherein man should be exalted or praised or glorified. I see no reason why the opinions of worldly-wise men should be trusted in and exalted. How can those who are destitute of divine enlightenment have correct ideas of God's plans and ways?

I am willing to be taught by Him who created the heavens and the earth, by Him who set the stars in their order in the firmament and appointed the sun and the moon to do their work. I need not go to infidel authors. I choose to be taught of God.

- **Heart Education**

It is right for the youth to feel that they must reach the highest development of their mental powers. We would not restrict the education to which God has set no limit. But our attainments will avail nothing if not put to use for the honor of God and the good of humanity. Unless our knowledge is a steppingstone to the accomplishment of the highest purposes, it is worthless.

What we need is knowledge that will strengthen mind and soul, that will make us better men and women.

Heart education is of more importance than the education gained from books. It is well, even essential, to obtain a knowledge of the world in which we live; but if we leave eternity out of our reckoning, we shall make a failure from which we can never recover.

It is not well to crowd the mind with a class of studies that require intense application, but that are not brought into use in practical life. An education of this kind will be a loss to the student. For these studies take away his desire and inclination for the studies that would fit him for usefulness and enable him to fulfill his responsibilities.

If the youth understood their own weakness, they would find in God their strength. If they seek to be taught by Him, they will become wise in His wisdom, and their lives will be fruitful of blessing to the world. But if they give up their minds to mere worldly and speculative study, and thus separate from God, they will lose all that enriches life.

47. Importance of Seeking True Knowledge

Far more than we do, we need to understand the issues at stake in the conflict in which we are engaged. We need to understand more fully the value of the truths that God has given for this time and the danger of allowing our minds to be diverted from them by the great deceiver.

The infinite value of the sacrifice required for our redemption reveals the fact that sin is a tremendous evil. Through sin the whole human organism is deranged, the mind is perverted, the imagination corrupted. Sin has degraded the faculties of the soul. Temptations from without find an answering chord within the heart, and the feet turn imperceptibly toward evil.

As the sacrifice in our behalf was complete, so our restoration from the defilement of sin is to be complete. There is no act of wickedness that the law will excuse; there is no unrighteousness that will escape its condemnation. The life of Christ was a perfect fulfillment of every precept of the law. He said; "I have kept My Father's commandments." John 15:10. His life is our standard of obedience and service.

God alone can renew the heart. "It is God who worketh in you both to will and to work, for His good pleasure." But we are bidden: "Work out your own salvation." Philippians 2:13, 12, A. R. V.

- **The Work That Requires Our Thought**

Wrongs cannot be righted, nor can reformations in character be made, by a few feeble, intermittent efforts. Sanctification is the work, not of a day, or of a year, but of a lifetime. The struggle for conquest over self, for holiness and heaven, is a lifelong struggle. Without continual effort and constant activity there can be no advancement in the divine life, no attainment of the victor's crown.

The strongest evidence of man's fall from a higher state is the fact that it costs so much to return. The way of return can be gained only by hard fighting, inch by inch, every hour. By a momentary act of will, one may place himself in the power of evil; but it requires more than a momentary act of will to break these fetters and attain to a higher, holier life. The purpose may be formed, the work begun; but its accomplishment will require toil, time, and perseverance, patience and sacrifice.

Beset with temptations without number, we must resist firmly or be conquered. Should we come to the close of life with our work undone, it would be an eternal loss.

Paul's sanctification was the result of a constant conflict with self. He said: "I die daily." 1 Corinthians 15:31. His will and his desires every day conflicted with duty and the will of God. Instead of following inclination, he did God's will, however crucifying to his own nature.

God leads His people on step by step. The Christian life is a battle and a march. In this warfare there is no release; the effort must be continuous and persevering. It is by unceasing endeavor that we maintain the victory over the temptations of Satan. Christian integrity must be sought with resistless energy and maintained with a resolute fixedness of purpose.

No one will be borne upward without stern, persevering effort in his own behalf. All must engage in this warfare for themselves. Individually we are responsible for the issue of the struggle; though Noah, Job, and Daniel were in the land, they could deliver neither son nor daughter by their righteousness.

- ## The Science to be Mastered

There is a science of Christianity to be mastered,—a science as much deeper, broader, higher than any human science as the heavens are higher than the earth. The mind is to be disciplined, educated, trained; for we are to do service for God in ways that are not in harmony with inborn inclination. There are hereditary and cultivated tendencies to evil that must be overcome. Often the training and education of a lifetime must be discarded, that one may become a learner in the school of Christ. Our hearts must be educated to become steadfast in God. We are to form habits of thought that will enable us to resist temptation. We must learn to look upward. The principles of the word of God—principles that are as high as heaven, and that compass eternity—we are to understand in their bearing upon our daily life. Every act, every word, every thought, is to be in accord with these principles.

The precious graces of the Holy Spirit are not developed in a moment. Courage, fortitude, meekness, faith, unwavering trust in God's power to save, are acquired by the experience of years. By a life of holy endeavor and firm adherence to the right the children of God are to seal their destiny.

- **No Time to Lose**

We have no time to lose. We know not how soon our probation may close. Eternity stretches before us. The curtain is about to be lifted. Christ is soon to come. The angels of God are seeking to attract us from ourselves and from earthly things. Let them not labor in vain.

When Jesus rises up in the most holy place, lays off His mediatorial robes, and clothes Himself with the garments of vengeance, the mandate will go forth: "He that is unjust, let him be unjust still: ... and he that is righteous, let him be righteous still: and he that is holy, let him be holy still. And, behold, I come quickly; and My reward is with Me, to give every man according as his work shall be." Revelation 22:11, 12.

A storm is coming, relentless in its fury. Are we prepared to meet it?

We need not say: The perils of the last days are soon to come upon us. Already they have come. We need now the sword of the Lord to cut to the very soul and marrow of fleshly lusts, appetites, and passions.

Minds that have been given up to loose thought need to change. "Girding up the loins of your mind, be sober and set your hope perfectly on the grace that is to be brought unto you at the revelation of Jesus Christ; as children of obedience, not fashioning yourselves according to your former lusts in the time of your ignorance: but like as He who called you is holy, be ye yourselves also holy in all manner of living; because it is written, Ye shall be holy; for I am holy." 1 Peter 1:13-16, A. R. V. The thoughts must be centered upon

God. Now is the time to put forth earnest effort to overcome the natural tendencies of the carnal heart.

Our efforts, our self-denial, our perseverance, must be proportionate to the infinite value of the object of which we are in pursuit. Only by overcoming as Christ overcame shall we win the crown of life.

• The Need for Self-Renunciation

Man's great danger is in being self-deceived, indulging self-sufficiency, and thus separating from God, the source of his strength. Our natural tendencies, unless corrected by the Holy Spirit of God, have in them the seeds of moral death. Unless we become vitally connected with God, we cannot resist the unhallowed effects of self-love, self-indulgence, and temptation to sin.

In order to receive help from Christ, we must realize our need. We must have a true knowledge of ourselves. It is only he who knows himself to be a sinner that Christ can save. Only as we see our utter helplessness and renounce all self-trust, shall we lay hold on divine power.

It is not only at the beginning of the Christian life that this renunciation of self is to be made. At every advance step heavenward it is to be renewed. All our good works are dependent on a power outside of ourselves; therefore there needs to be a continual reaching out of the heart after God, a constant, earnest confession of sin and humbling of the soul before Him. Perils surround us; and we are safe only as we feel our weakness and cling with the grasp of faith to our mighty Deliverer.

• The Highest Interests Demand Attention

We must turn away from a thousand topics that invite attention. There are matters that consume time and arouse inquiry, but end in nothing. The highest interests demand the close attention and energy that are too often given to comparatively insignificant things.

Accepting new theories does not bring new life to the soul. Even an acquaintance with facts and theories important in themselves is of little value unless put to a practical use. We need to feel our responsibility to give our souls food that will nourish and stimulate spiritual life.

- **A Personal Knowledge of Christ**

"Every word of God is pure: He is a shield unto them that put their trust in Him. Add thou not unto His words, lest He reprove thee, and thou be found a liar." Proverbs 30:5, 6.

We are not doing the will of God when we speculate upon things that He has seen fit to withhold from us. The question for us to study is: "What is truth, the truth for this time, which is to be cherished, loved, honored, and obeyed?" The devotees of science have been defeated and disheartened in their efforts to find out God. What they need to inquire at this time is: "What is the truth that will enable us to win the salvation of our souls?"

Christ revealed God to His disciples in a way that performed in their hearts a special work, such as He has long been urging us to allow Him to do in our hearts. There are many who, in dwelling too largely upon theory, have lost sight of the living power of the Saviour's example. They have lost sight of Him as the humble, self-denying worker. What they need is to behold Jesus. Daily we need the fresh revealing of His presence. We need to follow more closely His example of self-renunciation and sacrifice.

We need the experience that Paul had when he wrote: "I am crucified with Christ: nevertheless I live; yet not I, but Christ liveth in me: and the life which I now live in the flesh I live by the faith of the Son of God, who loved me, and gave Himself for me." Galatians 2:20.

The knowledge of God and of Jesus Christ expressed in character is an exaltation above everything else that is esteemed on earth or in heaven. It is the very highest education. It is the key that opens the portals of the heavenly city. This knowledge it is God's purpose that all who put on Christ shall possess.

To our ministers, physicians, teachers, and all others engaged in any line of service for the Master, I have a message to bear. The Lord bids you to come up higher, to reach a holier standard. You must have an experience much deeper than you have yet even thought of having. Many who are already members of God's great family know little of what it means to behold His glory and to be changed from glory to glory. Many of you have a twilight perception of Christ's excellence, and your souls thrill with joy. You long for a fuller, deeper sense of the Saviour's love. You are unsatisfied. But do not despair. Give to Jesus the heart's best and holiest affections.

Treasure every ray of light. Cherish every desire of the soul after God. Give yourselves the culture of spiritual thoughts and holy communings. You have seen but the first rays of the early dawn of His glory. As you follow on to know the Lord, you will know that His going forth is prepared as the morning. "The path of the righteous is as the light of dawn, that shineth more and more unto the perfect day." Proverbs 4:18, R. V., margin. Having repented of our sins, confessed them, and found pardon, we are to continue to learn of Christ until we come into the full noontide of a perfect gospel faith.

48. The Knowledge Received through God's Word

The whole Bible is a revelation of the glory of God in Christ. Received, believed, obeyed, it is the great instrumentality in the transformation of character. And it is the only sure means of intellectual culture.

The reason why the youth, and even those of mature years, are so easily led into temptation and sin is that they do not study the word of God and meditate upon it as they should. The lack of firm, decided will power, which is manifest in life and character, results from their neglect of the sacred instruction of God's word. They do not by earnest effort direct the mind to that which would inspire pure, holy thought and divert it from that which is impure and untrue. There are few who choose the better part, who sit at the feet of Jesus, as did Mary, to learn of the divine Teacher. Few treasure His words in the heart and practice them in the life.

The truths of the Bible, received, will uplift the mind from its earthliness and debasement. If the word of God were appreciated as it should be, both young and old would possess an inward rectitude, a strength of principle, that would enable them to resist temptation.

Let men teach and write the precious things of the Holy Scriptures. Let the thought, the aptitude, the keen exercise of brain power, be given to the study of the thoughts of God. Study not the philosophy of man's conjectures, but study the philosophy of Him who is truth. Other literature is of little value when compared with this.

The mind that is earthly finds no pleasure in contemplating the word of God; but for the mind renewed by the Holy Spirit, divine beauty and celestial light shine from the sacred page. That which to the earthly mind was a desolate wilderness, to the spiritual mind becomes a land of living streams.

- **To Be Given to Our Children**

The knowledge of God as revealed in His word is the knowledge to be given to our children. From the earliest dawn of reason they should be made familiar with the name and the life of Jesus. The very first lesson given them should be that God is their Father. Their very first training should teach them to render loving obedience. Reverently and tenderly let the word of God be read and repeated to them, in portions suited to their comprehension and adapted to awaken their interest. Above all, let them learn of His love revealed in Christ, and its great lesson:

"If God so loved us, we ought also to love one another." 1 John 4:11.

Let the youth make the word of God the food of mind and soul. Let the cross of Christ be made the science of all education, the center of all teaching and all study. Let it be brought into the daily experience in practical life. So will the Saviour become to the youth a daily companion and friend. Every thought will be brought into captivity to the obedience of Christ. With the apostle Paul they will be able to say:

"God forbid that I should glory, save in the cross of our Lord Jesus Christ, by whom the world is crucified unto me, and I unto the world." Galatians 6:14.

- **An Experimental Knowledge**

Thus through faith they will come to know God by an experimental knowledge. They have proved for themselves the reality of His word, the truth of His promises. They have tasted, and they know that the Lord is good.

The beloved John had a knowledge gained through his own experience. He could testify:

"That which was from the beginning, which we have heard, which we have seen with our eyes, which we have looked upon, and our hands have handled, of the Word of life; (for the Life was manifested, and we have seen it, and bear witness, and show unto you that eternal life, which was with the Father, and was manifested unto us;) that which we have seen and heard declare we unto you, that ye also may have fellowship with us: and truly our fellowship is with the Father, and with His Son Jesus Christ." 1 John 1:1-3.

So everyone may be able, through his own experience, to "set his seal to this, that God is true." John 3:33, A. R. V. He can bear witness to that which he himself has seen and heard and felt of the power of Christ. He can testify:

"I needed help, and I found it in Jesus. Every want was supplied, the hunger of my soul was satisfied; the Bible is to me the revelation of Christ. I believe in Jesus because He is to me a divine Saviour. I believe the Bible because I have found it to be the voice of God to my soul."

- **Wonderful Possibilities**

It is our privilege to reach higher and still higher for clearer revealings of the character of God. When Moses prayed, "I beseech Thee, show me Thy glory" (Exodus 33:18), the Lord did not rebuke him, but He granted his prayer. God declared to His servant: "I will make all My goodness pass before thee, and will proclaim the name of Jehovah before thee." Verse 19, A. R. V.

It is sin that darkens our minds and dims our perceptions. As sin is purged from our hearts, the light of the knowledge of the glory of God in the face of

Section 5: The Essential Knowledge

Jesus Christ, illuminating His word and reflected from the face of nature, more and more fully will declare Him "merciful and gracious, long-suffering, and abundant in goodness and truth." Exodus 34:6.

In His light shall we see light, until mind and heart and soul are transformed into the image of His holiness.

Wonderful possibilities are open to those who lay hold of the divine assurances of God's word. There are glorious truths to come before the people of God. Privileges and duties which they do not even suspect to be in the Bible will be laid open before them. As they follow on in the path of humble obedience, doing His will, they will know more and more of the oracles of God.

Let the student take the Bible as his guide and stand like a rock for principle, and he may aspire to any height of attainment. All the philosophies of human nature have led to confusion and shame when God has not been recognized as all in all. But the precious faith inspired of God imparts strength and nobility of character. As His goodness, His mercy, and His love are dwelt upon, clearer and still clearer will be the perception of truth; higher, holier, the desire for purity of heart and clearness of thought. The soul dwelling in the pure atmosphere of holy thought is transformed by intercourse with God through the study of His word. Truth is so large, so far-reaching, so deep, so broad, that self is lost sight of. The heart is softened and subdued into humility, kindness, and love.

And the natural powers are enlarged because of holy obedience. From the study of the words of life, students may come forth with minds expanded, elevated, ennobled. If they are, like Daniel, hearers and doers of the word of God, they may advance as he did in all branches of learning. Being pure-minded, they will become strong-minded. Every intellectual faculty will be quickened. They may so educate and discipline themselves that all within the sphere of their influence may see what man can be, and what he can do, when connected with the God of wisdom and power.

- **Results of Receiving God's Word**

This was the experience which the psalmist gained through a knowledge of God's word. He says:

Blessed are they that are upright in way,
  Who walk in the law of Jehovah.
Blessed are they that keep His testimonies,
  That seek Him with the whole heart...
O that my ways were established
  To observe Thy statutes!
Then shall I not be put to shame,
  When I have respect unto all Thy commandments.

Wherewith shall a young man cleanse his way?
  By taking heed thereto according to Thy word.
I have chosen the way of faithfulness:
  Thine ordinances have I set before me.
Thy word have I laid up in my heart,
  That I might not sin against Thee.
And I shall walk at liberty;
  For I have sought Thy precepts.

Open Thou mine eyes, that I may behold
  Wondrous things out of Thy law.
Thy testimonies also are my delight
  And my counselors.
The law of Thy mouth is better unto me
  Than thousands of gold and silver.

O how love I Thy law!
  It is my meditation all the day.
Thy statutes have been my songs

In the house of my pilgrimage.
Thy testimonies are wonderful;
  Therefore doth my soul keep them.
The opening of Thy words giveth light;
  It giveth understanding unto the simple.
Thy commandments make me wiser than mine enemies;
  For they are ever with me.
I have more understanding than all my teachers;
  For Thy testimonies are my meditation.
I understand more than the aged,
  Because I have kept Thy precepts...
Through Thy precepts I get understanding:
  Therefore I hate every false way.

Thy word is very pure;
  Therefore Thy servant loveth it.
The sum of Thy word is truth;
  And every one of Thy righteous ordinances endureth forever.

Great peace have they that love Thy law;
  And they have no occasion of stumbling.
I have hoped for Thy salvation, O Jehovah,
  And have done Thy commandments.
My soul hath observed Thy testimonies;
  And I love them exceedingly.

I have longed for Thy salvation, O Jehovah;
  And Thy law is my delight.
Let my soul live, and it shall praise Thee;
  And let Thine ordinances help me.
Thy testimonies have I taken as a heritage forever;
  For they are the rejoicing of my heart.
  Psalm 119:1-6, margin, 9, 30, 11, 45, 18, 24, 72, 97, 54, 129, 130, 98-104, 140, 160, 165-167, 174, 175, 111, A. R. V.

- **An Aid in the Study of Nature**

He who has a knowledge of God and His word through personal experience is prepared to engage in the study of natural science. Of Christ it is written: "In Him was life; and the life was the light of men." John 1:4. When Adam and Eve in Eden lost the garments of holiness, they lost the light that had illuminated nature. No longer could they read it aright. But for those who receive the light of the life of Christ, nature is again illuminated. In the light shining from the cross, we can rightly interpret nature's teaching.

He who has a knowledge of God and His word has a settled faith in the divinity of the Holy Scriptures. He does not test the Bible by man's ideas of science. He brings these ideas to the test of the unerring standard. He knows that God's word is truth, and truth can never contradict itself; whatever in the teaching of so-called science contradicts the truth of God's revelation is mere human guesswork.

To the really wise, scientific research opens vast fields of thought and information. The ways of God as revealed in the natural world and in His dealings with man constitute a treasury from which every student in the school of Christ may draw.

The real evidence of a living God is not merely in theory; it is in the conviction that God has written in our hearts, illuminated and explained by His word. It is in the living power in His created works, seen by the eye which the Holy Spirit has enlightened.

Those who judge of God from His handiwork, and not from the suppositions of great men, see His presence in everything. They behold His smile in the glad sunshine, and His love and care for man in the rich fields of autumn. Even the adornments of the earth, the grass of living green, the lovely flowers of every hue, the lofty and varied trees of the forest, the dancing brook, the noble river, the placid lake, testify to the tender, fatherly care of God and to His desire to make His children happy.

Section 5: The Essential Knowledge

- **Nature: A Key to Divine Mysteries**

As the student thus contemplates the things of nature, a new perception of truth comes to him. The teachings in God's great book of nature bear testimony to the truth of the written word.

In the plan of redemption there are mysteries that the human mind cannot fathom, many things that human wisdom cannot explain; but nature can teach us much concerning the mystery of godliness. Every shrub, every tree bearing fruit, all vegetation, has lessons for our study. In the growth of the seed are to be read the mysteries of the kingdom of God.

To the heart softened by the grace of God, the sun, the moon, the stars, the trees, the flowers of the field, utter words of counsel. The sowing of the seed carries the mind to spiritual seed sowing. The tree declares that a good tree cannot bear evil fruit, neither can an evil tree bear good fruit. "Ye shall know them by their fruits." Matthew 7:16. Even the tares have a lesson. They are of Satan's sowing, and, if left unchecked, spoil the wheat by their rank growth.

Fathers and mothers, teach your children of the wonder-working power of God. His power is manifest in every plant, in every tree that bears fruit. Take the children into the garden and explain to them how He causes the seed to grow. The farmer plows his land and sows the seed, but he cannot make the seed grow. He must depend upon God to do that which no human power can do. The Lord puts His own Spirit into the seed, causing it to spring into life. Under His care the germ breaks through the case enclosing it and springs up to develop and bear fruit.

As the children study the great lessonbook of nature, God will impress their minds. As they are told of the work that He does for the seed, they learn the secret of growth in grace. Rightly understood, these lessons lead to the Creator, teaching those simple, holy truths that bring the heart into close touch with God.

- **A Lesson of Obedience**

God's laws for nature are obeyed by nature. Cloud and storm, sunshine and shower, dew and rain, all are under the supervision of God and yield obedience to His command. In obedience to the law of God the spire of grain bursts through the earth, "first the blade, then the ear, after that the full corn in the ear." Mark 4:28. The fruit is first seen in the bud, and the Lord develops it in its proper season because it does not resist His working. So the birds fulfill God's purpose as they make their long migrations from land to land, guided through trackless space by the hand of infinite power.

Can it be that man, made in the image of God, endowed with reason and speech, shall alone be unappreciative of His gifts and disobedient to His laws? Will those who might be elevated and ennobled, fitted to be colaborers with Him, be content to remain imperfect in character and to cause confusion in our world? Shall the bodies and souls of God's purchased inheritance be hampered with world-bound habits and unholy practices? Shall they not reflect the beauty of Him who has done all things well, that through His grace imperfect man might hear at last His benediction: "Well done, thou good and faithful servant: ... enter thou into the joy of thy Lord"? Matthew 25:21.

God desires us to learn from nature the lesson of obedience.

Ask now the beasts, and they shall teach thee;
And the birds of the heavens, and they shall tell thee:
Or speak to the earth, and it shall teach thee;

And the fishes of the sea shall declare unto thee.
Who knoweth not in all these,
That the hand of Jehovah hath wrought?
With God is wisdom and might;
He hath counsel and understanding.
Job 12:7-9, 13, A. R. V.

Blessed is the man whose delight is in the law of Jehovah...

He shall be like a tree planted by the streams of water,
That bringeth forth its fruit in its season,
Whose leaf also doth not wither;
And whatsoever he doeth shall prosper.
Psalm 1:1-3, A. R. V.

The book of nature and the written word shed light upon each other. Both make us better acquainted with God by teaching us of His character and of the laws through which He works.

- **Education in the Life to Come**

The education begun here will not be completed in this life; it will be going forward throughout eternity, ever progressing, never completed. Day by day the wonderful works of God, the evidences of His miraculous power in creating and sustaining the universe, will open before the mind in new beauty. In the light that shines from the throne, mysteries will disappear, and the soul will be filled with astonishment at the simplicity of the things that were never before comprehended.

Now we see through a glass, darkly; but then face to face; now we know in part; but then shall we know even as also we are known.

49. Our Great Need

The knowledge of God that works transformation of character is our great need. If we fulfill His purpose, there must be in our lives a revelation of God that shall correspond to the teaching of His word.

The experience of Enoch and of John the Baptist represents what ours should be. Far more than we do, we need to study the lives of these men—he who was translated to heaven without seeing death, and he who, before Christ's first advent, was called to prepare the way of the Lord, to make His paths straight.

- **The Experience of Enoch**

Of Enoch it is written that he lived sixty-five years and begat a son; after that he walked with God three hundred years. During those earlier years, Enoch had loved and feared God, and had kept His commandments. But after the birth of his first son he reached a higher experience; he was drawn into closer relationship with God. As he saw the child's love for its father, its simple trust in his protection; as he felt the deep, yearning tenderness of his own heart for that first-born son, he learned a precious lesson of the wonderful love of God to man in the gift of His Son, and the confidence which the children of God may repose in their heavenly Father. The infinite, unfathomable love of God through Christ became the subject of his meditations day and night. With all the fervor of his soul he sought to reveal that love to the people among whom he dwelt.

Enoch's walk with God was not in a trance or a vision, but in all the duties of his daily life. He did not become a hermit, shutting himself entirely from the world; for he had, in the world, a work to do for God. In the family and in his intercourse with men, as a husband and father, a friend, a citizen, he was the steadfast, unwavering servant of God.

His faith waxed stronger, his love became more ardent, with the lapse of centuries. To him prayer was as the breath of the soul. He lived in the atmosphere of heaven.

As the scenes of the future were opened to his view, Enoch became a preacher of righteousness, bearing God's message to all who would hear the words of warning. In the land where Cain had sought to flee from the divine presence, the prophet of God made known the wonderful scenes that had passed before his vision. "Behold," he declared, "the Lord cometh with ten thousands of His saints, to execute judgment upon all, and to convince all that are ungodly among them of all their ungodly deeds." Jude 14, 15.

The power of God that wrought with His servant was felt by those who heard. Some gave heed to the warning and renounced their sins, but the multitudes mocked at the solemn message. The servants of God are to bear a similar message to the world in the last days, and it will also be received with unbelief and mockery.

As year after year passed, deeper and deeper grew the tide of human guilt, darker and darker gathered the clouds of divine judgment. Yet Enoch, the witness of faith, held on his way, warning, pleading, and teaching, striving to turn back the tide of guilt and to stay the bolts of vengeance.

The men of that generation mocked the folly of him who sought not to gather gold or silver, or to build up possessions here. But Enoch's heart was upon eternal treasures. He had looked upon the celestial city. He had seen the King in His glory in the midst of Zion. The greater the existing iniquity, the more earnest was his longing for the home of God. While still on earth, he dwelt, by faith, in the realms of light.

"Blessed are the pure in heart: for they shall see God." Matthew 5:8. For three hundred years Enoch had been seeking purity of heart, that he might be in harmony with heaven. For three centuries he had walked with God. Day by day he had longed for a closer union; nearer and nearer had grown the communion, until God took him to Himself. He had stood at the threshold of the eternal world, only a step between him and the land of the blest; and now the portals opened, the walk with God, so long pursued on earth, continued, and he passed through the gates of the holy city, the first from among men to enter there.

"By faith Enoch was translated that he should not see death; ... for before his translation he had this testimony, that he pleased God." Hebrews 11:5.

To such communion God is calling us. As was Enoch's must be their holiness of character who shall be redeemed from among men at the Lord's second coming.

- **Experience of John the Baptist**

John the Baptist in his desert life was taught of God. He studied the revelations of God in nature. Under the guiding of the Divine Spirit, he studied the scrolls of the prophets. By day and by night, Christ was his study, his meditation, until mind and heart and soul were filled with the glorious vision.

He looked upon the King in His beauty, and self was lost sight of. He beheld the majesty of holiness and knew himself to be inefficient and unworthy. It was God's message that he was to declare. It was in God's power and His righteousness that he was to stand. He was ready to go forth as Heaven's messenger, unawed by the human, because he had looked upon the Divine. He could stand fearless in the presence of earthly monarchs because with trembling he had bowed before the King of kings.

With no elaborate arguments or finespun theories did John declare his message. Startling and stern, yet full of hope, his voice was heard from the wilderness: "Repent ye: for the kingdom of heaven is at hand." Matthew 3:2. With a new, strange power it moved the people. The whole nation was stirred. Multitudes flocked to the wilderness.

Unlearned peasants and fishermen from the surrounding country; the Roman soldiers from the barracks of Herod; chieftains with their swords at their sides, ready to put down anything that might savor of rebellion; the avaricious taxgatherers from their toll booths; and from the Sanhedrin the phylacteried priests—all listened as if spellbound; and all, even the Pharisee, and the Sadducee, the cold, unimpressible scoffer, went away with the sneer silenced and cut to the heart with a sense of their sins. Herod in his palace heard the message, and the proud, sin-hardened ruler trembled at the call to repentance.

In this age, just prior to the second coming of Christ in the clouds of heaven, such a work as that of John is to be done. God calls for men who will prepare a people to stand in the great day of the Lord. The message preceding the public ministry of Christ was: "Repent, publicans and sinners; repent, Pharisees and Sadducees; 'repent ye: for the kingdom of heaven is at hand.'" As a people who believe in Christ's soon appearing, we have a message to bear— "Prepare to meet thy God." Amos 4:12. Our message must be as direct as was the message of John. He rebuked kings for their iniquity.

Notwithstanding that his life was imperiled, he did not hesitate to declare God's word. And our work in this age must be done as faithfully.

Section 5: The Essential Knowledge

In order to give such a message as John gave, we must have a spiritual experience like his. The same work must be wrought in us. We must behold God, and in beholding Him lose sight of self.

John had by nature the faults and weaknesses common to humanity; but the touch of divine love had transformed him. When, after Christ's ministry began, the disciples of John came to him with the complaint that all men were following the new Teacher, John showed how clearly he understood his relation to the Messiah, and how gladly he welcomed the One for whom he had prepared the way.

"A man can receive nothing," he said, "except it be given him from heaven. Ye yourselves bear me witness, that I said, I am not the Christ, but that I am sent before Him. He that hath the bride is the bridegroom: but the friend of the bridegroom, which standeth and heareth him, rejoiceth greatly because of the bridegroom's voice: this my joy therefore is fulfilled. He must increase, but I must decrease." John 3:27-30.

Looking in faith to the Redeemer, John had risen to the height of self-abnegation. He sought not to attract men to himself, but to lift their thoughts higher and still higher, until they should rest upon the Lamb of God. He himself had been only a voice, a cry in the wilderness. Now with joy he accepted silence and obscurity, that the eyes of all might be turned to the Light of life.

Those who are true to their calling as messengers for God will not seek honor for themselves. Love for self will be swallowed up in love for Christ. They will recognize that it is their work to proclaim, as did John the Baptist: "Behold the Lamb of God, which taketh away the sin of the world." John 1:29. They will lift up Jesus, and with Him humanity will be lifted up. "Thus saith the high and lofty One that inhabiteth eternity, whose name is Holy; I dwell in the high and holy place, with him also that is of a contrite and humble spirit, to revive the spirit of the humble, and to revive the heart of the contrite ones." Isaiah 57:15.

The soul of the prophet, emptied of self, was filled with the light of the Divine. In words that were almost a counterpart of the words of Christ Himself, he bore witness to the Saviour's glory. "He that cometh from above," he said, "is above all: he that is of the earth is earthly, and speaketh of the earth: He that cometh from heaven is above all... For He whom God hath sent speaketh the words of God: for God giveth not the Spirit by measure unto Him." John 3:31-34.

In this glory of Christ all His followers are to share. The Saviour could say: "I seek not Mine own will, but the will of the Father which hath sent Me." John 5:30." And," declared John, "the Father giveth not the Spirit by measure unto Him." So with the followers of Christ. We can receive of heaven's light only as we are willing to be emptied of self. We can discern the character of God, and accept Christ by faith, only as we consent to the bringing into captivity of every thought to the obedience of Christ. To all who do this, the Holy Spirit is given without measure. In Christ "dwelleth all the fullness of the Godhead bodily. And ye are complete in Him." Colossians 2:9, 10.

- **God's Promises**

To all who are willing for self to be humbled are given God's promises:

"I will make all My goodness pass before thee, and will proclaim the name of Jehovah before thee." Exodus 33:19, A. R. V.

"Call unto Me, and I will answer thee, and show thee great and mighty things, which thou knowest not." Jeremiah 33:3.

"Exceeding abundantly above all that we ask or think," will be given unto us, "the Spirit of wisdom and revelation in the knowledge of Him," that we "may be able to comprehend with all saints what is the breadth, and length, and depth, and height; and to know the love of Christ, which passeth knowledge," that we may be "filled with all the fullness of God." Ephesians 3:20; 1:17; Ephesians 3:18, 19.

This is the knowledge which God is inviting us to receive, and beside which all else is vanity and nothingness.

www.ingramcontent.com/pod-product-compliance
Lightning Source LLC
Chambersburg PA
CBHW070131080526
44586CB00015B/1648